The Meaning of Apricot Sponge

The Meaning of Apricot Sponge
Selected Writings of John Tripp

Edited by Tony Curtis

Parthian
The Old Surgery
Napier Street
Cardigan
SA43 1ED
www.parthianbooks.co.uk

First published in 2010
© John Tripp Estate 2010
All Rights Reserved

ISBN 978-1-906998-18-9

Cover photograph: © John Tripp Estate
Cover design: www.theundercard.co.uk
Typeset by books@lloydrobson.com

Printed and bound by Dinefwr Press, Llandybïe

The publisher acknowledges the financial support of the Welsh
Books Council.

British Library Cataloguing in Publication Data

A cataloguing record for this book is available from the British
Library.

Contents

At the Rainbow's End
A Selection of Prose Contributions to Magazines

Fringe Diversions
A Selection of Literary Criticisms and Reviews

No Peace for Dando
Uncollected Fiction

The Seed of Dismemberment
A Dialogue Verse Play for Radio

Appendix

Foreword

John Tripp and Dylan Thomas swam in the same sea. He may not have been as famous as his elder compatriot, nor as talented. He never visited America either. But in terms of volume his output was similar. He had comparable dealings with the media, read well on stage, had a voice that was good on the ear, drank gallons, had the same kind of difficulties with money. The two of them swam in the Welsh sea, a sea which surrounded a Wales which meant something, a place that was not England.

In his cups John Tripp would chant a personal mantra. 'I was born in Bargoed in 1927 and I want to know why.' Those near him heard it so often many could imitate him perfectly. Familiarity through the years allowed the words to lose meaning. But for John this statement remained as real as it could be. The birth in Bargoed gave him a Welsh legitimacy. Better than Cardiff, to some as remote as Llanystumdwy. Among the younger writers he mixed with, the 1927 made him an elder if not quite a statesman. The 'I want to know why' gave him purpose. A questioning of life he could write about, a realisation that it was all a joke that put him up there with the nihilists, allowed him to be as offensive as he wanted to anyone and everyone. And he did this often. The tales of Tripp half-cut are legion.

When he returned to Wales from London in 1969 he brought with him a twinkle of big city achievement, an air of having done more than we provincials had, even if, when you examined his London-Welsh fame, you found it to be largely full of air. Tripp, on stage at the Reardon Smith that year, more fitted the image of the writer who wrote because he had to, the bohemian, the poet driven, than did any of his fellow Anglo-Welsh literary travellers.

His years in Cardiff at a heady time for the changing world were accompanied by two girlfriends, a shed of booze, and a formidable output of performable, energised, engaging and highly readable verse. The life of the bar which John chose meant spending copious amounts of time in the company of those who also drank. A daily watching of the clock moving towards stop-tap, talking about nothing and everything to anyone who'd listen, poet of the people, far nearer the ground than most in academia, a hater of pretence and of those who would 'not recognise a poem if it came up behind and bit them'.

In the Welsh back bar of the Conway (as it then was, well before its present open-plan reconstruction) JT would hold court. Here he could surround himself with patriots, Welsh-enthusiasts, and many of the young writers who also found themselves there, hunting for the Cymric beat generation and the place where poetry, art and life crossed. Mike Povey, Geraint Jarman, David Callard, Fred Daly, Huw Morgan, Peter Tinniswood, Mici Plwm, Mike Stevens (singer). JT never saw himself as godfather, although as he'd achieved and largely the rest of us had not, he had some status. *Diesel to Yesterday*, *Loss of Ancestry*, *Province of Belief*, and then the rumour of inclusion in the poetry world's shit hot product of that decade, *Penguin Modern Poets*.

He was on the side of the young and the explorer rather than the great and the good who'd already arrived. I met him in the mid-sixties when I was starting up what was to morph into an international journal at the cutting edge of new verse, *second aeon*. JT contributed his work, readily, enthusiastically and for free. Ormond wouldn't do that, he complained to me. Although John Ormond subsequently did, just not with same open-heartedness nor in the same quantity. John Ormond was someone JT would measure himself against. They both drank nightly at the Conway, Ormond in the front bar among the locals (he himself lived in Conway Road), JT mostly with the rebels in the back. 'I'm going in there to sort him out,' John declared one evening when someone among us had been complaining (with no foundation, as history would reveal) about Ormond lording it with the hoi polloi in the front and never being willing to mix with us raggedy edge pushers and new beginners in the back. 'Who does he think he is? What's he actually published? I'm going to tell him.' We watched across the bar, expecting to witness what was to become a typical Tripp display of shouting, amazingly personal insults and gesticulated diatribe. Tripp, our man, the only Anglo-Welsh poet on the books who understood the new generation. Instead all we witnessed was the two of them quietly talking. Ormond bought JT a drink. JT drank it. 'Yeah, I told him,' JT said to me later, 'but he's not so bad.' JT, man of the even hand. Ormond and he later appeared in the same volume (27) of what was to turn out to be the last gasp of *Penguin Modern Poets*. Ormond the measured, the man who took care. Tripp the rager who let it flow.

Over at *second aeon* things were hitting the mainline. The magazine, which had started with a mere ten pages, was now running to hundreds. Contributions were coming in from everywhere that poetry mattered. John enjoyed being in the middle of it. He saw himself as a sort of Anglo-Welsh version of Charles Bukowski, the prolific Los Angeles American who churned out speech-patterned poetry about drink, drudgery and love. As books and scripts from Buk arrived (and he really was a prolific sender) I'd share them with John. *Erections, Ejaculations, Exhibitions and General Tales of Ordinary Madness*, his short fiction, and *The Days Run Away Like Wild Horses Over*

4

The Hill, his poetry. There was something about the sheer speed and the in-the-gutter content of these books of which John approved.

I'd already tried to align John with the beat-life drunken energy of J. P. Donleavy's *The Ginger Man*. When Donleavy visited Cardiff Tripp was set up with a pocketful of notes and a assignment to make the great man at home. JT, the nearest we had in Wales to Sebastian Dangerfield, hero of Donleavy's infamous book. But that had failed, unfortunately. Donleavy turned out to be a tweed-wearing early-to-bed non-drinker. JT was allowed to keep the dosh. Instead he became a Bukowski fan. 'Anything new come in?' he'd ask. I eventually gave John Buk's address: 'Ask him yourself,' I said.

In 1972, overrun by the sheer volume of small press (and for that matter big press) poetry publications arriving at my Maplewood flat, I appointed John reviews editor. This meant that Tripp would turn up on a regular basis, get me to take him to the Pineapple for a pint, and then leave with great bagfuls of books and pamphlets. He'd write them up on his famous, misaligned, red and black ribboned typer. JT exhibited a world view in his published comments and enjoyed the wildness and chaos of much of the American material which crossed his desk (although he never did have much time for the concretists and the sound poets). This mass of new material arriving daily in turn kept his poetry open. John's work in *second aeon* at this time, 'A Day in the Life of the Welsh', 'Return' and 'The Shepherd's Tale', in their ease of telling and their performable rant, show evidence of a man who had read Carlos Williams, Ginsberg and the beats, the New York school and certainly Charles Bukowski.

Being able to turn the material out, enjoying the association with the avant-garde and the frothingly new that *second aeon* lent, John was a regular contributor. Between issues 11 and 21 he is in every number. Living round the corner helped. He was once seen at a snack bar in Cardiff market wearing a newish brown suede coat. Mine. 'Finch gave me this as payment for the poetry,' he told enquirers. First I'd heard of this, but I let it pass. And the tales of the thank you note left in two-inch high magic marker on the wallpaper across our chimney breast are also true. 'He'll probably sell that to the National Library,' he told Glyn Jones when that lovely man complained to John on my behalf.

In addition to the *second aeon* contributions I also published two John Tripp books. For John there was something about the immediacy and the freedom of the small press that appealed to him. Christopher Davies, for all their hard-backed precision, were somehow too formal. Throughout his publishing life JT remained open to the alternative way of doing things, as Tony Curtis's Edge Press would subsequently find out.

second aeon's first Tripp title was *Bute Park and Other Poems* (1971). It evolved in much the same way as did his later *The Inheritance File* (1973). A few Cardiff-centric poems were expanded, on request, and a pamphlet put together. The photographer Barrie Rendell and I took JT around the city and through Bute Park itself shooting illustrative pictures. 'The whole is a little document of one person's observations in a certain place at a certain time, and of fondness for his habitat in an unfashionable, philistine, but warm and generous city,' wrote John in his introduction. On occasion the snap came first. JT standing outside Huxley's Surgical Goods shop counting his money as if he were about to enter to buy himself a truss or some of the Durex boldly advertised in the window led to the poem 'Caroline Street'. JT shown moodily in Ted Hughes pose on the railings of Roath Park Lake, the Scott memorial visible behind him, gave us 'Lakeside'. 'At the big houses of the solvent... at this hour they are making cocktails.' John, with the world always somehow against him.

The Inheritance File, its hardback publication aided through the sponsorship of the industrialist and poet Cyril Hodges, was a far grander affair. A book of poems about writers. John had written a couple and published them first in *second aeon* and then in *Poetry*

Wales and *Planet*. I encouraged him to write more, got Martin Dutton to illustrate the results – Proust with heavy moustache, Solzhenitsyn with his dark Russian sneer, Dylan Thomas with skyscrapers behind, a totally invented and rural looking John Clare. The book was splendid in style, printed on good paper, and bound as well as anything the commercial boys could manage. It was, however, less of a critical success than it could have been. 'Young poets whistle in the tunnel / to keep their spirits up, and the editors / wait patiently for a breeze of change' (from 'Letter to a Poet – for Charles Bukowski'). There were suggestions that John had not been entirely original in *The Inheritance File*, had lifted lines, stolen verses, had been seen at an exhibition of the notebooks of twentieth-century greats copying things down. A recycler ahead of his time.

As a public reader of poetry John had few contemporary equals. This was the seventies, of course, with performance poetry yet to evolve. In fact the very idea that poetry might also be entertainment was in some quarters perceived as a challenge. JT, Harri Webb, Herbert Williams and others were at the heart of the poetry and pints movement, the recitation of in-your-face and usually funny poems in bars. Verses interspersed with songs from the likes of Heather Jones. No one worried if the audience came and went, occurrences frowned upon at the more sedate readings of the traditionalists.

John had a reputation as a drinker, a man who would forever be borrowing money to fund the next pint and then insulting the donor for being alive. He was known to fall asleep in the readings of others and to leave restaurants either without paying or by collecting the tips for himself. Public scenes in pubs late at night were commonplace. Yet I never saw him fall off stage or stumble his words. A Tripp poetry reading was seriously done. There was order in the selection, entrainment and information in his introductions and perfection in his delivery. Drink later, not before. Be seen in the streets with a pint in your hand, fine, but read with clarity first. Audiences loved him.

John wore the broken rifle badge of War Resistors International on his left lapel and held strong opinions, delivered in his poetry, about the substance of Wales and the need for our independent place in the world. These were two things which should have aligned him readily with political activists and given him space on television. But somehow this anger against the monster next door failed to translate into any sort of action. For most of his time among the young and the new JT talked about poetry rather than politics. I wonder how much of his declared left-wing radical position was posture rather than belief. Both of the great loves in his life were Tory ladies. JT was never seen marching (not against the Vietnam war nor the bomb) and, as far as I know, was never a card-carrying member of a political party. In later life (in his case a short later life) he took to the enjoyment of long country pub lunches, visits to tea shops in coastal resorts, car journeys along rural lanes, claimed to have taken up wine, and grew a salt and pepper Harold Macmillan moustache.

Not that any of this prevented his regular relapses into writerly alcoholic haze. That's something that stayed until the end. The whisky bottle on the couch when he died. The ranting sandwich-throwing, drunken ghost that returned at his Welsh Union of Writers organised wake in 1986 at the Gower Hotel in Cathays. It's a memory that stays with all who knew him – the poet who walked a tightrope and the man who often ended up falling down.

Peter Finch
October 2009

10

Introduction

> His art was blunt inside its shattering glove,
> his spleen well thrust against a failure of the heart.
> He offered no quarter to the grubbing merchants of cant.
> But did his scarecrow vision of flesh and spirit,
> his flapping arms that terrified the crows of sin,
> ever let in a glimpse of golden cornland?[1]

John Tripp's poem biography of 'Caradoc Evans Revisited (1878–1945)' first appeared in *The Anglo-Welsh Review* in the autumn of 1973 and those closing lines have more than a passing element of autobiography, of self-knowledge. Tripp's own art, his poems, stories and articles, could be blunt. Tripp himself offered no quarter to those he felt were traders in cant and hypocrisy. John Tripp's anger, often expressed in venomous language and aggressive behaviour, did indeed terrify the crows of sin, but also too often those who wished him well. His arms and tongue flapped, sometimes to great effect and sometimes to no purpose. And what 'golden cornfield' did the later writer himself walk through?

This new selection of unpublished and uncollected writings brings the work of a neglected writer into the public arena[2]. The wit is sharp – John Tripp was the Clive James of Wales's television reviewing – the

11

humour is broad and infectious; the passion is still keen and engaging. In poetry, fiction and social commentary John Tripp's was a voice which for twenty-five years engaged with and articulated the concerns of Wales.

I have chosen to illustrate these qualities by bringing together some of his uncollected poems (the *Selected Poems* is still available from Seren Books) together with two seminal poems from the *Selected*. Many of these were provided by Fay Cornes, to whom I am indebted. Also here are some of the poems he intended for publication in a pamphlet we had planned together, *Intervals of Heat*, which never appeared, and two poems from a Peter Finch publication which has been long out of print. The reviews of other writers and the autobiographical pieces are taken from the magazines of his time in Wales – *The Anglo-Welsh Review*, *Arcade* and *Planet* – all of which he wrote for generously and frequently. His radio play, broadcast in 1972, appears in print for the first time and underlines his passion for the cause of Welsh independence.[3]

I knew and worked with John Tripp for the last twelve years of his life, and when I accepted the invitation from Peter Finch at the Academi to give the 2009 Gwyn Jones Lecture I was encouraged to re-examine John's work and my relationship with the man and the writing. In this introduction I will consider both the poems and the prose, fiction and what we now call creative non-fiction, a term which he would surely have taken to task. I will illustrate three broad themes or concerns in his work: War, Sex and Food. They are continuing and central issues for John Tripp's writing and his life and this selection supports that approach.

John Tripp was born in Bargoed in 1927. He grew up with his parents in Whitchurch, Cardiff, while his father Paul Tripp worked as a blacksmith at the Oak Tree Forge in Taff's Well, a business which he ran until 1969 and the building of the A470 by-pass meant that it was compulsorily purchased. John left Whitchurch Senior School and after a course in commerce at technical college he got a job as a junior clerk at the BBC in Cardiff. During the last years of the war he worked there in a variety of roles and was involved in creating sound effects for programmes, including *Children's Hour*. He was called up for National Service where 'boredom was worn like a second skin',[4] but did not complete training until the war was over. His experiences of drilling, followed by the tedium of clerking in a succession of army pay offices, would inform the 'For King and Country' poem sequence and other poems in which he cast a cynical eye at the life of the military; though he was genuinely passionate about the real business of war and was, no doubt, affected by the experiences of his father Paul,

13

who had served in the Great War, including several years on the Western Front where Lloyd George had 'paid the butcher's bill.'[5] He had survived and Tripp's family had not suffered 'the long solitude of widows / and spinsters'.[6] One of the pensioners John sees at the side of Roath Park lake in Cardiff

> ... wears the ribbons of calamity
> on his jacket – still ram-rod proud in an age
> when the evidence is stacked against it.[7]

And there is a reluctant pride acknowledged by the poet; something which that 'one soldier of goodness and truth', David Jones, would surely have understood.[8]

In fact, the tedium of his National Service years made a contribution to the education of this most notable autodidact.[9] Though he writes that he frittered 'my lean 19th year / among the reek of latrines and bolt-oil / in the bleak scooped uplands of Epynt',[10] he had plenty of time to read and, indeed, he wrote his first poems in barracks in Edinburgh, some of which were performed at army shows.[11]

After John's demob he discovered that there was no work back at the BBC in Cardiff and he moved to London, 'Dylan Thomas's "capital punishment"',[12] to work as a despatch clerk and record tester in the overseas service of the BBC there; in 1951, at the age of twenty-four, he became a news researcher and sub-editor and worked in these roles for some seven years. These were the years of drinking at the fringes of the famous: W. R. Rogers, Francis Dillon, Rene Cutforth and 'Louis MacNeice at the Cock', though 'I never approached him, being nothing much / at the Old Beeb, and he / seemed formidable... holding a glass / and looking at the world from a distance / through half-closed eyes.'[13] That could pass for a description of John himself in his later years.

John Tripp then joined the Young and Rubicam advertising agency and worked on the Maxwell House coffee campaign among others. He later worked as a journalist in London and from 1960 as a Press Assistant for the Indonesian Embassy. From that time he began to publish his poems more widely – in *Tribune*, *Poetry Wales* and *The London Welshman*. He became friendly with Tudor David, the editor of *The London Welshman*, Bryn Griffiths, Robert Morgan and Sally Roberts, who together formed the Guild of Welsh Writers, which was later absorbed into the Welsh Academy. One member 'who was a former undertaker from the Rhondda... who had been a tank-driver in the International Brigade in Spain... had plenty of money and took me once to a French café in Soho for snails, which we scooped out of the shells, dipping up butter, garlic and parsley sauce with bits of brown bread, and drinking a carafe of Riesling. Then through that

15

afternoon we drank a Martinique rum called St James, calvados (apple brandy from Normandy) and Southern Comfort bourbon which was stickier than I thought it would be, with ice and ginger ale and a slice of orange. It was a memorable day.' The 'capital punishment' was mitigated by such sophisticated sixties attractions. Contrast that with the fare he experiences on a 'Border Run' poetry gig back in Wales: 'We stopped at a Berni's sort of inn and had a shrivelled steak with one unripe tomato, smallshot peas and a mound of chips, which helped to fill us up. I think the red plonk was a Berni vinegar.'[14]

There were also visits to meetings of The Group at Edward Lucie Smith's house in Chelsea, where 'Juicy-Myth, in his Aquascutum dressing-gown' and 'Banjo Hamilton held court'.[15]

On Fridays we would gather at Lucy's
He squatting like a Buddha well fed
While my eye kept shifting from poetry
To a poetess I wanted in bed…

Tea cups clinked, marzipan offered round
As the poets stabbed absent friends.[16]

Wales was beginning to call him back from those horrors where 'the Muse was kept / Locked in the cold deep-freeze' and where one might be 'fanged by mad dogs / of the metropolitan mafia'.[17] It was also the case that London was becoming hectic and expensive and his work meant that he was often 'panting to ulcer deadlines'.[18] Following a Commonwealth Poets Conference in Cardiff in 1965 Tripp had had a poem included in the anthology *Young Commonwealth Poets* and his first selection of poems was published the following year as the second of Meic Stephens's Triskel pamphlets. Of *Diesel to Yesterday* John Stuart Williams said, 'His alien years have made him passionately conscious of his roots' with 'an exile's keen feeling for his own land'.[19] John Tripp attended the annual general meeting of Yr Academi Gymreig in 1968, where it was agreed to form an English language section. He returned to Wales in 1969 – 'I'd bought a single back to the beginning, / where people live at room temperature / and shopgirls call you "love"' – much encouraged by the award of an Arts Council bursary. He had poems included in the Stephens and Williams anthology *The Lilting House*[20] and attended the launch in Swansea. Things must have looked promising. He contributed the first of three poems to the 'Dial-a-Poem' scheme that began in 1970 and 'An Elegy for England' received 996 calls.[21]

On Valentine's Day in 1970, after a reading in the Angel Hotel (organised by JT) with Dannie Abse, Gwyn Thomas, Harri Webb, Roland Mathias, John Ormond, Raymond Garlick and John Stuart Williams, John Tripp met again Fay Williams, who worked as Meic Stephens's assistant at the Arts Council; they had first met at the launch of *The Lilting House* in Swansea in the summer of 1969.[22] Despite the difference in their ages – he was 42 and she was 23 – they formed a close relationship which lasted for some years. Things must have looked promising.[23]

For the next two decades he tried to carve out a living as a freelance writer and served as an executive member of the English language section of Yr Academi through to my time as Chair of that organisation in the mid-1980s. He undertook as many readings as he could get and accepted many magazine commissions, though none was well paid. He also appeared on an HTV arts programme, *Nails*, in which he hoped to celebrate the arts and also rail against 'the problem of the Coca-Cola/Coronation Street ethic creeping into the potentially great township of Cardiff'.[24] He even once worked as a film extra on a shooting of a production of *Sir Gawain and the Green Knight* at Cardiff Castle. In seventeen years of living back in Wales he never moved out of his father's house and both of them and the property grew old and time-worn together. He died of a heart attack in that bungalow in Whitchurch in 1986.

John Tripp never owned his own property, he never drove a car, did not have any substantial possessions, save his books and manuscripts. He never entered that state of marriage when 'two people set out on the journey / of custom and habit', though he could be, and certainly saw himself as, a romantic man.[25] His education was elementary, supplemented by evening classes at Morley College, though he often implied that he had been a full-time student there.[26] He was, however, an autodidact of considerable breadth and depth, knowledgeable in terms of current affairs and reading seriously among the English poets and his own Anglo-Welsh tradition. His return to Wales was prompted by political problems in Indonesia and therefore difficulties at the Indonesian Embassy. He left there to work for a further three years at the Central Office of Information as an information officer, North American Desk, but wished to return to Wales. He was also drawn home by his growing commitment to Wales and the promise of a new sense of independence in his homeland. But Wales could not sustain him as a professional writer: his occasional articles for the press, polemical pieces, poems and short stories for *The Anglo-Welsh Review*, *Arcade*, *Poetry Wales* and *Planet*, at which magazine he served as Literary Editor between 1973 and 1979, and brief sessions on radio and television were not the steady income he really needed. These were the early days of Arts Council supported poetry readings and John Tripp's power as a performer of his work also gave him a small, steady income from regular invitations to read.

19

Still, Wales let him down; his homeland did not live up to his expectations, especially after the referendum vote in 1979. That was a catastrophe for John Tripp from which his spirits and sense of purpose never fully recovered.[27] Much of his early poetry and creative non-fiction had been directed at the cause of Wales's independence and fuelled by a perceived sense of grievances against England, 'the slow choke of a race'.[28] Indeed, much of his poetry was marred by the forces which powered it. As Sally Jones observed, 'so much concern and so much violence, untempered by a sufficient irony, comes at last to seem perhaps too loud, too monotonous'.[29] John Tripp himself came to acknowledge that when, in a letter to *Poetry Wales* in 1980, he said, 'One sees now that a large slice of this poetry is now dated. In my own case it was written very fast in fulminating heat, disgust, outrage and despair... but this didn't seem to matter against the larger issue of a nation going down the drain.'[30] He characterised the Wales of the sixties and seventies as a 'social, political and cultural shambles', and in the face of that challenge John Tripp shouted and railed.[31]

His position as an Anglophone poet also proved a dilemma: he was an

... 'Anglo', dipped in England's sewer,
worse than a Michigan tourist, odd as an Eskimo,

20

roaming like a campless Arab
through the heart of his people.
All that his fingers touch, his mind bites at,

give voice to Wales,
all his verse will strain to bridge the gap.[32]

John Tripp felt as angry as Harri Webb, Meic
Stephens, Raymond Garlick and R. S. Thomas about
the political condition of Wales, but unlike the younger
poets – Peter Finch, Gillian Clarke and Nigel Jenkins –
he did not learn the language and, like his character
Thomas, Tripp feels an outsider at the National
Eisteddfod, no matter how vehemently he campaigns.[33]

It is easy now to regard such loud expressions of
outrage as dated, from our position of living in a post-
Assembly, bilingual Wales, but who knows what effect
a firebrand like Tripp might have had in galvanising
protests in the decade before he returned to Wales, the
decade that saw the drowning of Treweryn blinked
through a largely indifferent House of Commons?
Instead, he was caught up in London in a succession
of jobs, working to make a living. If at the end of his
life the nationalist stance he had struck appeared
forlorn, it is also the case, as Nigel Jenkins has pointed
out, that John Tripp was certainly aware of the new
problems in Thatcher's Britain, in which was created
'a vulnerable "under-class" ... without any obvious
future' whose plight was 'private individual, almost

invisible'. They were 'the marginal people in our botched society'.[34]

Such acute observations articulate a real concern which resonates up to the end of the first decade of our new century.[35] In my review of what was to be his last collection, *Passing Through*, I wrote: 'Tripp is still the greying knight in rusty armour in search of a grail one knows will prove to be battered and tarnished.'[36] I also wrote that 'John Tripp finds it harder and harder to stay fresh, to find in his language and in its rhythms the means to jolt himself and his reader into the expression of feelings which are undoubtedly there, under the skin.' In an earlier review of *The Loss of Ancestry* Roland Mathias had concerns that there was 'a lack of sufficient verse structure: discipline, one feels, might cramp the quickness of the next hit'.[37] John Ormond in his introduction to the *Selected Poems* emphasises this point with his call for more 'slow left-arm spinners' rather than the bouncers that Tripp sent down the page, sometimes unrelentingly. Tripp acknowledged this himself: 'I tried to oblige / but the language cherry reared up / again, wide of the off-stump.' In my review I single out 'Connection at Bridgend' as the most successful poem, with its near-absurdist sense of the need to make connections in order to confirm the meaning of living, for as John says:

... We are in it
together, until the last buses go out.
One by one they leave the bays.

Having caught the diesel to yesterday, in the last year of his sixth decade it may be that the poet feels he has latterly missed the bus.[38]

John Tripp was often short of money, sometimes blatantly borrowing and leaning on friends for food, transport and shelter. He would rail against the lot of the poet, too often peripheral to the flow of society. As John Ormond remembered, 'he could burst into barely-controlled rages which would offend strangers and half-acquaintances and try hard the patience of friends'. At the same time, Ormond 'never sensed any great sadness in him; rather the quiet of a man who had eaten a sustaining if somewhat frugal meal at the table of life's joys.'

I was to discover both aspects of the man from 1974 when I moved back to Wales to my first job in higher education. I included John Tripp in the exhibition of poetry manuscripts which I organised in the South Glamorgan College of Education in 1975 and published his work in the magazine *Madog*, which I tried to base there in the late seventies. In my 'poem for John Tripp'[39] written after the tragic, early death of a friend my wife and I had known at Swansea University, I wrote:

John, we are under the weight of this thing
And we wol sleen this false traytour Deeth
clench the fist around the pen, we riotoures three:
you and I and the third – our dead friends and fathers,
on the road, at the desk, looking over our shoulders.

John had lost his mother Muriel Tripp, 'the most powerful influence on his life',[40] in 1966:

I wanted to run
the other way, but was hemmed
by convention. My father coughed
and the long line shuffled to the brink
as she was lowered into clay.[41]

My father had died in 1978, an event which saddened John, though I think they had not met more than once, because my father was not much older than John and, strangely, in photographs had more than a passing resemblance to the poet. John empathised with my family's grief to a surprising degree. In *Passing Through* John included 'Poem for a Father', which was dedicated to me.

He misjudged the hung dust
of sorrow, how it lingers
in rooms, on a road or beach,
at the edges of celebration.
What we see is how they looked

24

and laughed, the way they walked
towards us, their arms opened wide.

I am sure that the poem has moved at its conclusion
to a confessional poem about John's own feelings, his
continuing grief for his mother and the knowledge that
given his father's age he would surely be left alone.
Certainly, that death brought us closer together.

In my fictional account of a bizarre poetry reading
trip to Pembrokeshire we both undertook a few years
later I have the Tripp character Griffiths say: 'I write
in order to slow the whole thing down – I want to
catch death by the balls.' That is probably a quote or
paraphrase of John; it certainly represents in my mind
or imagination his defiance in the face of mortality.[42]

It is difficult at this distance to recall precisely
where John Tripp aligned himself between the poles of
anger and frustration in the face of mortality and the
vagaries of the modern world. He latterly dressed
rather shabbily and seemed to present a persona that
was out of time with contemporary life in the late
seventies and early eighties. At the same time, this
rebellious outsider could express real interest and no
little knowledge of the finer things in life, particularly
concerning food, drink and women. He was 'an
occasional connoisseur / Of hotel fitments and
glimpses of the soft life'[43] and relished the opportunity
to enjoy those after the austerity of the war years and

the grim fifties. Tripp wanted to cut a dash, live high on the hog, to paint the town with a bobby dazzler on his arm. He walked the walk and wrote the life that was rarely achieved in his own: though on rare occasions he proved that 'he was an extremely good ballroom dancer'.[44] On Valentine's Day, two days before he died, John sent two cards to Jean Henderson, the second inscribed 'Love to the Tory girl in stylish wine-coloured shoes – Jx'.[45] How many men remember the shoes a woman wears, how many men are that gallant?[46] John Tripp knows that despite 'the blade up the sleeve', the 'short innocence bolted in the best years', despite the children who 'connive at their own disaster', it is 'the rusted and priceless compass of love / that will crutch us home...'[47]

Although there have been detailed examinations of Tripp's poetry,[48] his fiction and creative non-fiction, perhaps because this has never been collected, has not been critically examined. Some pieces – for example, 'Death on the Appel Quay', 'The Reds are Coming', 'A Skirmish at Inch', 'Connection at Ust' and ' Day of the Pigs' – are characterised as 'factions' and struggle to rise above their role as polemical dialogues.[49] Calling these 'factions', perhaps John was recognising the problems he faced in developing ideas into convincing fictions.

Nevertheless, John Tripp undoubtedly wrote more prose than poetry and he took himself very seriously as a journalist, storyteller and commentator. His articles and reviews for *The Anglo-Welsh Review*, *Planet*, *Arcade* and the Newsletter of the Welsh Academy kept his name before the reading public in Wales and kept a trickle of money coming in. Almost all his prose and fiction has a personal angle, a sense of a stylist, a raconteur entertaining and informing. He is indeed 'a kind of Anglo-Welsh Philip Marlowe'.[50]

The story 'Apricot Sponge with a Sage', from which this book takes its title, was published in the magazine *Planet* in 1973.[51] Tripp goes to visit a sage in west Wales, within sight of Caldey Island off the town of Tenby, in order to put to him a question about the meaning of life. It is more casual than planned as Tripp is 'doing a travel piece for a magazine'. Perhaps this was based on the travel piece 'At the Rainbow's End' from two years before[52] when he had been disappointed by a modern Tenby of day-trippers and its shops full of tat; but also by the worst of the denizens, that 'lost platoon of empire loyalists clinging to the pathetic shreds of the wreck of Victorian values – the lace-and-gingham world of yesterday before everything blew up in the trenches. A world where everything was ordered, people knew their exact station and the morning breakfast gong preceded the kidneys and bacon under silver covers.' He is delighted to be replenished at 'a mock-Tudor cellar above the South beach' where 'to cheer myself up' he

27

enjoys 'snails, French onion soup, roast Lincolnshire duckling in orange sauce flavoured with Cointreau, creme caramel and fresh farm cream, Turkish coffee and good Burgundy'. Tenby was important to John: in an earlier poem he wistfully watched 'The Children at Tenby' build sandcastles, 'doomed medieval mounds' which 'soon the sea will come to smash'. The innocence and persistence of the 'hopeful engineers' cannot quite carry the portentous significance of the poem, but there is surely something of the Sage and the Sandeman Port Man about the philosophising Tripp:

> and every summer tomorrow they will build
> as they have done through the seasons at Tenby.

> As they have done through all the seasons at Tenby...

Of course, that is the meaning of life: to persist; to taste life, to ingest it as food, experience, language, warm bodies.[53] John Tripp knows that better than the Sage, who is glued to his Westerns on television and is served in his armchair by his cowed wife. In both the story and the poem derived from it,[54] the man of wisdom sitting under his 'three china ducks froze on the wall' not only fails to give an answer, he can only respond with an absurd, or absurdist, retort: 'What's the meaning of apricot sponge?' (this is shouted in upper case in the poem). In the poem Tripp is served with 'stew, Yorkshire pudding, and apricot sponge', but in the story they have 'oxtail soup, a big mixed grill with kidneys and mushrooms, an excellent apricot sponge soaked in sherry, followed by Gaelic coffee stiff with whisky and cream, and two bottles of cheap but potent Portuguese rosé'. Food is always an important signifier for John Tripp; it helps to locate a character's mood and social class, their spiritual health, perhaps. He also delights in descriptions of food and drink; he tastes the effects of language. Whenever possible, Tripp records meals that are far from 'sustaining if somewhat frugal'.

The Cistercian monks on Caldey Island are more pronounced seekers of truth and Tripp delights in discovering that they do not take parsimony to extremes. 'Somebody told me they lived only on potatoes, parsnips, swedes and cabbage while they meditated and made their perfume. But a local greengrocer who supplied them denied this and said the brothers lived well on red meat and plenty of fruit.' In both poem and story versions of the Apricot Sponge, John Tripp is examining his role as a writer and seeker for truth. The story is the more rounded, situated piece and in distilling the later poem, he has sacrificed much that was there to be savoured in the story's language and imagery.

His short autobiographical piece 'A Midsummer in

Treslothan'[55] relates a visit back to the relatives in Cornwall. In his grandmother's kitchen 'on the black polished range crouched a simmering stockpot that nourished itself round the clock'; 'the smell of fried bacon floated to the nostril, sizzling in the huge family pan'. There are 'jugs of cider... hunks of cheese and fresh radish... big beef pasties packed with swede... the almond smell of strips of pastry, with jam and yellow crusted cream'. This celebration of an abundance of food and hospitality contrasts with his solitary bacon sandwich in the late Bridgend poem:

> At last my bacon sandwich is done;
> it was something to look forward to,
> slicing a minute's delight into the murk.

And bacon has the significance for Tripp of Proust's madeleine biscuit. It is also a social indicator. The 'haughty crone' in the tea-shop in his story 'A Visit to Miss Quilp' utters the words 'bacon sandwich... as if they were held in a pair of tongs'. And in 'Waste at Astey's', the first poem from the sequence 'Life under Thatcher', that grim depiction of the city of Cardiff in a seventies economic freefall, he says,

> I live in a country
> like the crummy kitchen
> behind a posh restaurant,

the cockroaches the customers
never see.
> Something festers here,
> a bowl of cherries
> where the rainbow ends. [56]

In the time of the miners' strike the valleys people he meets say

they were fuelled
on chips, baked beans, sardines,
corned beef, apples and Pro-plus pills.

At a roadhouse an 'old man asks for free burnt crackling / off the cold pork, and is refused'. At a poetry gig in The Golden Cross pub he is 'surrounded by paintings of oxtail soup / and lumps of meat out of [Francis] Bacon'. Tripp hates 'the encroachment of the Wimpey empire.'[57] In the accelerating commercialisation of the seventies and eighties he holds to the importance of the poet: 'the writing of poetry is as important today as it ever was, perhaps more so in a brittle, materialistic, fish-finger time'.[58]

In several of his unpublished later poems John has what we call now a green agenda: in 'Battlefield' (which has the scored-out titles 'Scars' and 'The price') he records a post-industrial scene:

... a machine-shop
with broken neon flickering,
an oildrum floating in a pool
its rainbow slick spreading on top...

All the scars of enterprise abandoned.[59]

At Dowlais he finds 'this enormous sadness' where once there was 'green order'. In the prose-poem 'Gwaelod-y-Garth' the hill that became a mountain in a later film looms over the site of Paul Tripp's forge. But now there is the M4 to the south, 'Ivy clutches a crumbled wall; frail stone skeleton of barn or outhouse; charred door. Distant occupation. Generations of family. Thin smoke spirals from a last chimney.' The poet realises that on this hill he is above the 'turbulence' which blows elsewhere and he has the beginnings of a Romantic insight: 'For a moment, I gaze at the green pleasing surface of things.'

He attends a 'Barbeque, Pentyrch' organised by the Welsh nationalists 'raising funds for their hectic cause'. There 'A fat lamb / turns on the skewer, / reminding us of roasted martyrs'. Despite the confusion of causes and the faint absurdity of such an event – 'A small detachment of tories arrive / like cavalry among the Cheyenne' – again the poet feels an essential goodness in the village, something worth fighting for:

The unmown grass waves on the lawn
above this silent, shuttered village
cupped snugly in the low hills –
safe for a day from the pickaxe
and piledriver – one small community
                                        Under the stars.

He is proud of the 'Trust' which preserves rural Wales
against 'the black explorers', and whose efforts in
protecting the countryside and wildlife ensure the 'the
swallow's swoop, swift's flick... through emerald
dawns and country dusk'. This is the naturalist side
of the louche city boozer, the man who was the boy
who saw

a kingfisher dive like a blue-green streak
clean through the water and out again
with lunch in its beak, then glide
to its fish-boned hole in the bank.

at his father's 'Walnut Tree Forge'.[60]

Just as the Sage in Pembrokeshire was glued to his
telly, so was John Tripp when he was at home in
Whitchurch, for his television column in *Arcade*
magazine ran for the length of that magazine and gave
John a sounding board once a fortnight for almost two
years. He wrote: 'Most people are waiting for
something wonderful and significant to happen in

their lives: love, money, happiness, success, even fame. The rest of us watch television.'[61]

This was the period of that doyen of TV critics Clive James, whose column was the first thing one flicked through to read in the *Observer* every Sunday. Sharing one's responses to a television service that was itself shared by a large section of the population provided a real opportunity to affect opinion and create cultural debate; now that is impossible since digitalisation and the vast multiplication of channels.[62] John Tripp's *Arcade* column has the same barbed wit and serious commitment to the debate about Wales as much of his other writings. He is fulsome in his praise of Wales-produced programmes such as BBC Wales's *Grand Slam* – 'that classic Paris weekend rugby romp from Gwenlyn Parry and John Hefin which could be repeated every year for the next 10' – but, John, it was, it was.[63] And *The Life and Times of Lloyd George*, written by Elaine Morgan and in which Philip Madoc was 'excellent'. Lloyd George was 'more philanderer than philosopher, a force of nature rather than a patient pragmatist'. He was 'like something out of Caradoc Evans – the cloak of convention covering the morality of a hot tomcat'.[64]

John admires the professional polish of Vincent Kane and David Parry Jones and clearly lusts after Eiry Palfrey – 'She looks as if she'd like to ask you in to see her etchings.'[65] Still, he was more often outside of this charmed circle of media stars: 'I've pressed my nose more than once against the windows of the pricey Gibson's and Harvesters restaurants in Cardiff and watched the fat cats of Welsh TV (both channels) gorging themselves on snails, pigeon pie and apricot sponge, washed down with Portuguese rosé, Cordon Bleu cognac and Cointreau. Maybe that very day they have produced more telly garbage for the people, and they know it, but any sliver of conscience or responsibility ends the moment their mouths close on the flavour of succulent wood pigeon. By the time they've reached the brandy, who cares?'[66]

In one rare critical response to the fiction of John Tripp, Karen Worthy in *The Anglo-Welsh Review*[67] reviewed *The Thinskin Award* and pronounced that 'Tripp's vision is an ironically bleak one, but he strikes a true note in his implicit appeal against idealism and romanticism. While his work is marred by rather silly attempts to draw sex into the narrative at every possible opportunity, if this were eliminated he could concentrate on developing his lucid and at times very witty prose into a more coherent and stimulating form.'

That was in 1978 when I had published four stories by John Tripp: I had run in a rather naive, half-hearted way a small press called Edge Press and John's was the sixth, and final, pamphlet in the series.[68] *The Thinskin Award* included 'Dic Tidy's Mistake', 'A Surprise

35

Ending' and 'A Visit to Miss Quilp', as well as the title story. The impulse behind Edge Press was a general frustration at the limited outlets for new fiction in Wales.[69] John shared that feeling and was pleased to contribute four unpublished stories; stories which he felt would not have found a home elsewhere because of their explicitly sexual subject-matter and language. Certainly, we both thought they were risqué by the standards of the day. They are, admittedly, far from completely successful, but at that time, and even thirty years on, I recognise in them Tripp's typical moments of satire and turns of wit.

In the title story a perennially unsuccessful playwright called Carmarthen Thomas finds that he has been shortlisted for the Thinskin Award, 'worth £500 and a trip to the States'. Not deemed important enough to be invited to dine at the Napoleon or the Caprice, Thomas joins Duckham the impresario and Stacy, his lieutenant – 'two PR sharks' – at the modest Asti's restaurant.[70] Even this proves to be a treat – a pork chop washed down by a Chateaubriand which 'tastes like sheep-dip' – to Thomas, who exists on a diet of 'soup, bread, potatoes, sardines, Marmite, Bovril and tea'.

Thomas comes from the same stock of characters as 'Deadwood Jones' and in such no-hopers John Tripp is expressing his disdain for the cultural and literary elite who judge scribblers such as he, but also his association with the writer as unrecognised outcast. Carmarthen Thomas is a hopeless case: 'A man who could write a five-hour epic about Oliver Cromwell with a cast of a hundred, and who had asked for Olivier or Burton to play the lead, must be either a genius or a lunatic.' Nevertheless, Tripp has a grudging admiration for the man's chutzpah.

In 'Dic Tidy's Mistake' Dic, who runs an inherited printing and stationery business, is cuckolded by a Wife of Bath woman known only as 'the cow'. Dic 'was called Tidy because his face was pink (some said from the gin) and soft, and he was always sprucely dressed, favouring pricey Donegal tweeds that he'd kept smart for many years, check Viyella shirts and wool ties, a gold Hunter in his waistcoat pocket, good Clarks brown boots, and sometimes sporting a plaid deerstalker with a red ribbon tying the ear-flaps.' I recall that John Tripp himself took to wearing a deer-stalker at times. Dic also had 'another concession to vanity' – the 'dyeing of his grey hair with Tunisian henna – which led some unkind villagers to suspect, mistakenly, that he was a queer'. Where John Tripp is usually content to characterise a person by some item of dress, behaviour or meal, Dic Tidy is the most fully described fictional character, albeit in a slight piece of fiction, and exemplifies Tripp's strategy of using food and dress to establish a character.

'A Surprise Ending' relates the narrator's brief affair

with the Irishwoman whose love-making was 'a bit frigid' and whose cooking was 'tragic... if we ate in her flat, it was usually a sort of sad, tasteless hamburger thing floating in a pink sauce, followed by prunes or orange jelly, though now and again we had nice raspberry almond slices'. The poor sex, if not the cooking, is shortly explained by the Tripp/narrator's coming unannounced across her engaged with a 'nest of lesbians' in her flat. He is traumatised and lives on through years of 'bungled, unsatisfactory affairs' and solitude.

The fourth and final story, 'A Visit to Miss Quilp', has the Tripp/narrator visiting a faded poetess who lives near Tintern Abbey. He overcomes his disappointment at being unable to buy a bacon sandwich at the 'café-cum-craft-shop' – 'We only serve home-made cream teas at this time of day' – and enjoys with Miss Quilp 'a bowl of watery soup produced, she said, during the making of an Irish stew; then a sliced raw onion and radish with running liquid Camembert nicely on the turn, and a Hovis crust, followed by a piece of cherry tart and a mug of milk'. Then, to the accompaniment of some 'great fast Vivaldi' and most of a bottle of Hine brandy, two stiff ones poured into balloon glasses, he enjoys Miss Quilp herself, who changes from 'a solitary, forgotten poetess of 50 to a ravishing sex-object of 30 before my eyes'.

Of course, it's probably partly autobiographical and

partly a middle-aged male fantasy. Miss Quilp has the last word: 'After all, one writes poems to give a little pleasure, fundamentally, don't you think?' Tripp is signing off this little stapled sampler with a wink; though the point is, characteristically, a serious one. John Tripp used to refer to his performance pieces as 'squibs' – short and packing a quick punch. *The Thinskin Award* stories are in that vein. Sometimes, overwhelmed by the complexity of life, politics, sexual relationships, the speed of the modern world, John Tripp fired off these short sharp volleys at the stagecoach that was leaving him behind.

Some years after *The Thinskin Award* John and I talked about publishing a sequence of poems he'd written over a decade before as a one-off pamphlet from a briefly resurrected Edge Press. Intervals of Heat is a group of sixteen poems concerning sex.[71] As John said in his putative foreword:

> Some of these poems and prose-poems were written to see how far one could go in accurate, acceptable description of the sexual act, plus its peripheral concerns. They are also partly dedicated to the notion that sex can be fun, with numerous delights in store for the inventive and the experimental. I was interested in the *technical* details of intercourse – that ancient and difficult craft to reach a simultaneous orgasm or unilateral female satisfaction, which places a heavy

responsibility upon men, even when they are fortunate enough to be cherished by patient women. Therefore the seemingly frivolous attitude of the male performer in these pieces (and he is no chauvinist pig) is basically serious. I hope women readers will enjoy them, too, and remember that it takes two to tango.

In writing them I also tried to make up a fresh vocabulary of description in order to pull away from the stale, tedious usage of the cheap novelette, the tavern and the barrack-room.

Tripp's language and argument here is central to understanding his attitude to sex. Remember, this was after sex had been invented 'in 1963, between the Chatterley trial and the Beatles' first LP'.[72] Larkin goes on to say, 'alas, too late for me'. Well, John Tripp was determined that was not to be *his* epitaph.[73] Larkin in poems such as 'Sunny Prestatyn'[74] and 'Be This the Verse'[75] had broken through any remaining barriers of language and taste. It was Larkin, close to being made Poet Laureate at the end of his life, who said 'They fuck you up, your mum and dad', not John Tripp: in fact John Tripp deliberately avoids using the word 'fuck' in these poems. He prefers the verb 'to Roger'; his sexual organ is a 'sword', a 'ramper', 'my tom'; the woman's is 'her door', her 'slit', 'her warm covered queen'.

Determined to be taken seriously in this writing

about sex, he intended the following as epigrams to the pamphlet:

'It was only a brief coupling, an act so insignificant that it's difficult to see how the large concepts of pleasure and sin could ever be associated with it.'

        – Simone de Beauvoir

'Sex is something I really don't understand too hot. You never know *where* the hell you are. I keep making up these sex rules for myself, and then I break them right away.'

        – J. D. Salinger, *The Catcher in the Rye*

'Men's instincts are gross; women are in demand and always will be.'

        – Margo St James, head hooker of US
        prostitutes' organisation COYOTE
        (Call Off Your Old Tired Ethics)

'No sex without responsibility.'

        – Lord Longford

It is clear that John Tripp wanted these works and their potential publication to be taken seriously. He is at pains to balance the seriousness of the issues involved in sexual relations with the undeniable pleasures involved.[76] And those pleasures need to be recognised as implicated, if not strengthened, by the

41

guilt felt in sexual conduct and the potentially serious social and personal repercussions of the act.

However, it is a difficult tightrope to walk and the contents list of *Intervals of Heat* immediately complicates and undercuts those serious intentions, for here is a litany of naughtiness:

Sandbowl Thrusts
Conceit of Power
Military Ram
West Turret Lay
Grubb's Complaint
Angel in Cardiff
Acefinger
Jane Russell at the Old Beeb
Centrefold
Zip
Dalliance at Tinkinswood
The Cats of Palma
Diolch, Hector Fellatio
Reversal at Freshwater East
Horizontal Shuttlecock
Dream of Lush Ladies

That has the wit and humour of a Peter Finch found-poem-list. As do the acknowledgements he gives, for some of these poems, he claims, were first published in *Paradise*, *Red*, *Michigan Runner*, *Screwdriver*, *Knave*, *Madog*, *Cosmopolitan* and *Experience*. Well, at least *Madog* was correct, for I published John in that short-lived magazine based at the Polytechnic of Wales. No other poems from *Intervals of Heat* were published in Wales, I think.

Judging these *Intervals of Heat* is as problematic as judging much of his other work. There is the sense of speed, the journalist's snapshot impressions. There is the rough and ready, or not so ready, form or roughed up shape.[77] The easy image and metaphor occur alongside glints of impressive originality.

'The Diesel to Yesterday' was still the train that John Tripp rode. There is a steady yearning for lost times, forgotten manners and customs and yet, at the same time, a willingness to gaze benevolently out from his carriage at the liberation of language, the freer expression of sexual mores and the liberation of women. The poet's two love affairs as a mature man back in Wales seem to be characterised by genuine feelings and a healthy sense of equality. 'The gnarled bard'[78] was never to find solace in marriage or a settled home, there had been neither the time nor the opportunity for children, but he was, it appears, a sexually liberated romantic.

Of 'Mrs Pankhurst's granddaughter', who is 'a sex grenade hurled out of the dust / of Victorian diaries', he asks, 'Where have you been hiding for centuries?' and notes that 'She has wiped out... playing second fiddle to men'.[79] He is also disarmingly honest about

43

the dangers of a self-deluding man inadvertently playing in 'a good Thurber-style tragicomedy based on the male "change of life" syndrome where the literate, passionate antihero, on his way to meet the devastating cleavage or micro-skirt, slips on a banana skin and chips a disc'.[80]

In *Intervals of Heat* and in other works, it is clear that Tripp's sexual interests were by no means predatory; he sees sex as a game between equals. He is embellishing memories, no doubt, but is also anxious to celebrate his sexual history. The callow youth who was pulled away from the clutches of the prostitute by his knowing Redcap in the late 1940s was escaping a woman 'used and misused again / by troops awash with booze'; she was 'history's doxy', a 'Poor lady / abused to the end'.[81] The Colonel's stepdaughter who becomes a prostitute in London and whose top stair creaks as Tripp enters is a victim of abuse, incest, it is rumoured. Hers has been 'a passage of rumpled sheets'. He is aroused, then ashamed and angered by the situation.

Even in the earlier years as a journalist in London he realised

What animals we were
even inside our town suits
through this interval of intense heat.[82]

44

And he follows the poem in the typed manuscript with an explanation of this assignment as a freelance writer for *Truth* magazine to cover the visit of an American *Playboy* cover-girl: 'we praised the girls even if we mocked the tinsel world they were part of. There was no cynicism in our responses to these remarkable beauties, who had to be seen to be believed, who invariably left us stunned.'

In 'Zip' from *Intervals of Heat* he describes with some relish the predilections of 'some kinks' but there is something less than prurient, something refreshingly honest about his own celebration of 'the unzipping of a woman's boot'.

> But me? Give me the ripping sound
> Of little bits of knitted steel
> Grooving like lightning down a boot
> Through soft and flexible leather.

And after a boring shift of night duty at 'the Old Beeb' he remembers seeing 'The remarkable California sexbomb' Jane Russell walking through the foyer to her waiting car,

> a long black Cadillac
> with coachwork by Vega of Madrid
> that would reach the Savoy within minutes.

> Stunned at the entire gorgeous marvel
> I remember my shades slid to the tip of my nose
> and something moved inside my trouser.[83]

Surely, that is more Leslie Phillips's 'Oh, I say!' than prurience. She was a remarkable woman and John Tripp celebrates her and details the glitz of that American-International lifestyle. In 'Conceit of Power' Tripp fails to follow through with sex after succeeding in inviting a beautiful Irish woman back to his 'loft / at the dead end of town'.

> Try as I might
> the bad roger wouldn't rise.
> She groaned and lit up a Benson,
> dropped back into her shift
> and kissed the culprit.
>
> ... leaving
> a red-faced spoiler frowning,
> much humbler with his power gone.[84]

The poet is a player in the oldest game, but it is a level playing field and he catalogues his failings as well as his successes. It is so from the beginnings in his National Service days:

> The best looking cook I ever saw,
> she met me at the back of her kitchen

after Lights Out, and we had it there
against a brick wall. She was gifted
in her method, helping a young soldier
to pass his apprenticeship...[85]

Indeed, in all the poems from the *Intervals of Heat* sequence John Tripp is at least as much sinned against as sinning: and he delights in it. After a 'West Turret lay' he asks:

- Are you OK, Rachel?
- What do you think?
We buttoned, smoothed, combed and tidied
then ran to beat the clock and keepers
before the gates shut. If this
was being wanton, wayward and reckless
we liked it.

Life's risks and the writer's scribbles are both ploys to 'beat the clocks and keepers before the gates shut'. That is what John Tripp's two encounters with Sandeman Port man, written decades apart, impress upon him. On the second occasion, on Tripp's forty-third birthday, Old Sandeman 'had a Mini outside, a portable Japanese / television set and two blondes'. The poet, though his mouth is 'an obsolete old Bren gun' has 'covered many lines / with perishable verse, two weddings / three funerals, four friendships / and the love of my life'. This time Sandeman creeps 'backwards through the door, muttering, clutching his apparatus of frivolity'. Tripp says, 'Oddly enough, I felt sorry for him.'[86] And that indicates a degree of confidence, a sense that the writer has been working to some purpose. In what was to be his final commentary John Tripp looked back at his work and the core of its purpose: 'I wanted, ideally, in my poems to create a terse, epigrammatic commentary on the Wales of today, its ramshackle beauty and sadness, its cultural and political predicament, its pride.'[87] He certainly did that and, as I hope to have shown, he did more, reflecting on public and personal lives in the post-war years, the place of the individual in a post-industrial society and the stress and joys between men and women. He wrote, 'A poet's delight and sadness / must be feminine'.[88]

John Tripp was a writer of energy but variable quality and control; few of his contemporaries are not subject to a similar judgement. Both strengths and limitations are as exhibited in his uncollected and unpublished prose and poetry as they are in the published writings. And I have, I trust, offered in this collection a range sufficient to recognise and celebrate that writer who 'walked the tightrope', as Peter Finch says. John may never have determined the meaning of apricot sponge, but he relished the taste. Perhaps he would have welcomed his judgement of Geoffrey Grigson[89] as an epitaph for himself and his own work:

Mark him, young poets in the city.
He has much to teach, against the clock,
packing beauty into the murk.

Notes

[1] All poems quoted are collected in *John Tripp – Selected Poems* edited by John Ormond, (Bridgend, Seren, 1989) *SP* unless otherwise indicated; or *Collected Poems 1958-78* (Swansea, Christopher Davies, 1978) *CP*.
[2] There is clearly more work to be done on this writer. This present volume is annotated within the bounds of the publishing brief and to the best of my ability at this time. It will be for others to build on what I and Nigel Jenkins in his Writers of Wales book have done and then to conduct a more exhaustive study of John Tripp – his work and his significance in his period. My hope is that this book will encourage others in the field.

[3] See also the notes to accompany "Seeds of Dismemberment" in this present book. In the early 1970s JT had ambitions to be a playwright.

[4] See "Farewell to a Shambles" for this and other details of his National Service in *Planet* 28, August, 1975.

[5] "Lloyd George" *The Loss of Ancestry* (Llandybie, Christopher Davies, 1969).

[6] "Is There Still Honey for Tea?" *Passing Through* (Bridgend, Poetry Wales Press, 1984).

[7] "Lakeside" from *Bute Park and other Poems* (Cardiff, Second Aeon, 1971).

[8] "A David Jones Mural at Llanthony" *SP* p.97.

[9] Nigel Jenkins has done research into the myths and facts of John Tripp's education, particularly the Morley College years. See *John Tripp* in the Writers of Wales series, (Cardiff, UWP, 1989) pp.23-28.

[10] The poem was called "My lean eighteenth year".

[11] This and other early details are confirmed by the unpublished beginnings of a biography written (with corroboration from John Tripp) by Fay Williams (Cornes), his companion in the early days after his return to Wales in 1969, a copy of which she kindly sent to me. Fay adds: He was trying to encourage me to write and he thought a good starting point would be a biography. He even gave me a little notebook on which he wrote: "For use only to recount anecdotes and to write little intimate portraits of writers, etc.".

[12] From "Indonesian Interlude" in *Planet* 22.

[13] *Passing Through*.

[14] *Planet* 34.

[15] From "Who's In, Who's Out" a poem from the Fay Cornes

(Fay Williams) collection of mss shared with the present author in 2008.

[16] "The Last at Lucy's", a poem never collected, but published in *Welsh Voices – an anthology of New Welsh Poetry* ed. Bryn Griffiths (London, Dent, 1967).

[17] "Geoffrey Grigson at the Purcell Room" in *The Inheritance File* (Cardiff, Second Aeon, 1973).

[18] From the poem "Nash Point" in the Cornes collection of mss.

[19] John Stuart Williams's introduction to *Diesel to Yesterday* (Cardiff, Triskel Press, 1966).

[20] *An Anthology of Anglo-Welsh Poetry 1917-67* published by Dent in 1969 with an introduction by Raymond Garlick.

[21] There were further "Dial-a-Poem" recordings: January 8, 1971 (499 calls) – "Bard of Winter (in memory: for R. Williams-Parry)" (*Anglo-Welsh Review* Autumn '71, Vol.20, no.45) and *Poems '72* ed. John Ackerman, Gwasg Gomer, Llandysul); and 7 December, 1973 when John read "Otter". In addition, it should be noted that JT made other recordings: 1972 "Dial-a-Poem" (Wren Records).

Side 1: John Tripp ("Elegy for England"), Tom Early, Sam Adams

Side 2: Gwyn Williams, Gillian Clarke, J.P. Ward.

Other JT recordings include the 1975 LP - "Poets of Wales" Argo Records (the Decca Record Company Ltd) recorded on behalf of the Welsh Arts Council in association with the British Council.

Side 1: Gwyn Williams, Glyn Jones, Roland Mathias

Side 2: Emyr Humphreys, Harri Webb, John Tripp ("Lincoln 1301", "On my Fortieth Birthday", "Soliloquy"), Gillian Clarke.

[22] Tripp had met her at a "Dial-a-Poem" recording with John Ormond in the January of 1970. (Confirmation of several personal details regarding this period have been supplied by Fay Cornes (nee Williams) in telephone conversations and correspondences with the author in 2008).

[23] Fay Cornes writes: "I was still living at home with my parents when John and I met but, in January 1972, I bought a flat in Curlew Close, Whitchurch, which was just off Manor Way. Obviously, John often stayed the night and enjoyed using the flat when I was at work if he wanted some peace and quiet to write. But apart from a toothbrush and the odd item of clothing, he did not move in and I never asked him to! At that time we both liked our independence despite being madly in love. In any case, I do not think he would have wanted to leave his father on his own. By the way, he often used to write letters to the *Western Mail* and *South Wales Echo* from Lloyd Llewellyn, Curlew Close, Whitchurch."

[24] See "Viriamu Jones Slept Here" in *Planet* 20. I think that the title was suggested by the John L. Hughes novel *Tom Jones Slept Here* which he had previously reviewed in *The Anglo-Welsh Review* Vol.21. No.47, 1972. See also "Folly before midnight" in *PT* – "They tucked us away in a late/late slot: after the clowns/and before the weather forecast." JT appeared in this programme in 1973 and began presenting it the following year.

[25] "Pontypridd Wedding" from *The Province of Belief* (Llandysul, Christopher Davies, 1971).

[26] For this and many more insights and information I am, of course, indebted to Nigel Jenkins's excellent volume on John

Tripp in the Writers of Wales series (Cardiff, University of Wales Press, 1989).

[27] See also "Breaking the Past" *PT* – I knew I was tired/of the Past, that great/haunting – and guilty/because I was tired."

[28] "The Governors" in *TLA*.

[29] Writing in Poetry Wales (quoted by Nigel Jenkins p.56).

[30] *Poetry Wales* 15, Spring, 1980.

[31] In the interview from *Common Ground* ed. Susan Butler (Bridgend, Poetry Wales Press, 1985).

[32] "Outsider?" from *TLA*.

[33] C.f. "The English at the Eisteddfod" in *Planet* 18/19. Also, my chapter "Grafting the Sour to Sweetness: Anglo-Welsh Poetry in the last twenty-five years" in *Wales: the imagined nation* ed. Curtis, (Bridgend, Poetry Wales Press, 1986).

[34] *Common Ground* p.191.

[35] In Nigel Jenkins p.100.

[36] In *The Anglo-Welsh Review* No.79, 1985.

[37] *The Anglo-Welsh Review* Vol.18 No.42, 1970.

[38] In "Night with the English Society" the poet feels that he had failed to connect with the undergraduates at Aberystwyth: "They were so solomn and sad/that nothing would do but my grey head/sacrificial on a platter, my screwed/mind and mushy hearty offered up in woe/from some solipsist room." Cornes collection.

[39] From *Preparations* (Llandysul, Christopher Davies, 1980).

[40] Quote from his childhood friend Peter Owen (to Nigel Jenkins – in *NJ*).

[41] "Pantmawr" *SP* p.72.

[42] "H.M.S. Cassandra" in the selection *Considering Cassandra* (Llanrwst, Gwasg Garreg Gwalch, 2003). That incident aboard the naval frigate in Fishguard harbour informs John's poem "Defence of the West" in *SP* pp.93-4.

[43] From my poem "Thoughts from the Holiday Inn" first published in *The Last Candles* (Bridgend, Seren, 1989).

[44] Jean Henderson in *Planet* 56, 1986.

[45] It is interesting to note the significance of Valentine's Day. Fay Cornes confirms that, "John was the most romantic man I'd met."

[46] Ibid.

[47] "Thoughts at Llandaff" from *TPB*.

[48] See of course Nigel Jenkins and also a more recent survey by Patrick McGuinness in *The New Welsh Review* No.68, 2005 "Poetry at the Checkpoint".

[49] All published in *Planet* – numbers 39, 30, 43, 36, 49/50.

[50] As Jermey Hooker characterises him in his review of *CP* in *The Anglo-Welsh Review* No.65, 1979.

[51] *Planet* 15, January, 1973.

[52] *Planet* 5/6, Summer, 1971.

[53] Even his final companion Jean Henderson does this in her account of their last day together when "He had mulligatawny soup and a roll, and myself fish and chips, most of the chips filched for a golden retriever and a tabby cat he welcomed extravagantly and who joined us at the fireside to make an instant family." from "Tripp's Last Day" in *Planet* 56, 1986.

[54] *CP* p.126.

[55] *The Anglo-Welsh Review* Autumn 1973, Vol.22 No.50.

[56] From *Selected Poems* pp180-189.

[57] From "Casualty" a short story from *Planet* 17.

[58] "Round the Poets" a review article in *Planet* 16.

[59] These poems were in the possession of Jean Henderson who kindly gave me copies. It is probable that John Ormond read and rejected these for the *SP*.

[60] P.151 *SP*.

[61] *Arcade* 10 – 20th March, 1981.

[62] John Tripp would have been delighted at the success of Jaci Stephen, who he knew as a young writer in Cardiff, in this work and dismayed by the abrupt ending of her *Daily Mail* column; the digitalisation point being cited as the reason for deeming the role of the TV critic redundant.

[63] *Arcade* 11 – 3rd April, 1981.

[64] *Arcade* 12 – 17th April, 1981.

[65] *Arcade* 5 – 5th January 1981.

[66] *Arcade* 11 – 3rd April, 1981.

[67] *Anglo-Welsh Review* No.63, 1978.

[68] The others had been by Alan Perry, Madeline Mayne, Mike Jenkins, a prose-poem sequence of my own called "Out of the dark Wood" and, most remarkably it seems now, Charles Simic's first British publication.

[69] Tripp published three stories in Sally Jones's Alun Books series in the following year: "Last Day in England" (Port Talbot, Alun Books, 1979). The two other than the title story – "No Peace for Dando" and "Go Home Davy Tuck" – were collected in *Pieces of Eight* ed. Robert Nisbet (Llandysul, Gomer, 1982)

[70] There's an echo of Astey's in the "Life under Thatcher" sequence. Both pieces may date from the 1970s.

[71] I had included one of these in an issue of *Madog* magazine which I'd founded and edited, published by the new Polytechnic of Wales.

[72] Philip Larkin's poem is still often quoted as a key text in understanding both the poet himself and the mores of the 1970s.

[73] Copies of the poems and the accompanying notes are all in the possession of the present author.

[74] Published in *The Whitsun Weddings* (London, Faber, 1964).

[75] From *High Windows* (London, Faber, 1974).

[76] JT's handwritten note to me reads: "Dear Tony, Herewith *Intervals of Heat* – extended slightly revised version, with insertions and deletions but still OUTRAGEOUS. Good. If, when the time comes, you make a beautiful job of it I'll buy you a bottle of Campari. Best, John – Please acknowledge receipt." The bottle of Campari refers to our adventure aboard the frigate in Fishguard harbour: see my story "H.M.S. Cassandra" in *Considering Cassandra* (Llanrwst, Gwasg Carreg Gwalch, 2003).

[77] Interestingly, in his review of J.P. Ward's Second Aeon pamphlet *from alphabet to logos* he castigates Ward's experimentations with form and concrete, games-playing poetry, arguing that Ward should stay in, "the traditional trench without going over the top towards the rattle of experimental machine-guns. ... Come home, come home, John Ward, to the good old-fashioned stanza! Language and poetry need you!" *AWR* Vol.24. No.52, 1974.

[78] "The gnarled bard undergoes fame" *CP* p.83.

[79] "Mrs Pankhurst's granddaughter" from *PT*.

[80] "The way the Biscuit Crumbles" from *Planet* 26/27, 1975.

[81] "Lady of Devizes" from *For King and Country* (Swansea, Swansea Poetry Workshop, 1980).

[82] "Centrefold" from the unpublished *Intervals of Heat* manuscript, undated.

[83] "Jane Russell at the Old Beeb" from *IH*.

[84] There is a very explicit poem about oral sex and menstruation in the *NLW* mss collection – "Red Date in Solva".

[85] "Military Ram" from *IH*.

[86] "The Return of Old Sandeman" *SP*.

[87] *Common Ground*.

[88] From "Writer in Schools", a poem in the Cornes collection.

[89] From *IF*.

Farewell to a Shambles

A Selection of Autobiographical Writings

Midsummer in Treslothan

In my grandmother's kitchen at Lower Farm there was a dip in the stone flags, the floor rose and fell at intervals. Slabs of fat pig hung salted on hooks from the ceiling above sackfuls of leek; on the black polished range crouched a simmering stockpot that nourished itself round the clock.

On a crisp Cornish morning on the farm, between Redruth and the sea, the smell of fried bacon floated to the nostril, sizzling in the huge family pan. I would wake in the dormer room, as basic as a puppy, to the delight of that smell, drop quickly into my cords and vault down the ten worn steps to five home-cured rashers on a plate, with fried bread. Eight would sit at table, and sometimes twelve, if the four hands borrowed from neighbouring farms were there for the sowing or harvesting. If June was warm, and it usually was, each part of the land was exciting and busy, and appetites were up. I'd take jugs of cider out into the fields, with hunks of cheese and fresh radish, for the uncles and their friends. The wide crops were waving, when a breeze came, like the long golden mane of a hundred palaminos. No corn was as ripe as the corn on Lower.

After we returned from morning service at

Treslothan church on a Sunday, the farm filled with the waft of baking bread. (Contrary to popular belief, even the most religious farms in the Godfearing West did not rest on the Sabbath.) My small Granny, squinting through her half-lens spectacles perilously brinked on the end of her nose, slid the loaves on a steel scoop out of the oven. I used to watch her, bringing the same patience to baking bread and feeding her brood as she brought to the ironing-board, with the steam off the hissing flat reeking of good flannel as she unpicked the stray tifflins* in fading light from the dairy window. The big beef pasties packed with swede burned on a subtle onion whiff to the edge of perfection. In a linen bag, these folded-over slits of pastry, running with vegetable juices pulled from the allotments of Beacon, would be snapped by my young hungry fangs. The delight when one's teeth closed over a pasty, and started chewing, was almost indescribable.

One of my uncles, Matthew, left the farm to be apprenticed to a bookbinder in Truro, where he soon distinguished himself as a layer of gold leaf and fancy trimmings on valuable books. I used to visit him in his neat, narrow little Georgian house in a back street of the cathedral town. He was a middle-aged bachelor by now, but still loved to dress up in fine peacock clothes.

* South Cornish dialect: ends of cotton-thread.

His mother, my grandmother, would pretend to faint when she saw his latest purchases from the best shops in Truro or Plymouth. I remember one superb outfit he wore – a raspberry-sherbet-coloured blazer, of dramatic and unprecedented flair, and well ahead of its time. It had a belted back, brass buttons, box-pleated scalloped patch-pockets and deep centre venting. With this he had biscuit cord breeches, calf-length brown leather laced-up boots, fawn waistcoat, a ruby pin in his pink cravat, and on top of the entire show he sported a subtle-check deerstalker with a red ribbon tying the earflaps. The whole ensemble was his tailored ideal which he had been seeking over a number of years, and now he had found it in a smart new haberdasher's. He spent most of his spare cash on good clothes. It was his one indulgence, a quirk which his mother never quite understood. He was considered slightly odd by the other brothers, despite his nimble skills, but as time went by this reference took on a rough burnish of affection.

Sometimes he let me come with him to the back of Amos Jennings's grocery shop, to that part of the premises reserved for the consumption of liquid refreshment. Here he drank cider and chatted to his cronies, while I drank lemonade and kept quiet. He was a very active, domesticated man, doing all his own cooking and cleaning. He had a keen sense of humour, too, but the fear and boredom of growing old sometimes showed through. His locked-out prowler, scratching at the window, was death. He disliked visiting hospitals or going to funerals, and was fond of telling me to make the most of my youth. I never listened to him, of course.

At home he sat by the wood fire and sucked his old Dunhill briar, thinking. His nose was a gigantic hook, the pride of a family with splendid Roman specimens, seemingly efficient for skewering meat or for putting golf balls. Once he took me upstairs to his working loft to show me his tools. In this cramped place he put 22-carat gold leaf on book covers, using eyebrow-tweezers to pick it from between ricepaper diary leaves, blowing it unwrinkled and cutting with a blunt penknife so as not to hurt it, then rolling it flat on the spine with a little heated wheel held over a spirit flame, and cleaning the strip in benzine until it shone bright in the dim loft. Many fine volumes and folios came under his pampering hand, and he was much in demand by collectors and restorers in Plymouth and Bristol. A full day of this craft, by sunlight or lamp, would bring him downstairs to supper, with Mozart or Schubert on the primitive horn, and then he would have a last pipe of Erinmore before his tired eyes closed.

Occasionally he drove me in his trap back to Treslothan to visit the rest of the family. The hamlet was in a sort of cul-de-sac, a track between laurel which curved onward to the inland dunes, past steep-pitched thatch over the mullioned windows of old cottages. You could hear the sounds of pigeons fluttering and sheep cropping around the stones of the Wesleyan church. Long unmown verges resisted the farm wagons trying to get down there, and the paths were always cleared by scythe and hook. The hedgerows were a rioting clot of parsley and vetch, the wide orchards a burst of pale rose blossom with crab-apples on the green floor, and the dwellings sat squat against the wind off the distant sea. I have never known a place so tucked away from change.

Now, half a lifetime later, I remember above all else the pleasant holiday smells of Cornwall – the oil-wick lamps and the candles guttering in their wax at dusk, carbolic soap in the farm wash-houses, fresh ironed linen, pungent tobacco from pipes and smelling sweet in jars, whiff of pasties and stews, and the almond smell of strips of pastry with jam and yellow crusted cream.

Lost bits of yesterday, when a family was knotted in a love they seldom showed, or mentioned, even at funerals. When the bread was real, and the fat pigs hung salted from the rafters.

Ferret and Weasel

When I was a boy I thought nature was fairly kind, with her woods and fields, cows and sheep, the smell of new-mown hay and fresh dung. This was before I met creatures with vindictive streaks – things like ferrets, and others of that particular filth.

The hob (male) and gill (female) were here when the Romans lived, rampant through the medieval borders, and dying in the roads and lanes if their keepers lost them. They were bred centuries-deep for destruction, trained to hunt vermin that were vermin themselves. They rutted with wild polecats to make two yearly broods of blind and sightless kittens.

The little pink-red eyes, slit with malice, betray their deadly cynical albino stock. They possess no knowledge of love or its power to tame them, and the sexual lives of hob and gill are merely clockwork hunger mountings, coming round like a peasant's supper. All they know are the soft, defenceless bundles which are targeted for rapid squealing death. These they rip, glutted to the eyeballs. Digging out the rabbit-holes, they sometimes find brave bucks who may stand and fight, while the whimpering does are pelting to a quicker death in the steel traps or from the farmer's gun. I saw a ferret, full of rabbit, get up on a tree-stump and bite a feathered mess of bluetit that was swinging from a cake-bag.

My grandfather, a Cornish farmer – an earthy, practical man, decent and unsentimental – kept one pampered in a hutch and fed twice a day on bread-and-butter sops, rabbit and fowl liver. He muzzled the spoilt killer by looping and knotting twine about its snout, or the thing would have bitten a finger off. You can only stop it acting in a terrible manner by pressing a thumb just about the eyes, which can almost put it to sleep and prevent its mad career through the world.

I knew of a farmer's son who clutched one beneath his shirt and next to his skin and sent him into a garage to kill a rat. That rat was big and king of his crowd, but like a sparrow against a hawk, torn within seconds to a crimson shredded strip. Even when the boy had flung his pet in a reinforced aluminium sack, still it was biting, teeth gnashing and jaws working for more taste of the recent turbulence.

Ferrets are long carrion land-eels, they can wriggle through insect spaces to their meat, move like grease, and are worth a pack of Russells. They are equal to the weasel and stoat, their brothers in high stink.

In value the weasel is only a scrap of furrier's pelt, a remnant trimming for a wrap. But he is another gangster from the womb, of extremely bloodthirsty disposition, as vicious as anything in Britain on four legs. Before his carcase is flung on a heap, his rampage through field and stream is a long suck and feed on blood and warm fresh meat. He is nine inches of reddish-brown disaster to rat, mouse, vole and frog. Rooks and crows are nothing to him, and an owl is merely a staid lump in a tree. He will eel up a bush or hedge for thrush and blackbird eggs, and swim about a mile to a pike ruin.

He is a killer for joy of it. He will slaughter a granary of rats and then look around to see if he's missed one, before settling down to his huge supper. His jaws clamp, he takes them at the skull's base, with teeth dug in the brain. Once, in North Wales, a hawk was found with a weasel's skull still locked to its throat. Chased by a fox, he will stop to kill a chicken, for the hell of it, gnawing the head off. I saw one come grunting from a rabbit burrow, mouth dripping, then slide to some mole mounds for more plunder. Packs have been seen to hunt on moonlight nights in the west and Wales, dancing in a crazy scamper behind some terrified hare. Packs have also been known to attack a man. Even single and alone, a weasel will jump for the cuff or throat if he is cornered and sees no exit.

In residence, slum dwellings suit him best: a sheep carcase, hollow rotted tree-stump, hedge-root of crud and dropping, crumbled wall crevice, any abandoned fish-hole in a bank. The louder the stench the more he purrs. His nursery of bulge-eyed bandits nest flat-headed at the back of the hole.

His campaign of ferocity is endless, he only stops for rest and sleep. Such a stinking thing, after his festival of blood, can end as ermine on a prince's cape.

Both ferret and weasel are old guests at the coronation of foulness. Law cannot silence them extinct, or remove their talent. It is too late, unfortunately, to complain of their peculiar skills in the sad landscape.

Farewell to a Shambles

Planet's literary editor takes a nostalgic look at his time in the Royal Welch Fusiliers.

When Robert Graves was a young officer in the Royal Welch Fusiliers in the first war, he saw another subaltern sent off battalion parade because his buttons read 'Welsh' with an S instead of 'Welch' with a C. *Welch* referred them somehow to the archaic North Wales of Henry Tudor and Owain Glyndŵr and Lord Herbert of Cherbury, the founder of the regiment; it dissociated them from the modern North Wales of chapels, colleges, the radical upstart Lloyd George, Liberalism, the dairy and drapery business, slate quarries, and the tourist trade. The regiment was really an English one, with a Welsh veneer, and led by obedient, foxhunting monarchists.

We conscripts from Glamorgan, in the crucified south, didn't want to go down the pits as 'Bevin boys' unless a chinless wonder from Eton or Harrow went down with us, so we had to go into the Fusiliers or Borderers for a few years. (One of my schoolmates, who decided to go down a pit instead of into the army, went bald within a year; he blamed the sweating tightness of his miner's hat, which didn't let his hair 'breathe'). My intake at Dering Lines, Brecon, in the summer of 1945, after they'd dropped the Bomb, included two of my best friends from the same school, and a batch of hard cases from the reformatory at Quaker's Yard in Merthyr Vale, which made some of the English Borstals look like Sunday Schools. We cared nothing for tradition or military glory and already had the mark of dedicated anarchists, or militant nationalists of the future. Literature seemed very far away then, from that dump, and so did every other art. Poetry had no place among the harshness, bullshit and insensitivity, ruled over by a bunch of neo-fascist NCOs.

One platoon sergeant, Hopkin by name, was block-thick and sadistic, with rubbery lips and small pig eyes like blue ice, the original martinet out of *Beau Geste*. After an hour's drill, he'd march us up to the butts to pick mushrooms for his wife, who was stuffing herself with chocolates in the married quarters. I tried to find toadstools to poison both of them, but was too scared. Dead sheep were littered all over the hill, accidentally shot or victims of mis-aimed grenades. A beef-faced farmer, whom I always liked, would curse loudly in Welsh at us military killers as we trudged through his cattle pancakes: 'Fuck off out of it!' he'd shout. They say he waited ten years for a few pounds of compensation from the blimps, who had ruined his traditional way of life.

We had a fledgling second-lieutenant, Rhys-Prosser, a county scion from Monmouth, who lost an arm trying to retrieve an unblown stick-bomb. It was such a useless bravado act. (I often wondered: what misfortunes to come, of career and girls, stemmed from that missing limb?) Still, he didn't get his matrimonial chances ruined as one Fusilier captain did on a range up north. They wanted to call it an accident, but his unit was packed with rebellious lads from Liverpool and Birkenhead who hated officers. Poor sod. He really belonged in a novel by Lawrence, or a chapter from Evelyn Waugh.

I remember once we had to form a burial party for an officer who had been killed in a range mishap. Four of us dug a hole in a copse on an upland not far from his house. The poplars dripped as the coffin, draped with a Union Jack, was shouldered off a gun-carriage. We almost dropped it as one of us slid in the mud. Our capes were drenched, our boots caked, and there was this continuous drizzle and much slithering about as the box was lowered on straps. The widow's black stockings were splashed with mud. Then a bugler blew a Last Post, piercing and eardrum-banging on the morning air, and riflemen discharged their blanks as the little knot of mourners waited under the dripping trees for the thing to end. We covered him up, flattened out the earth, slung spades and rakes on the jeep, lit fags and sludged back to the camp through sopping fields in the pouring rain. I remember what sheer misery felt like on that day, making me wonder, not for the first time, if there was any sense in anything.

Down in Triangle Wood lay the bayonet pits – fat sandbags on old railway sleepers – and a corporal-instructor, Mad Jack Price, the wild man from Abergavenny. Jack was hatchet-faced and thin as a willow, he'd never heard a shot fired in anger, but he kept to the antique Crimean textbook of death by cold steel. 'Stick it in 'em, lads!' he screamed as we charged the sandbags all through the morning with our short pig-stabbers. He was my first encounter with an uncertified lunatic.

Up at Brecon we slept on pallets where beetles, or 'black pats' as they were called, lived in the straw. There were also cockroaches in the canteen. We were a mixed crew, an unlikely but interesting assortment of bully-boys from the ports, illiterate farm-hands, clever students who got sorted out later on for higher rank, and callow bundles of shock like myself from Capel Ebenezer. There were a couple of quiet, dazed boys who'd had a rough time against the German SS in the Reichswald Forest, and were just resting before getting their tickets. The physically underdeveloped were sent away to get themselves built up, and those who couldn't read or write went back to school – all at the army's expense. Nervous cases, like homesick 'wet-beds', were usually moved from an upper to a lower bunk to receive a taste of what they, poor devils, dished out. This, amazingly enough, seemed to cure them, unless they were too far gone as mother's boys, in which case they were toughened up on a special course by hard but sympathetic sergeants. Sometimes this failed, too, and then they were 'stabilised' as waiters in the officers' mess, or sent home for good as impossible material.

I always felt rather sorry for them, poor blighters. Some had led very sheltered lives indeed, spoiled and tied to apron-strings. A Welsh infantry training centre was no place for them. It was an early lesson in self-sufficiency, and in how to get on with other people, or go under. There was no egotism here, and not a scrap of sentiment. We were in the short-term game of survival, doing as little as possible for an alien Crown, and wanting nothing so much as to get the hell out within four years.

The summer rain dripped on the Lines, boots crunched on the concrete in our prison in the hills. It was always like that, preparing for a war we never went to. Not that we were particularly keen to see foreign parts where bullets were flying. We weren't professionals, and it had nothing to do with us. At the time, there was a nasty scuffle going on in Greece between royalists and communists, and some of our blokes were sent out to fight for the king's men, being conned into believing they were preventing the dismemberment of Christendom. Others were shipped off to Indonesia, where the Dutch (ousted by the Japs) were trying to creep back after three centuries of colonial rule, behind the coat-tails of the British, who still believed in empires then. One of my friends, a good boy from Rhymney, was killed out there – 10,000 miles from home – for no apparent reason. Nobody found out whether he was shot by a Dutchman, a Jap or an Indonesian. God knows what his parents thought.

Fortunately, I had bad feet and stayed in Wales. Boredom was worn like a second skin: we ate slops and drank cocoa, darned our socks, cleaned our guns, ironed the itch out of our trousers, sewed our Welch buttons with a C, whitewashed the coalhouse, weeded the CO's lawn, and saluted anything that moved, including a tin-leg major in the Royal Ulster Rifles with fruit-salad all over his chest who fell off his bicycle every time he tried to return a salute with one hand and steer the bike with the other. The only excitement was watching Lana Turner or Jane Russell on a crackling screen in the camp cinema; and borrowing Hemingway or Greene from the mobile library. Once a fortnight the butcher barber, an ex-policeman from Llandrindod Wells, who was thin on top and hated anyone else having hair, skinned our skulls closer and closer to a replica of Yul Brynner. Most of us had heads of skin, which, as discipline gradually slackened, slowly bloomed into American crew-cuts. I began to actively loathe the army, its monstrous crushing of individuality, and its habitual whim of sending young men to some unpronounceable place to get killed by strangers. In my brutally short three-score-and-ten, I wanted time to do better things, not to waste it in this mindless, emotionless, unobserving stagnation. We did everything to avoid the army's meaningless notion of work. Here, in a fertile green hollow of farmland north of the Beacons, the once-proud Welsh regiments of the line were reduced to a skiving remnant.

When I went there I was young, respectable as a lay preacher, stunned by foul language, strapped in my Calvinistic Methodist (or Galvanised Messtin) straightjacket. I soon learned to curse and to drink draught Bass, dance with buxom Naafi wenches, and to waste my lean 18th year among the smell of latrines and rifle-oil in the high broken hills of Breconshire.

*****

As time crawled by, they couldn't find anything for me to do in the infantry, so I was shunted about the country on attachment to various unprepared units until I landed in the notorious 107 Field Pay Detachment, under a swine of a major named

Tucknott, at Devizes, which had a permanent garrison, eight pubs, a big duckpond and a corn exchange where the three town harlots were available at the Saturday night hop. One slight advantage I had over the mixed Cockneys, Geordies and Jocks in this pick-up pantomime was the piece of 'black crap' stitched to the back of my tunic collar. This was a flash: a fan-tail bunch of five black ribbons, each two inches wide, seven and a half inches long, and ending in a dove-tail. The angle at which the fan was spread had been exactly regulated by regimental convention, and only the Royal Welch were privileged to wear it. When I was doing a short, pointless Sten-gun course with D Coy., 3rd RWF in a disused cinema at the bottom of a side street in Aber, an old regular told me that the Royal Welch were serving abroad in the 1830s and by some mischance never received the order abolishing the flash, which used to keep pig-tail grease off the collar and tie up the knot. Anyway, it was a good conversation gambit with women. You asked a girl for a jig, and nine times out of ten she'd inquire about the black crap. Then, with any luck, sweeping her along with tales of your own valour and how you won the flash for shooting 50 Krauts, you were soon away into the Durex-strewn lanes if you fancied it. Some of us served our modest, and clumsy, apprenticeship to the Act in the back streets of Devizes. (You could have a good night out on a quid in those days. I was paid about five shillings a day, plus a small allotment for my next-of-kin.)

Inside the cold Nissen huts at the camp, heated by inefficient coke-stoves, we worked out allowances for soldiers' wives whose husbands had deserted or simply disappeared. Pathetically the abandoned spouses wrote in pencil or crayon, asking for funds, on the backs of Tate & Lyle sugar packets or brown wrapping paper. This was where the military dregs went, right down to the bottom of the barrel when their regiments spewed them out. We had poor feet, squints, glass eyes, stammers, unhappy childhoods, and the aspect of criminals looting on the run. But we could add up pounds, shillings and pence, were literate, and could write formal letters to these destitute women.

The Taff barrack-room was full of conscripted bookies, failed officer-material, and the smoothest spongers on earth – the despair of colonels and chaplains from Colwyn Bay to Penzance. I knew then that none of us would enter the ministry or speak to the Cymmrodorion or the Welsh League of Youth. Most of the officers were sick bankrupts, physically downgraded, and seeking refuge from tenacious creditors. In the guardroom there was a tough Royal Scot ex-sniper who was permanently under arrest for continual desertions. He used to chew brand-new Gillette razor-blades to entertain us, in exchange for jugs of beer we smuggled in from the Naafi. The rim of his tongue was serrated with old wounds which he received while serving his apprenticeship to blade-chewing.

Yet, somehow, within that morass of inferior soldiery, decency lurked – 50 men were boxed in gruff warmth through a year of fraternal tedium, sex-starved, encircled by meaningless paper and files, and waiting like caged beasts for their own bugle of release. I remember some of them even now, including a bookmaker's son from Swansea who went on to make a small fortune out of the punters and lost it all playing poker over two weekends in London.

I was demobilised in an old shed at Woking, in Surrey, given an ill-fitting suit and trilby, some money, cigarettes, sweet ration, and my old greatcoat to keep. As soon as I came out of the demob centre I was pounced upon by kids and spivs for my sweet-ration and suit. Thus, the vultures always wait, everywhere. One bad soldier of the king had done his duty, pursued at the end by civilian scroungers. I remember I felt tired, not knowing where the years had gone, not knowing what lay ahead. I had begun, at 21, to harbour grave doubts about the nature of human existence. I even lost my new trilby, which blew off on the escalator in the underground at Waterloo.

Indonesian Interlude

About fifteen years ago I was out of a job – in London, Dylan Thomas's 'capital punishment', and a depressing enough place in winter without being unemployed. I had left the news division of the BBC after five years of night-shifts and foreign crises, which had seriously affected my digestion – a complaint that is still with me, and for which I always carry a little tin of assorted pills for dyspepsia, flatulence, acidity and heartburn. Since returning to Wales, the combined tensions of patriotism and literature have not improved my condition.

I took a temporary job writing blurbs for obscure books in the basement of the Bodley Head, under the pavement, and then spent a few months as a copywriter with an American advertising agency, working on the Maxwell House Coffee account – a traumatic experience which I would not recommend to my dearest enemy, although they did give me three books of luncheon vouchers as a Christmas bonus.

One bitter cold day, strolling in Grosvenor Square, I happened to be passing a tall, redbrick Georgian residence with a board outside saying 'Embassy of the Republic of Indonesia' and a red-and-white flag hanging limp. (All I knew about Indonesia was that it was a vast archipelago of scattered islands, had once been the Dutch East Indies, and had fought successfully for independence against the Dutch and their temporary British allies after World War Two and more than three centuries of colonial rule.) On impulse, I walked inside. It was all chandeliers, cream walls and red carpet. I asked the receptionist if I could see the man in charge. The ambassador was out, he said, but I could see his number two. This gentleman was dusky and charming, with a black fez on his head and a small red star in his buttonhole. I asked him if he could employ me. He could, and I started work next day.

It was a criminally underpaid job, even for those days, but it was different and interesting, and carried certain perks in the form of a monthly supply of duty-free drink and cigarettes – two vices which are with me to this day. I was called a Press Assistant, writing propaganda in English for the extreme left-wing Indonesian government for distribution in West Europe. They would pass me reams of rubbish typed in pidgin-English from their European news agency in Amsterdam and I would have to condense and re-write it for British and continental consumption. If there wasn't enough news for the six sheets, I used to make it up: it was always fairly safe to mention another inflammatory speech by a Marxist-Leninist cabinet minister, or a shipload of wheat and machine-tools from the US or the Soviet. Much of the material they gave me read like the speech of an excitable Pakistani immigrant trying to explain something to a customs-man. The late Dr Sukarno was in power then in Djakarta, playing a dangerous game between Russia and America, and his megalomania, his crackpot political and economic concepts, and his endearing misuse of the English language ran riot through the tape-machine. Really, in many ways it was the worst sort of hack-work, except for those more creative paragraphs when one could use the imagination to invent news items.

Sometimes, if there was a crisis out there – and there was about one a quarter – I arranged for the BBC and ITV crews to come with their interviewers to question the ambassador. These interrogators seldom did their homework and were constantly looking for the imminent downfall of Sukarno. Usually, they dropped in between visits to two other embassies of countries that were in a shambles. But the oiled ambassador was crafty, like most trained diplomats, and marvellously evasive, leaving the interviewers with the impression that Indonesia was one of the most stable places on earth. He merely smiled, quite blandly, drumming his fingers on his knee-cap and falling into long silences, which the television people had to cut. During his tenure, he must have cost the BBC and ITV a lot of money in wasted film.

Despite my lowly status at the embassy, there were social compensations. The Indonesian diplomats and their minions were nice, friendly people, apart from one sinister air attaché who came and went: he was a dedicated anti-European and had a vicious streak. They would invite me to their houses in Hampstead and Swiss Cottage, surrounded by platoons of delightful children, for enormous dishes of curry and rice, or lumps of burnt mutton on skewers like the Turkish kebab. Then they would grill me about Wales and the Welsh, whom they thought lived somewhere beyond the Irish Sea, mysterious and shrouded in fog. I must admit I rather liked this picture they had of us. I don't think I ever quite convinced them that we were only a three-hour train ride away from Paddington.

One evening the Queen of England was supposed to come to dinner at the embassy. The Indonesians went to a lot of trouble and put up the cipher 'H.M.' with a gold crown over her private lavatory, along a corridor, but forgot to include western toilet-rolls, because, being good Moslems, they wouldn't let paper touch their backsides but used water kept in Coca-Cola bottles. Unfortunately, the function was cancelled for some official reason. I would have liked to have seen the ensuing confusion if the lady had wanted to go to the privy.

Another time, a trade delegation came over from

Java to negotiate a contract for some military trucks and helicopters with an English firm. After the deal was signed, two of the Indonesians asked me if I could procure girls for them. I said no, I couldn't but I could show them a good night out. We went to the fleshpots of Soho, but they were soon bored and said they fancied something more 'homely'. I took them to the London Welsh Club down in Gray's Inn Road, where they seemed perfectly happy dancing with respectable girls from Swansea and Aber and drinking orange squash. One of them, a grave and handsome army captain, made a great hit in his immaculate biscuit-coloured uniform with epaulettes and medal ribbons and 'Indonesia' lettered in red on his shoulder. The uniform, a crisp combination of American flamboyance and Russian austerity, oddly reflected his country's political confusion.

I remember their favourite militant poet, a black-bearded character who looked a bit like a younger Asian Ezra Pound, flying into London for some cultural junket. He was the Yevtushenko of Sumatra, honoured in his own land as much as Waldo, Gwenallt and Williams Parry in Wales – a man who was a guerilla leader in the long revolution against the Dutch and had a few bullet scars to show for it. His poetry was of a blistering vehemence against America, capitalism and all forms of colonialism: great broadsides of rage and bitterness which still sounded pretty explosive even in a toned-down English translation. The Indonesians lapped it up, and looked upon him with a mixture of love and awe commonly reserved for political patriots like Castro or Nehru. He was very pro-Chinese and took some of us to a restaurant called the Peking for an excellent meal of bamboo shoots and pancakes. I informed him that the proprietor was not a communist, but had come from Hong Kong with his entire bourgeois family. This didn't seem to deter the poet, who attacked his food with gusto. He asked me why the Welsh, unlike the Irish, had not risen against their oppressors. I told him we had no air force, an answer which seemed to satisfy him. Later, he went up to Oxford to give a stormy reading and was reported to have fallen foul of the remnant of empire Tories in the university, who abused him for his communism, and of the Magdalen literary aesthetes, who vilified him for his poetry. He didn't like Oxford at all. In fact, when he got home he wrote a lengthy tirade against the 'feline cockroaches' of England's premier university.

One of my friends at the embassy was a Londoner, Peters, with a cubby-hole on the top floor, almost in the attic. If he had gone up much higher, he would have been working on the roof. From this crow's nest he saw everything that was going on. Peters had been with his beloved Indonesians for twenty years, ever since the embassy was a small poky office in a back street off Notting Hill. He was a sort of 'fixer', to use the American term. Anything difficult, from obtaining a special brand of chocolates for the ambassador's lady, to making arrangements with BOAC to fly home the body of a deceased member of the Indonesian community, would be referred to Peters' miraculous flair for getting things done. He was a remarkably efficient gift to the embassy, which paid him reasonably well and gave him a princely supply of whisky and tobacco. Passports, visas, purchase of cars, cocktail receptions, Foreign Office contacts, clandestine meetings – all came under Peters' control at some time or another. The last I heard of him, he had opted for premature retirement and gone to live in the remote countryside.

Peters was the lieutenant of a head of administration, Hassan, who was so security-conscious that he kept a double-lock on his sanctum door and would have screened his own grandmother without a second thought. I don't think he trusted anyone except himself, and probably ran a check on his own credentials from time to time. If he'd had his way, he would have fortified the embassy with barbed-wire and machine-guns. His in-tray was always full of confidential personnel files and once I was actually allowed to handle them while he ticked off the security-ratings. This was roughly the equivalent of receiving the *Good Housekeeping* seal of approval.

Fortunately, Hassan was on leave when the press attaché and myself went to a gloomy private club in the cellar of an eighteenth-century house off the bottom of Villiers Street, near Charing Cross and the river, to meet a freelance journalist named Mower. This thin fellow looked like the spy who came in from the cold. I honestly thought he was a character out of le Carré or Deighton as he kept glancing over his shoulder to see if a man from MI5 was behind him. He showed us, furtively, a pale blue piece of cardboard wrapped in celluloid, with his name typed on it and a signature below it in red biro. I expected him to bring out a Minox or a midget tape-recorder at any moment. I recall that he had an elliptical habit of speech, a kind of shorthand, resorting to oblique allusion as if the poor baffled press attaché understood every word. He wore a scuffed British warm, and downed a few glasses of Vouvray while the attaché sipped Vichy water. Mower wanted money from the embassy to visit Indonesia to write a series of friendly articles for English papers. When the attaché said there was nothing doing, Mower switched his tack to the idea of acting as a diplomatic 'go-between', because at that time there was a breakdown of cordial relations between Indonesia and Britain due to trouble on the Borneo border. (Later, there was wild talk that Mower was really a cypher clerk from some obscure ministry in Lambeth who had been sent under a cover to ferret for military information in the 'confrontation' between Indonesian guerillas and British troops in North Borneo.)

It seemed too incongruous to me, in that murky London club, that this creep was probing a harmless Indonesian about partisan movements ten thousand miles away in the jungles. But he definitely reminded me of one of Graham Greene's seedier agents in a soiled mackintosh, meeting his contact in a Lyons teashop among the crusted ketchup bottles and passing the microfilm over. I saw him again twice, months later, walking with a man in a bowler hat down the Haymarket, and dining with an Oriental gentleman in a Mayfair restaurant hung with prints of the Italian lakes and straw chianti bottles.

Governments rose and fell in Indonesia, heads rolled, and the country sank into chaos, governed by a hopelessly inefficient communist-socialist-liberal coalition of hotheads, empty orators and corrupt merchants, under a theoretical system known as 'guided democracy', which was a pathetic attempt to steer a middle path between the two big power blocs. My own humble position in the embassy was eventually made untenable by the bewildering changes of directive when a military dictatorship took over and the easy-going embassy was suddenly staffed by unimaginative, ramrod soldier-diplomats who wore dark glasses and carried canes and told me to get my hair cut (they had seen too many films about the British Army in India).

Before these robots arrived, there was a sad farewell supper at the ambassador's palatial residence in Finchley. He and his colleagues had no chance to brood over the collapse of their martyred hero, Sukarno. The restlessness of dissolution was all about them; the air of disintegration was intense. Even the domestic staff, the cook, maids and waiters, had the quick, flurried reactions of those who hear the barbarians at the gate, and the pickaxe at the walls. They fully realised that the new regime would order most of them home within days; a few had already packed their bags. For some of them, it was the end of a twenty-year party. And that night at the residence, their English and other guests continued to dance soberly and sedately, as in the palm court of a sinking foreign ship.

Anyway, the new military, crop-headed diplomats were not interested in conversations about Wales and the Welsh, like their decent predecessors – only in the price of refrigerators in Selfridges and how many Jaguars they could ship home at a reduced rate.

That was all a long time ago, or so it seems. Where are my Indonesian friends now, I wonder? Some dead, I suppose, meeting violent ends in the upheavals out there. Or posted to other, less important consulates, out of the way. That London winter fifteen years ago, without a job, I should really have got on the first express going to Cardiff. But I'm glad I stayed a while longer, in that chaotic disorder of the embassy, surrounded by polite and baffled Asians who thought Wales was a far-off land wrapped in sea mists.

End of a Guild

In London in the mid-sixties, the left-wing weekly *Tribune* used to arrange poetry readings on alternate Thursday evenings in Regent's Park Library. The various cliques and factions of the metropolitan literary world would be present: the Lucie-Smith group, the Abse-Robson group (poetry and jazz), the Friends of MacBeth, plus hangers-on and members of less respectable crews who were scratching about in the little magazines. All seemed at odds with each other, intent upon their own ambitions. Lucie-Smith also had a salon in Chelsea, which was an excellent place to stay away from.

One night, I was reading in the library, and at the end a bouncy Welsh poet and ex-merchant seaman named Bryn Griffiths came up and asked me if I'd like to join a Guild of Welsh Writers he was organising. I liked the look of Griffiths, he seemed real and un-phoney. (Later, he edited the controversial anthology, *Welsh Voices*, which was thought not to be fully representative, but which still went into six or more editions and was a set book for A-level in schools.)

About a week afterwards, I met Bryn at the Cock Tavern in Great Portland Street, which Louis MacNeice used to frequent in his BBC days before and after he went to Lord's to watch cricket. Tudor David, then editor of *The London Welshman*, was there, full of mischief; dear old Prys-Jones, doyen of Anglo-Welsh poets; Robert Morgan, probably the best miners' poet since Idris Davies, and a prince of Taffs; Sally Roberts, of the gentle but steely touch, building her talent; and Tom Earley, kind poet from Mountain Ash who was doomed to live in the next best place, Bloomsbury, and was a most loyal member. We set up the Guild, with Prys as chairman, Bryn as secretary, and myself as treasurer – an unlikely choice, as money tended to run through my fingers like water. Tudor, Robert and Sally were the other three watchers on the committee. I remember Robert shouting: 'We're making history here tonight, boys!' This wasn't quite accurate, being an excitable over-statement, but we felt a bit thrilled at having founded a sort of club for literary exiles.

Soon, Welsh scribes in London and at home got to know of our existence and sent their £1 annual subscriptions to join. I had never heard of many of them – they included a doctor from Merioneth who hadn't written anything except prescriptions, and others who had only written letters home to their mothers. We had no real standards then, and I was reluctant to turn them away. One member was a former undertaker from the Rhondda who had been a tank-driver in the International Brigade in Spain. He probably had a good novel and a score of stories in his head, but unfortunately he didn't know how to write. He's dead now, and I always felt it was a pity he couldn't get it all down, or even tell it to someone else, who could have ghosted it and done an editing job. He had plenty of money and took me once to a French café in Soho for snails, which we scooped out of the shells, dipping up butter, garlic and parsley sauce with bits of brown bread, and drinking a carafe of Riesling. Then through that afternoon we drank a Martinique rum called St James, calvados (apple-brandy from Normandy), and Southern Comfort bourbon which was stickier than I thought it would be, with ice and ginger ale and a slice of orange. It was a memorable day.

Another member, from Builth Wells, always carried a dog-eared copy of the glossy American magazine *Cosmopolitan* with him, containing a short story he'd written years before. This was very bad manners, rather like toting a volume of your poems around with you. In those days I used to sit in Bloomsbury cafés at weekends, scribbling in a notebook full of fragments of poems, prose descriptions and overheard dialogue for stories.

I don't think there was one novelist among us. As is usual with Welshmen, most of us were sprinters, not long-distance runners. Tudor David published a couple of four-page anthologies in his magazine, Bryn got an Anglo-Welsh section into *Poetry Review*, and we did readings in bookshop basements in Charing Cross

Road, the London Welsh headquarters in Gray's Inn Road, and even in private houses in Neasden and Blackheath. Back home, Meic Stephens was running his Triskel Press, bringing out pamphlets and starting up *Poetry Wales*. His severity as an editor was well-known, but it was necessary to clear away much of the rubbish that was pouring in. He operated in a cultural wilderness then, but came back with a few blooms. I often thought of writers like the three Joneses – Glyn, Gwyn, and the late Jack – who between the wars and afterwards had worked in almost total isolation. The sudden 'second flowering' of the Anglo-Welsh, in their own backyard, must have pleased them like a good supper in a tavern after a long lonely walk.

Every other month the Guild held a social evening at the Lamb & Flag in Covent Garden, in an upstairs room. Sally laid on the bread and cheese, and I organised the wine and beer. At the last party, before we broke up, we had a barrel of very bad ale, and I complained to the management, but unfortunately a couple of gluttons had already sampled the atrocious filth, so I didn't have a leg to stand on when the witch-landlady demanded the full price. We never went there again.

At the parties, editors met eager poets, a bore with some essays up his sleeve pinned down a helpless victim, and a famous name held court in a corner. There were clever men with a future, as well as bumptious little fritterers with none. The salted biscuits and crisps crunched in the mouths of attractive women, as long-haired sponging pirates came in with their scarecrow girls. Cheap plonk spilled red down the shirtfronts and pullovers, and the bitter chugged from the barrels. The talk flowed on until midnight, all the scriveners jammed together in an outpost which somehow contained all that was most vivid to Wales. On the centenary of the landing of the Welsh settlers in Patagonia, the cultural attaché from the Argentine Embassy came to a Guild party to praise our ancient stock in fractured English. Being a professional diplomat, he was smoothly insincere and probably cared as much about Patagonia as Harold Wilson cares about the future of the Scillies. Once or twice the late B. S. Johnson appeared, looking solid but sombre as he sipped his wine and listened.

Another time a lady writer of crime-fiction came. She was plump and jokey, with an ego so huge that she didn't consider there were any other detective writers in existence, not even Chandler or Simenon. She didn't speak well of anyone who hadn't written favourably about her trivial work or done something to advance her career. I've never heard anyone so completely devoid of the self-critical faculty. An intellectual emptiness was unsuccessfully covered by a mono-tonous drip of insipid humour, with herself always at the centre of the stories. We were glad that old Griff, who kept an Aladdin's cave of books off St Martin's Lane, didn't stock her work.

My only regret was that the home Guild members seldom had a chance to enjoy our evenings, and I felt we were eating into their slice of subscriptions, even though we had managed to get a few of them published in magazines. Finally, we dissolved ourselves. In a hotel off the Strand, at a farewell party for Bryn before he left on his first Australian tour (this one was successful, but by the time of the second one, people with their notoriously short memories had forgotten him), we decided to dissolve the Guild into the English-language wing of Yr Academi Gymraeg. This was a small landmark, and we were happy about it, though I think most of the Welsh-language writers, understandably enough, still looked upon us as ex-colonial mongrels. Anyway, we had finished in London, and our little, friendly, delightful club, that we had built up from nothing, was over and done with.

Later, I couldn't find a copy of the instrument of dissolution to release our remaining few pounds from the Midland Bank, and to the best of my knowledge these are still in the account, accumulating scanty interest. One by one we drifted back to Wales: Sally to Port Talbot to work as a librarian and to write a beautiful volume called *Turning Away*, probably one of the best collections of poetry ever written by a

Welshwoman. Her quiet insights and perception, and her technical skill, are impressive things that we should cherish. The nearest I've come to recapturing the social atmosphere of the Guild is among her own crowd in the Port Talbot Literary Group, whose hospitality is massive and overwhelming. They run readings and lectures in four different restaurants and clubs, with good food and enough booze to float a rowboat. There is a warmth and generosity in the Afan valley that makes some other places seem like refrigerators. If you go to Port Talbot to give a reading or a talk at six o'clock on a Wednesday, you're quite likely to end up in the Neath railwaymen's club, housed in an old corrugated shed, at midnight on Friday. Another good place is the Conway Hotel at Llandaff Fields, where some of the regulars are almost part of the furniture, such as the erratic but gifted folk-singer, Ike Stevens, the small-press editor and publisher, Peewee Winch, the aspiring novelist and bird-fancier, Joshua Huws, and the blind piano-tuner, poet and mimic, Davy Seed. All are what are known as 'characters', well outside the rings of dull mediocrity.

As part of the Welsh literary evacuation from England, Ned Thomas gave up an editorship in the benighted Central Office of Information and settled in Tregaron; and Roland Mathias gave up a headmastership in the midlands and nested in Brecon. I came back to Cardiff, where my passionate friend of many years, Fanny Willems from Caerffili, was waiting at the station and waving a copy of *Poetry Wales*, as if the big breakthrough had finally arrived. Dedwydd Jones, a very handsome man who looks like a film-star, and an incredibly prolific playwright full of ideas and projects, came to Creigiau in Glamorgan to try his luck, which ran out about a year ago.

Then, later, Bryn Griffiths took the fast train to Swansea. He'd known a good run in London, being lionised in Hampstead and elsewhere as a sort of reincarnation of Dylan Thomas, a label which he personally detested, as he had his own particular voice. He came from the same town, and looked the part, but there the resemblance ended. The truth was far different, of course, from the image people had of him, but Bryn had received the red-carpet treatment for a season or two and, in a way, had been spoiled by the adulation of shallow fools, or the pilot-fish going ahead of the shark-packs of critics. That whole area of Hampstead, at that time, was given over to what I called the 'destruction school' of poetry, led by the vicious sycophants of Ted Hughes, who sometimes met in a divorced Irishwoman's flat off Heath Street. Nobody liked anybody else, and the combined smell of hate, cordite, heartlessness and flip dismissal was everywhere.

Back in Wales, what seemed to some talented mavericks to be a conspiracy of academic mandarins, the Calvinistic Methodists and Plaid Cymru was, in fact, a fresh Anglo-Welsh search for excellence, for a poetry that was actually difficult to write, presented problems, and cost the poet something ('The fascination of what's difficult', as Yeats said). It was an almost monastic safeguarding of standards, which really had nothing at all to do with political nationalism.

I still remember the Guild and its easy, fraternal warmth before the ice-age came. For once, during a period of two or three years, writers gathered together without stilettos of malice or jealousy, uninvolved in a stupid 'race for fame' – simply enjoying each other's company, getting on with their jobs, and asking nothing from one another but friendship. In a rough world where, in most quarters, serious poets are less regarded than dog-turds, it was something to be grateful for.

Viriamu Lewis Slept Here

A director on Harlech Television, a reporter with the *Observer*, the arts correspondent of the *Western Mail*, and myself were sitting around and chewing the fat among the faded plush and decadent elegance of the popular Conway Hotel, near Llandaff Fields in Cardiff. The four of us were involved in an abrasive 'arts' programme called 'Screws', which went out once a month from Pontcanna studios, tucked safely away into the late-night slot before the weather forecast. Somebody referred to us as the Epilogue Men. The director had said he wanted to purchase our minds (or what was left of them), and so we were let loose at night to astound Wales at some hour when most of its fortunate population were asleep. His head of programmes was a brave man – civilised, intelligent, unsqueamish, and not given to retreating from the juicy prospect of a skirmish with the 'respectables'.

Really, it was a fairly uncompromising programme for Wales, even if it only had an audience of about five – a belated attempt by some urban guerillas to stir up the entrenched, orthodox cliques and cabals who seemed, to us, to be ruining the very fabric of contemporary Welsh life, taking the spontaneous gaiety out of it and stamping everything in sight with the black deacon's mark of severity and solemnity. We were eager to blow a few amusing, eloquent, deflating raspberries. And in the process we hoped to examine ourselves, our own motives and dilemmas. Was my own patriotism, for instance – though seeming genuine enough to myself – unassailable without an intimate knowledge of my country's language and literature? Could I possibly be some kind of recently exiled, demoted mercenary still clinging to a lost Anglo-Welsh fort in Glamorgan? Wales to me meant landscape, Pembrokeshire, Tongwynlais up the road, the clubs of Ebbw Vale, a visit to Senghenydd, a drizzling, drunken Saturday with good boys in Merthyr, as well as the survival of its language and culture. For years I had been concerned, in poems and elsewhere, with the problem of the Coca-Cola/Coronation Street ethic, creeping like fungus into the potentially great township of Cardiff and its suburbs – a sort of spiritually neutral Gaza Strip of displaced persons, hopelessly un-Welsh, where nobody had roots or felt they *belonged*. It was even spreading to Swansea, that last, proud, insular citadel of the independent-minded Taff. 'The wasteland cometh,' I thought, 'fast as light...'

Sometimes, at Harlech Television, the situation was almost surrealist, with a touch of Monty Python; in a studio on one side of us, they would be rehearsing Emyr Humphreys' dramatised documentary of Saunders Lewis; on the other side there might be two

101

poseurs and talking-heads yapping at each other; while we poor corsairs in the middle would be trying to float a slightly reckless experiment in box-articulacy. What was also off-putting was the presence of a number of delightfully nubile young women shuttling like metronomes along the corridors. Not everyone approved of us, but we didn't mind.

At this particular time we were desperately short of ideas, and even went so far as to consider someone interviewing Milord Chalfont about the sale of Harrier jump-jets to the Spanish Navy. I had long thought of doing something with a fictitious poet I had invented, named Viriamu Lewis, who lived alone in Merioneth in total obscurity and had never received an Arts Council bursary or even a travel grant to Patagonia – a cruelly neglected discard, ignored by patronage, who died in poverty and despair.

Anyway, that night in the Conway Hotel I mentioned this notion of Viriamu, and the young *Observer* correspondent, who was the outspoken anchor-man on the programme, laughed his head off. (Working as he did for a quality London newspaper which occasionally specialises in sophisticated demolition or the complex spoof, the idea must have appealed to him. He himself was a tough, hard-boiled, cynical, completely professional reporter who should have been sending back hot copy in the middle of the French Revolution.) The sharp, rational arts correspondent of the *Western Mail* merely smiled, still hugging his own dream of a volume of literary criticism that would even keep Dr Leavis awake. Both were good, with excellent credentials, and they could turn a sentence as if operating a language lathe. Later, mulling things over in the director's white Edwardian flat, we knocked out a full bottle of Jameson's and I put forward again the idea of Viriamu. Sober as a judge, the director bought it, and asked me to deliver a 10-minute script.

Years before, I had met someone very much like the Viriamu I had in mind – at Cowbridge in Glamorgan. I'd had a tidy win at Chepstow Races (don't ask me how I got to Cowbridge) and met this character in the bar of the Bear Hotel. He was small, stocky, middle-aged, brown like a weatherbeaten nut, puffing a Woodbine, with Penguins of Pound, Orwell and Faulkner stuffed in his pockets, and also carrying a hardback about the worst tyrannies of Hollywood, which had the marvellous title *Nobody Ordered Wolves*. We chatted, sipping pink gins. He was trying very hard to get published, and had even put himself at the mercy of some lethal vanity press in Brighton which had extracted many pounds from him to print three of his poems in a bogus anthology. I thought he must be pretty naive, but I also felt that I was in the presence of integrity. Here was clearly a talented hermit almost at the end of his tether. I liked him, and could see that he was down on his luck, so I offered to stand him lunch. He took me in his rattling Morris banger down to some crummy restaurant in the Vale, where we had chop suey and a white fluffy cake for pudding. He was fond of quoting Wittgenstein over the table: 'The limits of my language are the limits of my world', or 'I am in a terrible state of mind of not being able to get over a particular fact' (presumably a reference to his own continued failure to appear in print), or 'What lies on the other side of the limit will be simply nonsense.' These statements were probably true enough, but he seemed to have a weakness for saying things out of context, as if they were ultimate truths. I suspected that the years of literary frustration had unhinged him. He showed me some passable examples of his work in a grubby notebook, as good as much of the stuff one sees in the better poetry magazines. At least it had form. I gave him the address of three editors, he thanked me, and I never saw or heard from him again.

Before the programme was recorded, the director of 'Screws' told a couple of his learned colleagues that he was going to do something on Viriamu Lewis. They nodded sagely, reluctant to admit that they had never heard of him. 'Yes, yes, of course,' they said, 'Viriamu Lewis. It's high time we did something on him.'

The director, crew and myself went up to Llandaff

to shoot some features of Viriamu's habitat in an old ramshackle barn we had chosen behind the director's flat, near a row of shattered greenhouses. It was a lovely summer's day, and the scene could have been in Provence or Palma. The shots that the cameraman was getting into his frame were like copies of impressionist paintings. The graphics people at the studios had made a very authentic blue-and-white memorial plaque, saying simply, 'Viriamu Lewis, Craftsman in Letters, Lived Here'. It was a masterpiece. We stuck this on the wall of the collapsing barn. Then, standing in front of a bramble, and later squatted on a stool inside the flat, I told the sad story of Viriamu. The camera roamed about, picking up the external bits and pieces of his life – the desk, manuscripts, books, pictures, cooking utensils, and his solitary bed. When we had finished, I went back behind the bramble bush and signed-off with a sly foxy grin. We considered that this would be sufficient for brighter viewers to realise that they had been spoofed.

After the transmission, a number of viewers were baffled, not quite sure that my contribution was a send-up. A few asked where they could buy Viriamu's works. Others, knowing it was a spoof, thought that the entire programme was, too, including a visit to the Lower Machen Festival – which sounded unlikely enough. What surprised me was that several eminent men of letters, who were supposed to be acquainted with every Anglo-Welsh writer since the Tudors, didn't detect that Viriamu was an invention, even though this was obliquely underlined at the end of the film.

I felt sure, in all humility, that the granite shade of Gwenallt was overlooking me, hugely displeased at such frivolousness. But it was because of the stark, very real presence of himself, Williams Parry and Idris Davies in my own mental landscape, that I had wanted to attempt this ephemeral essay for Harlech in the first place. I had actually known a few good writers who were too proud to apply for grants or social security and who had lived on the extreme edge of penury. Also, recalling the deeply pessimistic region within Gwenallt, Parry and Idris themselves, perhaps they might have agreed that the point was in the pointlessness.

Some nights later, I had a vivid dream about Viriamu, from which this little poem stemmed, several of the remembered lines being lodged within the dream itself.

The crew from Harlech, plus myself
went to see him in Merioneth,
racing the gear-wagon through deep
country. Gareth the stylish director
shot ahead in his Jaguar,
eager to meet the fabled Viriamu.

106

His old crumbling barn loomed
out of the high grass. 'Croeso'
he said at the shattered door,
fallen off its hinges. Gnarled,
and crusty, his face was seamed
by warm wind in a summer broiler.

'We've come to bring you the plaque, Viriamu,'
said Gareth. 'The blue plaque you so richly
deserved. We have covered the miles from the capital
like bats out of hell.'
Reverently he handed it over:
'A Craftsman in Letters lived here.'

Viriamu grinned with delight, showing us
his empty mouth, except for two stumps
gripping his Woodbine stuck in the gap.
'Is this from the Arts Council, then?'
he croaked. 'Is this the accolade
I've waited for so long?'

'No, no, Viriamu,' said Gareth. 'This is
from us, your friends, the people.'
'Thank Christ for that,' said Viriamu,
'I thought it was a gift from the deacons!'
as he fondled the blue-and-white plaque
and spat his wet Woodbine out.

'How's your masterpiece going?' I asked,
'How's the Muse?' He slid me a look
from the other side of the grave.
'Have some faggots and peas before you go,
have a drop of Jameson's, my lovelies.
You're the first human beings I've seen

since the snow blocked me in
last winter.' 'We have to go now, Viriamu,'
said Gareth as he gave him a packet
of king-size fags. 'Take this from me,'
the old man said. 'Remember me
by this.' And he plucked from the hedgerow
a single, perfect dog-rose.

Border Run

To warm myself up, I put a brandy into the coffee as I waited in the buffet for the train. On the way to the station I'd passed the old Bodega in St Mary Street where Williams-Parry used to get soaked now and again with a disreputable companion when he was in Cardiff. It didn't quite fit his image, somehow, but those who knew him assured me it was true. It was rather like hearing that Waldo Williams had cycled all the way to Wiltshire to see a church that Betjeman admired, which he actually did do.

Opposite me in the buffet sat a comely, early-middle-aged woman with a pleasing swell of bosom under her sheepskin coat. She was drinking a Screwdriver. I could have gone on looking at her without any pain, but then my train pulled in. It's always the same. Whenever anything nice is happening, like being left in peace to look at a rounded mature woman in full bloom, a train arrives to whisk me away somewhere.

Shorthouse beside me was silent. He was usually like that. He once told me that he had no opinions about anything, and I believe him. 'Be careful now,' he said. 'You know what to do?' He'd fixed up these readings, and liked to think he was taking care of me.

Poor sod, he'd gone on an Intensive Welsh crash-course in Aber for 10 weeks, and still couldn't say 'Diolch yn fawr' properly.

'OK, Short,' I said. I gave him 50p for some Brains SA, meaning 'special ale' but which we called 'skull attack' because of its power. It is one of the strongest bitters in the country, and has made mild-mannered men beat their wives and seasoned drinkers collapse. Shorthouse liked it.

I was going to Abergavenny first. The only thing I remembered about Abergavenny was a local scandal many years before, when a homosexual club was unearthed in the town. There was even a rumour that the men who painted white lines in the middle of the road had asked for a risk bonus. My connection there was an enthusiast named Yorath, who knew every writer on the western circuit. I'd never met him, but he tried to negotiate the best fees he could for us. The Muse can pay off sometimes, especially in America. There was one poet out there who made 1,000 dollars in a single day in a town no larger than Swansea, jumping cabs between colleges and ladies' clubs. You couldn't blame him; I've worked for 10 quid a week before now, left the job, then lived on that for a month. Just baked beans and chips. This poet's wife sued him for divorce and wanted the equivalent of 50 quid a week maintenance. So he had to stay famous and keep talking, poor bastard.

I looked through the train window. The landscape was pleasant – green, with lots of cows and sheep dotted about, and battered red and grey farmhouses. But I suppose you could die of boredom there as well as anywhere else. My grandfather had been an ostler around here somewhere. He was with the evangelist Evan Roberts and his five lady-friends during their tour of the Welsh valleys in the Revival of 1904. He was dissolute before his conversion, but sober as a deacon afterwards.

By the time I'd finished thinking about making money in America and my grandfather's conversion, the train had reached Abergavenny. On the platform a small figure was waving at me.

'Hello, I'm Yorath.'

He was an emaciated young man in faded blue denim and buried in brown hair. I could hardly see the flesh on his face, but his eyes were clear and far from hostile. His mouth was wide and his huge nose like a beak. He was so thin, I thought his bones would crack as he moved.

We had an hour to waste before the reading at the college, and Yorath suggested we go to some professor's house for preliminary cooking sherry. 'He's not a bad bloke,' he said. 'He could be useful if you keep in with him.'

'Useful for what?'

'Well, criticism, reviews, readings, that sort of

thing. You know what I mean.'

I knew all too well. He was talking about coteries. The provincial English arts machine had built up, over the years, a reputation for cliques and snobbery. If you weren't on an invitation list, you were dead. Some people regarded receptions and private views as the best sources of free liquor; others as esoteric rites of self-recognition, a mutual admiration club catering for an elite. Probably the truth lay somewhere between the two.

The prof's house was a rambling old place, with ivy and bramble everywhere. On a wall of the front room was a painting by Lely of Charles II's French bird, the Duchess of Kerouaille. The prof offered me a damp palm. 'Ah, Trigg,' he said. Physically he reminded me of a rabbity-looking fuss-arse I used to work with on the North American Desk at the London Information Bureau, who brought his own private box of salad for lunch every day and would accept no fact as gospel unless it was confirmed by at least three sources. I think he wore braces as well as a belt, and kept his money in a purse with an elastic band round it.

'Croeso,' the prof said. 'Are we going to have some saturation bombing today?'

I didn't know what he was talking about. Sometimes these academics spoke in riddles, in a kind of closed shorthand, just as their essays had to be read between the lines. They made you feel like a gate-crasher at an

112

exclusive party, about as welcome as a cow would be if it turned up at the headquarters of United Dairies.

There was one chopsy tutor present whom I knew from the old days of the dissolved Guild of Welsh Scribes in London, when we had riotous 'social evenings' at the Lamb & Flag in Covent Garden. I was digging at the time in the cosy house of Caradoc Richards the crowned bard, and his well-known blonde wife Millie, who looked like a Swede. This tutor, who'd written a very static novel about adultery on a tropical banana plantation, had once invited me to a reception in Soho given by the Canine Defence League, where the elderly president, Lady Tweedshag or something, got drunk on pink gin, and the late television knitting-instructor, James Norbury, brought his poodle along. The legendary Keido Rees, editor of Cymru, was there too; but that was long before his mild scuffle and punch-up with the Swansea bard, Butt Griffin, outside a pub in Hampstead High Street. It was a head-on collision between the out-going wave and the incoming one. Such are the odd, unlikely, slightly seedy footnotes to Anglo-Welsh literary history.

After three schooners of cooking sherry and the usual fractured shop-talk about who was in and who was out at the moment, we strolled over to the college. Just before we went inside, I wished I was back home in my room with a good book and Mahler on the record-player. Still, it was a living.

I was led into a room that was so small, it was like being in a cupboard. About 20 students were there, boxed-in. They'd been thoughtful enough to put a water-carafe and tumbler on the table. The prof made a short speech about the 'desperate nothingness' of life without poetry, but nobody in the audience seemed to care too much one way or the other. I noticed that the basic expression they all appeared to share was one of complete and utter boredom.

I unzipped my little bag, took out my books and a half-bottle of Hirondelle rosé, with the cork already eased, and poured some into the tumbler. There were chuckles from the audience, which sounded friendly. I read them my stuff, between sips of wine. It seemed to go down all right (the poetry, I mean). Nobody twitched or mumbled or screamed. At the end some clever twit asked: 'How did you become a poet?' I said I didn't wake up one morning and decide to be a poet; somehow poetry chose me as one of its lesser, though conscientious, representatives. There was room for variety. He seemed satisfied with this answer and sat down. Then a couple of them came up and asked me to sign copies of my books. One was a girl, a real mindblower. She was wearing a blue micro-skirt that showed off her plump thighs and shapely legs, and a low-cut blouse which she dipped so that I could take a good look at her deep cleavage as I signed. She stunned me, as all well-built young women do. The face, which was ordinary, didn't matter. If she'd known what I was thinking, she'd have written me off as just another male chauvinist pig, or a grubby middle-aged scribbler. I felt a bit like Prufrock, without the gentility.

'Let's get out of here, Yorath,' I said. 'I'm starving.' I'd had nothing to eat since scrambled eggs for breakfast. I said so-long to the rabbity prof and the nice micro-blouse.

Yorath had got a ramshackle car from somewhere for the drive to the second reading at Hereford. We stopped off at a Berni's sort of inn and had a shrivelled steak with one unripe tomato, smallshot peas and a mound of chips, which helped to fill us up. I think the red plonk was a Berni Vinegar.

I knew Hereford from the past, when I courted a girl there in a sad affair that quietly died on both of us, and remembered some of the inhabitants as reserved and neutral. It was often like that when you were in a border town. They either loved the Welsh like brothers, or loathed their guts. Border people, being neither one nor the other, had a habit of glancing over their shoulders as if they were being followed. Other literary practitioners had been on this particular run – Elias, Gormond, Morris, Harlick, Steven, Jones and Bebb – and all had complained of moments of blank coldness.

'Be careful,' Yorath told me. 'They're rather conservative here.' He sounded like Shorthouse, a reformer. But it was nice to know that a few people cared sufficiently about me to keep an eye on my conduct, even if their concern was almost interchangeable with a nagging wife's.

At this college, in the hall, they had a four-man group going that was blasting my ears off. I'd never heard such a noise, and I've heard some peculiar musical sounds in my time. This is a good start, I thought, but after about five minutes of bad riffing they shut up and disappeared from the scene, taking their shattering instruments with them.

Before I went on the rack again I needed to relieve myself. On the lavatory wall there were bits of typically student graffiti, like: 'Mr Gandhi, what do you think of western civilisation?' – 'I think it would be a good idea'; 'Othello was a bigot'; 'George Orwell was an optimist.' Also on the contraceptive-dispenser (unusual in a college) some wag had scratched: 'This is the worst chewing-gum I have ever tasted.' While I was pissing, I thought how cool many of these students were today: Johnny Cools, that's what they were. Most things to them were a bore and a drag. You name it, they'd yawn at it. Art was a bore, sex a drag; they avoided heavy dialogue like the plague, plus intellectuals, philosophers, and anyone else who didn't hang very loose and limp or slip silently in and out of scenes. They even had an imported North American jargon of their own – 'uptight', 'hassle', 'drift', 'split' etcetera. Their ambition seemed to be to hit the age of 30 then run.

A burly student came in, with the head of a Hereford bull printed on his T-shirt, and stood beside me in the next stall. 'I thought I'd drift over to hear what you had to say,' he said. 'I wanted to catch your act.'

'Don't put yourself out,' I said.

Back in the hall Yorath was waiting to tell me that they were going to tape the proceedings for the 'archives' and to introduce me to the head of the English department. This fellow had a face like an old totem-pole, all wrinkled and seamed and grooved and gnarled, criss-crossed from side to side with furrows. There was a lot of worry and living in that face. I thought of Somerset Maugham and Auden, who said of his own face that it looked like a wedding-cake left out overnight in the rain.

There was no tumbler on this table, and I recalled hearing of some American poet who used a thermos-flask for his booze, disguised as coffee. But I had a quarter-bottle of Martell left, and took swigs from that between poems. I read the stuff, varying it from the Abergavenny performance, to about 50 people. There was no intermission, and I was hoarse and sweating at the end, when they clapped quite loudly, even old Auden-Maugham. I thought: you can't fool students, even if some of them are among the most cocksure specimens on earth. They didn't like pretentious crap, or anyone fudging it up. Given a fairly false situation, I tried to be as honest and natural as I could, but the length of the applause still surprised me. Perhaps they liked the brandy-swigging.

Then the inevitable hairy berk stood up and asked: 'What's poetry, anyway?'

I gave him a frozen smile: 'Do you want a drink?' This was a right nutter, so I let him have it – the big gun I reserved for such occasions:

'No single definition will suffice. There's "the art of patterned language"; "emotion put into measure"; "language that implies more than it states"; "emotion recollected in tranquillity". Poetry generally represents imaginative speech in its greatest concentration. The boundary between poetry and prose is far from rigid, the distinction often being mainly formal.'

I paused for a moment, then turned the screw in: 'High claims have been made for the poet and poetry. Wordsworth believed in inspiration but saw the poet as "a man speaking to other men". He insisted that poetry should be written in a selection of the language really used by men. The idea of poets as dreamers out of touch with reality applies to few if any of the great poets, who have usually been men of rare perception, expressing their own responsiveness and that of their times in language not vague but precise.'

They seemed to accept that, including the berk. There was a short round of applause and I stepped down. Having been seen to have done my duty, Yorath gave me the 50-quid cheque for the two gigs and asked if I'd like to go to Auden-Maugham's house for supper. No, thanks. I just wanted to get back to my bed. I could feel the reaction coming, the blue mood, the melancholic post-reading deflation when all I wanted was to be alone. I wondered if this was to be my fate, scrabbling for small and medium cheques in cold halls, stuffy lecture-rooms, upper rooms of crumbling pubs and hotels, reading some poems I was tired of repeating, that seemed no part of me any longer.

Yorath drove me to the station, I said thanks, and went inside with my little bag containing the books and the empties. Ah well, I thought, back to the drawing-board, the desk and the local. Sometimes the poet seemed less important than the postman or the baker's roundsman – someone to be dumped at a chosen spot to communicate for a few minutes, then moved on to another hot seat, and finally sent back to wherever he'd come from. Was he equal to the doctor, teacher, clergyman, or architect? Who cared? I couldn't be anything else now, even if I'd wanted to. The fragile consolations were only inside my own head, as I munched a sandwich and waited in the evening rain on the platform at Hereford.

The Way the Biscuit Crumbles

The philosopher Wittgenstein once wrote in a letter to his friend Engelmann: 'I am in a state of mind that is terrible to me. I have been through it several times before: it is the state of *not being able to get over a particular fact.*'

I know what he meant. My mind isn't exactly in a terrible state, but the particular fact I'm unable to get over, as another Yuletide and New Year's Eve approach, is the cold one of growing older, and not very gracefully at that. I'm already more than half-way to Boot Hill. It's not just the odd twinge in the hip and back, or that policemen are looking younger and shorter, or that nearly every well-built woman this side of 55 looks desirable. It's not even the expressions of disbelief on the faces of some of the young when I decline to speak in monosyllables. No, it's worse than that: one experiences the non-alcoholic shakes for no apparent reason, and also strange unfamiliar feelings of apprehension. There is a sort of panic at not having done what you intended to do, and time running out. Self-confidence ebbs. Cracks appear in the formerly smooth, mature facade, even if you have the combined security of the Pearl and Prudential around your little stockade. Once, when I was dancing – if shuffling can be called that – with a young woman at Tito's club in Cardiff, I nearly ran out of puff and felt very undignified, not to mention receiving a three-day deafness in one ear due to the shattering amplification of the resident group. I decided then that there was certainly a generation gap as far as I was concerned. It gave me a stiff back and a deaf ear.

As Philip Larkin wrote: 'Life, no matter how we use it, it goes.' And it seems to go at such alarming speed. One thinks more about things that matter: death, solitude, loss, change, the past, our relations with each other, what remains of religion, and the coming and going of seasons. One becomes even kinder to, and more sentimental about, elderly people, children both nice and nasty, and *all* animals. Every day I remember to feed the birds.

Personally, I think it's a male version of the menopause – a strictly mental one, a change of life going on inside the skull, which only much later spreads to the loins. This is a theory most people look askance at, or don't believe, or don't wish to – especially women, at least the more insensitive ones who fail to see that when their men suddenly wilt at about eight in the evening, needing more sleep than the cat, and go berserk over modern poetry, Schopenhauer, or plunging necklines (a couple of years ago it was micro-skirts), this is the old meno-interval coming up. Sometimes these blokes take to walking the streets at night, without the dog, or stand looking at Llandaff Cathedral. Others take stock of their accomplishments, dislike what they see, and blame it on 'society' or being 'locked into the system' or their bourgeois puritan upbringing; they carry a whisky-flask for furtive nips, and start painting, sculpting, or listening to Bach. A few, who never cared before, have even been known to worry about the future of the Welsh language, and the causes of our mildewed inferiority. Some start looking for mistresses. All these are symptoms of the over-45 churn-up. Only last year I met a sober writer at a cocktail-party whose hand was shaking so much, he was spilling gin all over the carpet. 'What's the matter?' I asked. 'The wobblies, boy,' he said, transferring the glass but still spilling gin. 'The fifth-decade wobblies.'

My friends and fellow-writers are getting older. One can see it in the mellowing process, the preoccupation with domesticity, and some of the Welsh fire going out of their bellies. One or two suffer from ulcers, occasional breathlessness, lumbago, slipped discs, and various minor ailments. Our once-stimulating conversations often sag in the middle, and the verbal excitement has disappeared. All they require now is maximum peace and quiet. Also, I could not number those apathetic acquaintances who have become socialist-nationalist-anarchist-liberal-tories – most things to most men – squatting on the tidy fence. And in literary matters, I think a few editors are suffering from combat fatigue – too many manuscripts to read, too many words and 'undisciplined squads of emotion' flying about, bringing an understandable weariness to their spirits. In writing about their own land and people for so long, the veterans have won a sort of crippled dignity as recorders of decay, and consider – quite rightly in my opinion – that other themes are unworthy of serious treatment. (During a reading given by Welsh poets at the Mermaid Theatre in London some time ago, a lady in the audience asked: 'Why do you go on and on about the past?' One of the poets replied: 'Because we can't forget it, madame.')

In my own case, aggravated by the march of time, the 'wobblies' take the form of a vague unease manifested in bouts of mild insomnia (I was always a sound sleeper until I hit 40). Several people I know between 45 and 65 are incapable of getting what doctors used to call 'a good night's rest'. For years, one of them has read right through the seven volumes of Proust and then back again. By the time he's got to the end, he's forgotten what the beginning was about.

This is the age of the five A's: agonising, apprehension, anxiety, angst, and Anadin. People are eating tranquillisers or staying doped to the eyeballs, smoking less but drinking more, and at three o'clock in the morning – 'the long dark night of the soul' as doomed, romantic Scott Fitzgerald called it – many of them lie awake, thinking, their minds whizzing like flywheels. My own nocturnal habit is not to count sheep or Anglo-Welsh poets, but to list the names of characters in Henry James, who had a great talent for inventing unusual, memorable names: Ralph Touchett, Henrietta Stackpole, Guy Domville, Owen Wingrave, Densher, Croy, Stant, Quint, Theale, Verver, Monteith. The list is almost endless, and you can always dig up new ones. Often I recall some favourite, profound, comforting quotes, like 'The mass of men lead lives of quiet desperation' (Thoreau); 'Culture is so much steam off the galloping horse (Marx); 'Much is won if we succeed in transforming hysterical misery into common unhappiness' (Freud); or 'The fact that evil triumphs doesn't prove that evil is good' (Saunders Lewis). And sometimes I even try to remember distant, incoherent Saxon agricultural idiom: 'Git yer britches on, yer grit mawk, an sleg thet shite', or 'Futtle aht them ruddocks fore tha trunch felths'. You can pass the time, too, by thinking of all the people with whom you've lost touch, old love affairs, or compiling all the known ancient monuments in Glamorgan, which should soon drift you off to sleep. Where we live, things don't go bump in the night, but stray cats knock off the dustbin lid to get at the leftover fish-fingers, and there's a rusty weathercock swivel somewhere that's never been fixed, creaking in the wind. Now and again, my loose unease ('the black dog' Dr Johnson called it) arrives in broad daylight, and then I have to stay quite still, wherever I am and whatever I'm doing, for the time it takes to go away, which can occupy anything up to an hour.

A few years ago, in a sink of boredom and depression while working for the Central Office of Information, I was seriously contemplating a visit to a mind-bender, but was saved by reading Rilke, who thought that psycho-analysis was too fundamental a help for certain people, because it helped you once and for all, it cleared you up, and to find yourself finally cleared up one day might be even more helpless than the confusion you were in. A person can be quite worn out, anyway, by the self-analysis of others, by the absurdities of their constantly re-examined and re-evaluated lives – the endless introspection and fabricated complexity, picking away at their emotions and 'hang-ups' like itching scabs.

Another sign of slowly creeping senility is one's concern, in poems and short stories, with portraying assorted elderly men: old gnarled philosophers, bards, novelists, preachers, uncles, hermits and tramps. I may be in danger of becoming, to the exclusion of all else, a modest chronicler of the jettisoned and forgotten over-70s. These I use as mouthpieces, vaguely hoping that through them a few pearls of wisdom might drop out to give me some reinforcement and consolation on my own walk down the tunnel, where I'm whistling in the dark to keep my pecker up. One continually ransacks the memory for poems and stories. Perhaps the motive for recording selected scraps of the past is, as Graham Greene put it, 'to reduce a chaos of experience to some sort of order' – though I have long doubted whether a few pages of writing can really make sense, or bring any kind of order, out of the random and accident, the unpatterned chaos.

It was at the birth of the 'affluent society' that I was really made aware of the pathos of ageing, and the near-expendability of the old, by those posters and billboards put out by Macmillan's 'I'm all right, Jack' Tory administration of the '50s and early '60s. Its tatty slogan, 'You've never had it so good', was plastered all over those boards, which showed only two generations of a family – the young, successful, smiling father and mother with the mandatory son and daughter in a warm nest. But where were the grandfather and grandmother? Nowhere in sight. They were forgotten, discarded like a pair of old gloves or boots shoved away in a back room. The callous indifference of the cynical philosophy behind those posters gave me the shivers. The ad-men were pretending that anyone over 50 simply didn't exist. Kingsley Amis's recent short novel, 'Ending Up', is primarily about the physical and mental process of growing old. Everything in it is spare and accurate, the writing honed, shaved and clarified. This very funny yet very serious book is full of dread before the spectre of old age, the appalling threat of senility (you can almost hear the dragging tread of Holst's 'Saturn' in the background). But Amis doesn't waste his time ranting against the human condition: he manages to keep on top of his material, witnessing, observing, and although plainly awed by the unspeakable, his wit and intelligence combine to overcome it. Such, surprisingly enough, seems not to have been the case with poor Auden who, towards the end, despite achieving a mildly ironical tranquillity in his work, apparently experienced considerable distress in his life, often sinking into alcoholic and sexual indignity – utterly distracted and frantically restless and uneasy. The latter-day celebration of the comely, the ordered, the decorous and the domestic in his poetry, was belied by the touch of frenzy in his day-to-day living as oblivion came nearer.

Well, what does one do to escape, by-pass, or put off the encroaching nastiness of high middle-age, given that one already possesses a sense of reality, and compassion for those friends who decided to remove themselves, prematurely, from the scene? A sense of humour helps, like smiling when a bank manager reveals unaccustomed concern about your future finances, as if you were 21 again; or being able to shrug when your package-flight from Rhoose to Palma is cancelled by a wildcat caterers' strike and you have to spend your five days in Barry instead, wandering in the rain through the nightmare of Butlin's. But always try to do something *pleasant*, to relax tension, to prevent raising your blood-pressure or bringing on heartburn. (You may fail, as I do, but *try*.) Humour shouldn't be stowed away in the attic with yesterday's sepia album, but flourished in the face of most that life can throw our way. The trend of the modern temper may be towards gloom, despair, morbidity and resignation, but morose periods have come and gone before, through 20 centuries, along with ruinous decadence. When we moan, we would do well to recall happier phases in history such as the Black Death.

To my surprise, one or two of my companions have told me lately that I may be mellowing before my time, though not yet lugubrious, solemn or sombre enough to enter the chapel of tragic art. (Have you noticed that if one ever writes in a humorous vein, one has 'outlook'; and if in a tragic vein, one possesses 'insight'? I suppose the limitations of the serious, lighter writer's tools place him in a different category to the heavy Hamlet, going around looking like a tortured bard or death-warmed-up.) Some years back a reviewer in a Sunday paper wrote: 'The tragedy of age is not that a man grows old, but that he stays young', and there could be the base of a good tragedy in that semi-truth. But another semi-truth might be put in a reverse Shavian paraphrase: 'The trouble with youth is that it is wasted on the old', which could have the makings of a good Thurber-type tragicomedy based on the male 'change of life' syndrome where the literate, passionate anti-hero, on his way to meet the devastating cleavage or micro-skirt, slips on a banana-skin and chips a disc. At 50 he's a born loser, and while in hospital he's cuckolded by the milkman.

It's sad, but also funny, and if the injured hero has a sense of the ridiculous, he'll chuckle too. Where there's a scrap of gaiety, there's an indestructible piece of battered old hope. Algernon Swinburne, a pagan spirit who lived in Putney to be a crotchety 72, once wrote in a poem that he'd been set completely free from too much love of living, and from hope and fear. I don't think Algernon should have been envied, even if he did think up the marvellous title 'Atalanta in Calydon'. Anyone who thinks he's been freed from those things might as well spend the rest of his days playing one-armed bandits or listing the characters in Henry James, or joining those imbeciles and sweet idiots who think that happiness consists in wandering about in the sun on a spring day. (I'm sure I'd rather be on a heavenly raft with Groucho Marx than Swinburne.)

Now, in my middle passage, I prefer the old adage, 'It's later than you think' and try to do something about it, or what Hemingway said, enigmatically, on his 60th birthday: 'How do you like it now, gentle-men?' A middle-aged, English-educated American friend of mine, when informed by his young wife that he was no longer a very delightful sight, replied with a grin: 'Well, sweetheart, that's the way the biscuit crumbles.'

Radical Passing

A Selection of Uncollected and Unpublished Poems

Jet to Palma

It banks, dips, whines through fleece
for a long mathematical descent,
held tight by some unknown friend
with four gold strips on his epaulettes
and captive to fallible instruments.
Across shattered windmills and scratch-farms,
peasants in their donkey carts,
the sophisticated cruiser glides,
its ramping power throws the screeching engines
into reverse, braking on volcanic thrustback.
The human brain and the precision switches
slightly thud us on cushioned wheels,
and we are down.

Strapped in my dwarf seat, with cheap
Dimple and Embassy carton, brought a thousand
miles through the blue cirrus
above broad water and the Pyrenees,
I wonder if a poem could tribute
this miracle? Pictures put to paper
seem much less than this captain's skill
landing our frail skin-and-bone
intact on a baked playground.

Radical Passing

The old socialist was dying upstairs in the Stag,
propped on two big pillows under purple blankets.
It was the end of his agendas, the rough
committee meetings and freezing campaign rooms.
I went to pay my last respects
to a man who didn't need a parson
but wished to make the scaffolding of a will.
The doctor shook his head as I pencilled the names.

Downstairs in the bar two men were disputing
about what the old man had done,
how times had changed since then etcetera.
One was a Prussian boot, talking as though he liked
the sound of marching feet much more than sonatas;
the other wore a Clare College tie and kindness,
sensing that he wouldn't be there
but for old men like the one upstairs.

The Retreat in Gwynedd

The spent horses come up over the marram sands,
their hooves lifting in it. Along the sheep-runs
the bleating flocks scatter in front of them
and a goatskin drum beats the homecoming.
A hedge-layer stops his work and waves to soldiers.
In the turf smoke pieces of lamb are roasting on spits
and famished horsemen rip them off,
others drop down in the grass and go to sleep.
All day the useless pack-mules tramp the ridge
coming back from the battle, swarms of flies at their heads
with foot-soldiers stumbling behind them
and lice crawling in their jerkins.

The creaking carts of wounded are left lodged in sand.
The camp women have gone over to the foreign king
and his feral rabble. By lakeshore and deep bog
peasants go on milking cows and thatching roofs
while the grey survivors stump into the hills
and a nation is dying before cock-crow.
The foreign commander in his bright cape and hat
looks down from the ridge. He is confident
that his Sovereign Lord, Henry, by the Grace of God,
the Fourth of that name, will approve.
'They put up a good fight.'
He wheels about, rides back to his supper and bed.

A horn blows clear in an upland pass.
It is the fatal moment for a dipped flag,
for the old grudging earth of Gwynedd.
Pikes and cudgels lie in the cornfields
as rain drizzles down through the night
and smoke from the doused turf fires
drifts across silent Beddgelert.
The few horsemen cover the prince's start for Fflint
when he tracks away from his hafod,
a thin beard on his chin and his eyes sharp.
He turns in the saddle, against the skyline
and lifts one arm to stretch his cloak
in farewell salute. His soldiers watch him
bold against the sky, riding away ...

Patagonia

When they got off the tea-clipper
there wasn't a field in sight,
just thornscrub waste moaning with ice.
No methodist God waited cosy in Salem.

It was 1865: a bad year for luxuries.
They slept in caves, chopped the land,
put wood over their heads, met the Indians,
raised cattle and turnips.

They bred, as the gospel Welsh always breed
to bring more believers into purgatory,
jacking up chapels in the desert
and converting some of the Indians

to the Carmarthen concept. In time the language
blurred with colonial dago
so that their dogs and sheep knew it.
They survived the folly of their enterprise.

Now the roots sink to a century
on windy farms ringed by poplars.
Blue skies canopy the reward of effort
over roads hacked by the mad settlers.

Prinknash Abbey

It was a distant winter of snow and ice
when the monks humped their goods on a farmcart
down to the slapping water and onto a barge
towed by a chugging outboard over Caldey Sound,
then eastward by truck along potholed roads
to this retreat in a hunting lodge.
Twice a week through the razor months
a boat bumped the freezing quarry; nine hours between
                              Tenby and Gloucester,
a community was shifted from island to hill.

After mile upon mile of Cotswold stone
and the boredom of kempt verges,
this house has a shattered beauty
pleasing to the eye. History's bramble clamps
to its flaked façade and ivy creeps
comfortably up its seamed walls.
Oily commerce in the antique towns
gives way to this tumbledown nest of praise
propped in its ruin like verity,
hinting at hope. Peace taps at my stale spirit.

I look at their plain wooden bowls and spoons,
their pottery wheels with creaking pedals

smoothed thin by the instep. A green wafer
and a chipped carafe lie on the floor,
chill damp mixes with paraffin heat.
A portrait of Bloody Mary tilts on the wall,
a Tudor rose bedded in a rafter,
a cavalier's head cut on a mullion
and the Stuart arms crowned on the stair.
God was always a Royalist then.

This enclosure hid all the narratives
of men stumbling towards Christ –
lawyer, soldier, physician, clerk,
opting for prayer within a silence
where you heard a tile slip, a twig crack.
Potter and winemaker achieved a dusty fame.
On the creamwashed sides of the chapel
a monk brushed a splendour of curve and line
to show us the steps to Calvary.
Talent was humbly offered in the chalice of faith.

The brothers in their off-white cloaks
pace with open books on the unmown lawn.
One of them bends to a cupped cigarette
as I bid him good-day, then he stumps
to chime up the monastery bells
to the full octave. The noise
is prodigious, hammering my drums.

I watch the Roman Benedictines stroll away
to Vespers and Compline, to the odd calm
they have chosen, on an English hilltop.

R. S. Thomas

Greetings. I was a bourgeois
too, cushioned. They say
some of us squat
at your feet. You, I am sure,
would not be so unkind.
                    But show me
this muck and blood and harshness,
this rain and spittle and phlegm.
1 may find some good copy there.

Could I come visiting with you
in the evening, spend a few hours
over supper with talk of weather
and stock and farm prices?
I promise not to mention
souls or immortality
or the good life, which I secretly enjoy.

Down here we miss all that.
One is still alone, but it's dangerous
to be a recluse. Horizons
of industry thrust up, hovels
of vacancy, the chapels clang
with emptiness. At dusk, when the rain
falls, there is a great loom
of skull, that once was Wales.

Edward Thomas

He liked to crumble the soil in his fingers
and look at Wessex under tile and thatch.
A modest wish for most men,
but this was no ordinary man.

He walked a solitary track, loving both the maid
and hag of nature, her beauty and twisted form.
But his hands were grubbed in ink, and his days
were shut to simple fellowship.

His grief was a country he would never see,
home for the herd but not for him –
a ghost in the shattering landscape,
lonely against earth and sky.

He is out of reach of change
and the passing fad we worship to be thrown aside.
It is the hangman's joke of his end
I can't accept: the careless shell at Arras on his loving
                                                    mind.

Peninsula Tour

A rare bold December sun
blinded me at the windscreen
as we crunched off the red beach
of Manorbier, under the great ruin.

High-altitude jets crossed the pale blue,
butting headless trails like snail-creep
as we slickly perched on an ancient coast,
two ants mobile in speeding tin.

Flutter of pheasant into hedges
and up the slime banks at Barafundle:
its rotting signboard lay in mud
by Stackpole Quay, where the smacks bumped fish

long ago. I saw the bits of picnic
mess and plastic cup of summer

from there to wide Bosherston sands
and the limestone loft of Stack Rocks –

two crags lifting from the sea
breaking on the wine-streaked bulk
of St Govan cliff, a mariner chapel cut
in a cleft six centuries gone.

The shock orange sun was still smashing
the glass. We watched the last
blonde guttural panzers truck
from the ranges of Castlemartin

and the tractors and sheep return
to where they belonged.
Helicopter whirr and gunboom
faded to Freshwater West, the huge

round dunes bunkered in gorse
rolling back layer upon layer
like craters of the moon.
And then skidding through tunnelled driftsand

banked up to the roof
closing in for a wing-touch
as we curved the lost dunes
to washed sandrock at Angle,

the long blockhouse flat in the dusk bay
at the end of a westward shore
in ramshackle winter splendour,
at the end of history's province.

Nash Point

I have gone there on days of knuckle-duster
wind, just to listen to the sea slap,
or in pea-soup with invisible ships honking.
An austere sweep in the off-month,
it is good for quiet solutions or for exiles
taking a last blow before trundling to England.
Coming to the upland through twisting pocket Llantwit,
the big booming surfers crash on the jutted point,
a blueish-white foam rolling in below cliff tracks
once tamped smooth by black-patch smugglers' kegs.
The sheep-cropped turf is lush enough for Lord's
as I tread to the white coastguards keep
where a man could stock up for a winter
rummaging through neglected books
or scribbling long tracts on the Whigs
without panting to ulcer deadlines,
screened behind portholes for a season of peace.

A weathervane squeak on a rusted swivel
goes right through me like fork-scrape on plates,
and a sudden back-jerker roar when two jets
shoot up from Rhoose, ferrying the lucky to ski slopes.
The wet earth is flaking on my bootcap at the
                                        crumbled brink,
a yearly foot of it clipped from the landblock,
Time nibbling away at the Vale of Glamorgan.

Pleasure

On nights that qualified
for the huge record book of yawns,
my father gave me supper-treats
learned far back from his placid mother's
Cornish kitchen. This night he surprised
even me with a butcher's favour
of pork crackling layer done on a slow burn
for hours, in the hottest corner of the oven's
top shelf, underfat melting down the grill-pan
away from the low jets. It was dark
golden salty crisp nut-tasting,
with a heavy buttered crust
one of the best flavours on earth.

Afterwards we'd sit by the fire, replete.

I see him now
sucking his briar, old spry craftsman come to terms
with his casualty list, warming his album
at memory's embers.

Craftsman

I saw what were left of his tools
in a small loft where he put
22-carat gold leaf on book covers,
using eyebrow-tweezers to pick it
from between ricepaper diary leaves,
blowing it unwrinkled
and cutting with a blunt knife
not to hurt it, then
rolling it flat on spines with a little
heated wheel, and cleaning the strip in benzine
until it shone in the drab loft.
Many fine books came under his pampering hand.
A full day of this, by sunlight or lamp,
would bring him downstairs to supper,
Mozart or Schubert on the primitive horn,

and a last pipe
before his tired eyes closed.

146

He was missing down a Belgian lane
when riderless cavalry came back from the guns
in the last lunacy to prove the horse.
But I still keep samples of his golden work.

West Welsh Tale

My rich bulge-eyed aunt, Carmarthen Ann,
of notorious flint and vinegar, armpit reek,
boned my tub uncle down
to a shank. They said she'd scrag him
to a wizened Piggott, a prune jockey.
She lusted after his misery,
penned him long on the Irish staple
of jacket spuds, numbered the peas
and slitted the butcher for a copper.

Uncle, sea-salt vanishing in malnutrition,
was towed into dock and repaired
on broth and duff. They sent him
dapper up to Solva for strength
where he dandered through a blue-lined summer
in a punch of booze
and bedded a generous doxy.
He left her his portion of arable,

crocked Alvis and gold half-hunter.

Sloven Ann, raving, took up with a
bisexual epileptic gravedigger
who snailed by the hovel one day.
Later they found her stretched out cold
in tree-stump crumble on her string-chicken run.
The bent digger inherited everything.

Village Circuit

Eglwys Newydd at night...
At exact intervals the carriageway lamps
make a long orange necklace.
Every few minutes a Royal Air Force car goes by,
its learner-driver being night-tested.

I pass the semi-detached
of a storyteller –
neat, blue-and-white-fronted, concealing
extreme craftsmanship. I look over, and pass by.

Then a jug at the Fox & Hounds
in the Death Room, where locals

shift up a place when one of them dies
to make space for a younger man.

Then the old Rialto flea-pit
that now belongs to a coal-merchant
named Merry. I have one in the skittling Plough
with ninepins falling at the back.

Beyond St Mary's church
I pass the house of an editor
who got here from Pontypridd –
it is probably the only house
in a road of dentists and doctors
where Welsh is uttered. His car
is parked at the rear, but I do not stop.
The TV will be on, or the kettle, and I am not
one to invade a privacy.

The last of the trains
passes through Llandaff to Ponty.

At the top I can loop
back through allotments. The Forest Farm Dairy
is lit, with the Jones sisters
baking cakes for tomorrow.
(They have been there forty years.)
I have two in the Oak

among the old men and women,
look at the dogs being walked on the common,
go past the chapel graveyard
and up the suburban hill to our house, in darkness...

I feel pleased. Home is still home.

The Journey
(a prose-poem for Jeannie)

I saw her on the late train
as I walked down the restaurant-car,
bashing puritans on the head.
She was famous by now, this heroine of the shopping-
feud
who'd fought against the open-cast
                              in darkest Pentyrch.
She had nice blue eyes, wide apart,
and a figure that filled her red-
white-and-blue dress, zipped to the neck.

    Now she was attacking
her second steak, after belly pork
and crackling, roast turkey legs
and a piece of duck, with broccoli spears.

She felt peckish...

(This is the woman for me, I thought.)

She looked at me and smiled.
'Where are you going?' I asked.
'Away from the emotional cement-mixer,'
    she said as she nibbled an angel cake.
    'Where are you?'
'To a haven for the mediocre,'
    I said as she drew my astrology chart.
Then she stacked the bones of her dinner
neatly on a plate, finished her Bovril,
and we danced down the restaurant-car
to the disapproving frowns of the squares.

This lady had turned me on.
I could see we were destined to take
a short journey together through Time.

When we got off the train at Combe
we spent a year in a country hotel,
away from the supermarket names
and the bad vibrations,
surrounded by paintings and food,
listening to Mozart and staying in bed.
Now and again she looted the deep-freeze
and cooked us delicious meat.

Such is one accident of love
within the pattern we can never see...

Gwaelod-y-Garth

Above the valley, the M4, the mock castle,
   the brickworks, the viaduct pillars, and
   the trapped estates, picnic couples
   twitter in the fern. Circles of sheep-
   droppings at intervals; pyramids of
   whirled hunter dung, perfectly formed
   one on another, as if stacked from an
   ice-cream scoop. This pre-war Bournville
   cocoa tin, dented, rusty, a scrap of red-
   and-orange label. A flaking log wrapped
   with soft fungus.

Geese honk behind a fence, on a patch of
   scratched arable. Crows drop, big and
   black, where greaseproof bags and biscuit
   crumbs were left; their wings fan out
   across the disused gravel pit.

Thickets of thorn and bramble. Ivy clutches
   a crumbled wall; frail stone skeleton of

barn or outhouse; charred door. Distant
occupation. Generations of family. Thin
smoke spirals from a last chimney.

High up, on this long narrow twisting ridge.
    Fern. Sheep. Rust. Logs. Stone.
    Tumult fades down the slope. Turbulence
    blows elsewhere. Time hovers.

For a moment, I gaze at the green pleasing
    surface of things.

Trust

We traditionalists
in deerstalkers and tweed suits,
we mavericks
in creaking cords
believe in your title.

Trust.

Every time you halt the black explorers
squinting for a drift of coal-dust,

or a cipher with rock in his head
looking for a quarry,
you preserve for all of us
a piece of Wales.

'Our heritage',
these stretches of green,
are not a damp cliché.
Only you can build a ditch
between the destroyers and the open fields.

   Who one day, will thank you?
People;
and the roosting hawk, the bulleting thrush,
   the singular robin, and the guzzling crow.

Each time we tread the reserves,
beauty is salvaged from the garbage-can –
   and there we may mark again
   the swallow's swoop, swift's flick,
   woodpecker's drum and gull's trawl

   through emerald dawns and country dusk...

Writer in Schools

There you do not smell
ink, chalk and urine now –
that old foul mixture
hanging through the air of bad schools
abandoned in Victorian granite.

Today they learn under glass
with coffee bars and lecture cockpits.
The elbow-patch teachers are cynical,
gone grey in the boredom,
hopeless against plastic odds.

The boys like animal verse,
history and sport. The girls like love.
The boys glint at blood and force
and shuffle at introspection.
The girls spring to life for couples

who are tangled in passion
or botched in their alliances.
A poet's delight and sadness
must be feminine. I feel the girls
join me in a moment of bond.

Recital

Sherry beforehand, and elderly ladies
in hats squat in the armchairs
of the palm court, I expect to hear
violins scrape, to see dust on the piano.

For the generous cheque, I will offer them
their favourites: Tennyson, Brooke,
some Vernon and a carefully chosen
Reverend Thomas.

               It is nice here,
through the window a view
of Pulteney Bridge, and in the room
the last genteel remnant
of Edwardian England, smelling of moth-balls.

They appreciate form, and a passage
of traditional rhyme. In my waistcoat
with conservative tie and dark suit,
hair cut short to military length,
I just get by. They may forgive me
when I turn on the cold Welsh tap.

Who's in, Who's out

Juicy-Myth, in his Aquascutum dressing-gown,
is writing three columns simultaneously
and laying Oxford marmalade on his toast
in his Chelsea drum.

                 Banjo Hamilton
vanishes through the back door of the TLS
to avoid autograph-hunters. He can't wait
to edit more massacres. He is winning
control of poetry in England.

                 Juicy and Banjo
meet for lunch at the Trattoria Rump,
compare their black lists,
exchange faces and pneumatic drills
and slide out into the sun.

Tiff

They looked all right when they came in.
He ordered drinks and she sat down,
taking cigarettes from her handbag, lighting one.
He sat beside her and lit up.
She said: 'What's the matter with you?'
Friction was crackling in the air,
she was about to throw the riot act at him.

The rest of us were typical, ears cocked for invective,
the delightful whiff of sulphur.
'Oh for Christ's sake,' he said. Silence.
She sipped, puffed quickly, tapped twice on the ashtray,
he drank half his pint and drummed touchy fingers
on the table to the moaning muzak.
I could feel them raising the tension half an octave.

She wore a wedding ring, and they'd sniped through this
before – tired old hands at bicker and niggle.
They were damping down a public bomb on the brink.
He finished his pint and she drained her whisky.
He opened the door for her. She looked at him.
'What's the matter with you?'
we heard him say outside.

Sleeper into Waverley

Stiff from the overnight bunk, I blink
bloodshot at my host compatriot
who wants to steer me about the city
at this barbaric hour. The September dawn
is dour and taciturn, reflecting an image.
The red lion billows on the turrets
and the Black Watch pose for guests.
Tattoo of pipes and drum packs the Royal Mile.

The people are selling their heritage:
Scott's house and his turgid prose,
the bedrooms of Mary Stuart; even
their luckless Jacobite prince
if they could lift him from the bottom
of a Highland loch. Culloden and Cumberland
fade, along with the Clearances.
They sag under bourgeois provosts.

In Edinburgh I am still lost and bored.
I quit the murk of a fringe event,
glimpse a dark alley and go down it
to another shambles. They give me
fish and chips in the Grassmarket,
surrounded by chilling granite

among the mumbling beards and guitars.
Here our poems are ancient riddles,

our special concerns drop oddly
with an obscure thud. Blood and idyll
is being offered in the Assembly Hall
of the Church of Scotland. A Calvinist priest
threatens to show me the tartan sights.
I bundle up my clothing and postcards,
have a whisky below the crawling clock
and wait for the last train to Wales.

Kestrel

IA wide, hard wind was bumping at me
down the long shelf of cliff
when I saw him floating, hung sea-hunter
old as doom on his coast run,
drifting with remarkable eye
to sweep his lunch dunes –
the circle and dip from air, brake, hover,
inches off the sand for the strike
then a rabbit in his talon, hopeless,
beak finishing it, broken-backed

at once and swung up
and away over the point.

I shuddered slightly, and it wasn't
the wind. Shaken before nature
in its vast blood arrangements.
Was there a contender for that hooked bird
lording rock and dune?
Perhaps some creature unknown to us,
living in caves, made it afraid.
Perhaps only man, training it to come
to his steel-gloved fist, could destroy it in a fit of rage.

Taffy

We miss our dogs.
His soft snout and whiskers,
his tattered state from a wild night
with the farm bitches,
his ritual burying of the strange vol-au-vent,
the black-and-tan bundle at the end of my bed.

That proud battered head and arched back,
legs straight as honesty, and his tail up.

This was not the companion
that slipped away from my keeping
quietly in a cold January.
They give us everything,
we who can give so little in return.

Northern Railway Blues

A winter torture stored up for me
by the devisor of the medieval stretchrack
was the night at Crewe,
which comes to all of us, in the end.
I waited for the slow unheated connection
down the white Welsh border,
scuffing about in that abandoned hole
of the north, the Scots mail
two hours late in a blizzard
and knots of misery on the skidding platforms
                    at the entry to Siberia.

Here, you think, is where my malpractice
has brought me, at last, to this Cheshire freezepack
at this blue hour without hope.
All the fingers mark to retribution

in the shape of this moaning hag
approaching me now at four o'clock
of a December morning. She looks as if Christmas
never came to Crewe, splashing
fawn char in a cup, handing me a rock pasty
far from its Cornish base,
full of stale scrags enclosed by yellow crust.
I nibble into the concrete and sip the piss tea,
feeling worse than Dr Zhivago.
I check the lost snowtrains:
I am there till noon, all hope gone.
Nothing resembling light will seep
through to this rack for five hours
and then four more to shift us.

Our bodies may never be found.

Masks

In the time-glass, crow-feet gathering
and cramp in all parts of me,
I am still several persons
and cannot settle for whatever
is me. When the setting is right

for idiots, I play the fool,
and when the knife-intellects come
I can dust off my box of tricks
with an insight here, an apt quote
there, the brow thought-furrowed.
The jester that crouches inside me
juggles for the pretty court,
the undertaker beneath him
puckers a cynical mouth.

A blunt giggling understudy
always capers from the wings
to take over my sagging Hamlet –
that family paragon who has slummed
in a mile of gutters.
There is really no celebration
in this glass – only two bright eyes
dead in their sockets.

Conceit of Power

Once in a full moon
a poet without silver in his purse
may run into nice female weather,

sliding down a friendly wind.
Occasionally he may find a plum.

It came to me in a Tudor house
owned by a bald Welsh harpist
who plucked for a steady hour.
She shone with a tawny Mayo crop,
was full and curved, and ripe for smoothing.
I poured her a large cherry brandy.
– Isn't it boring? she said.

Awash on the hostess's punch
I flew her by cab to my loft
at the dead end of town.
In one swish her shift was away
and then her pink silks;
unbuckling before the collision
I trimmed her for my sword.
She waited with a sighing heave
as I hung to mount,
But my tom on the potent punch
was soft as mallow, and flopped
at her door. Try as 1 might
the bad roger wouldn't rise.
She groaned and lit up a Benson,
dropped back into her shift
and kissed the culprit.

It is a lesson hard to learn.
She had left by the bloodshot dawn,
chuckling to herself and leaving
a red-faced spoiler frowning,
much humbler with his power gone.

Military Ram

The best-looking cook I ever saw,
she met me at the back of her kitchen
after Lights Out, and we had it there
against a brick wall. She was gifted
in her method, helping a young soldier
to pass his apprenticeship, giving the lift
I needed for my penetrator
to make a clean entry. The problem of uprights
was solved by her good grip while I beavered away like
                                                a digger
with my concentration unfettered
by shifting weight, and the fear of slipping
out. She loved it swift and sudden
in what we called a fast ram, the sheer thrill
stemming from a fair imitation of rape –
almost an act of bulleting violence
with the tool turning into a weapon.

We locked there, more than once
against the old cookhouse wall,
me going like a fiddler's elbow
and she gasping and telling me how
to control position and rush her coming.

I remember her name to this day.
It was Gladys, and they promoted her
to officer-cook. She deserved it.

Zip

The sexiest sound of modern times
is the unzipping of a woman's boot
before her tights and silk come down,
before she drops to a floor
of grass or wood or carpet,
her dress in folds at her neck
and your thug going in at speed of light.
(Perhaps, for her, the nicest sound, is the unzipping
of her lover's fly.)

Once, in days gone by,
it could have been the sound of buttons

167

popping on a swelling bodice
in the panting silence prior to a mount.

Some kinks like a matronly bosom
sagging beneath a soiled trenchcoat;
a denim shirt with cleavage scoop;
a micro-skirt with glimpse of lower rump;
black French stockings with holes;
or a negress in purple suede.
I knew one furtive greaser
who loved a ruffled garter to slap
on taut elastic against a beefy thigh;
another came armed with fat cream-puffs
to squash on a strumpet's belly.
Some spend a life on the buttock hunt
or a search for hairy calves.

Such ferrets have peculiar ways
and pay high fees for the privilege.
But me? Give me the ripping sound
of little bits of knitted steel
grooving like lightning down a boot
through soft and flexible leather.

Jane Russell at the Old Beeb

I'd just come off a night shift
of boring Tests and weather forecasts.
Through expensive Polaroids
I saw the remarkable California sexbomb
walk flowingly oiled across mosaic tiles.

> The black hair
> come-to-sleep eyes
> sulky mouth
> famous unbelievable bust
> long legs tapering to ravishing ankles
> in sheer silk
> in goldleaf highheels

> and the clinging nothing of a thousand-
> dollar dress, with heaven underneath...

scribbling JR in the fanbooks
then in a flick disappearing
into the softness of a long black Cadillac
with coachwork by Vega of Madrid
that would reach the Savoy within minutes.

Stunned at the entire gorgeous marvel
I remember my shades slid to the tip of my nose
and something moved inside my trouser.

Dream of Lush Ladies

Gobbling lady you devour me
Nipples like rubber plugs
Sprout from a circle of bruised plum.
Some feed off my scrag-end of spirit
but you shrivel my poor codpiece.
I shift my bladdered sack
away from your renaissance curves
and your Hindu contortions
back to the cold English rut.
I shall toss in sheets till daybreak
to preserve my juice
and wait for endowed replacements.

The noose hangs in the attic
next to the waxed flypaper
black with wrecked squadrons of flies.
Wet spiders from a hedgerow dungheap
spit on the melted sugar lumps;
my cat licks a crusted saucer of sour cream.

I somersault to the squat turret
and see musketry puffs from its loopholes.
Hungrily the earth-mothers blush, panting,
pulling up their frayed skirts

for the delicious womb-shock.
Wasps buzz the hooked meat.

The blue clock fades its chime
in the distance as I switch
my stance to an ermine duchess
fumbling with my buttonfront.
Tongue-salt tells me the sea is near,
the sink of boot into marram.
Soot cakes her ivory teeth
and her marbled cheek
as her seamless gown slides to the lawn.

II

Dozing, I sieve experience
stripped in a fleshvat
as she billows over me
swimming in flesh, folding, uttering
then swallowing. I am a truffling pig,
feel sand, trickling from my boot
and the mixture oozing.

She cloaks herself,
a thigh-slash down the muslin sheath.
She clanks a skillet and pan,
she watches the percolator
bubbling under its glass lid.

Her ring glitters in the lemon shaft
flooding our bedcover.
I smoke in the butterhaze,
see her flaked red fingernails
and beaked nose,
a snail clamped to the rainbow mullion.
She stops the coffeepot, smiles
and lifts the fermented juice,
apricot light bouncing off the goblets.

A. E. Housman

I met a classics buff who knew him,
waving his cold wand: 'His passion
was laid carefully in the ice-box.'

The lyrical don could never comprehend
why his Shropshire boy was timeless.
Admirers bored him, he yawned and squirmed.

But still they kept it like a bible
while dandruff settled on his frock-coat
among the racks of flaked pavement.

As moss grew, the ice-level rose,
his wit dripped away like acid
in the cockpit and the ivy quad.

The gap was always too wide
between Passchendaele, one of the deadliest places
under the sun, and that cherry hung with snow.

He was only happy with a Latin sheaf
and a burrowing quill, digging for sweet logic
in some chronicle of lost order.

So how can it be, in these green border fields
where blue sky meets hill and turret,
he is the only poet inside my head?

English Crow:
A Laureateship in Animal History

You opened up a whole new tribe
wearing deerstalkers and tweed suits,
replacing vicious men with vicious beasts
Eliot saw the power and turned you loose.

Since then you've never looked back
as you carved a capricious swathe
through pages of blood. The pike-eating pike
floats full-bellied and replete

under the cynical roosting hawk
and the bulleting thrush. Life for a guzzling crow
is basic, it begins and ends
in loathing and the garbage-can.

The shattering of the lobster's carapace
into the harpoon-jaws, the endless red slush
of guts and skewering on talons,
the drilling by beaks like javelins.

The leopard gazes out at his fat future,
your taut muscled skill is bunched like a fist
behind the wild will to live, behind
the jitters on the lip of nothingness.

But how I wish, now and then, you'd mark
your own swallow's swoop, swift's flick,
woodpecker's drum and curlew's crawl
through emerald dawns and chiming seadusk.

One day in a lonely snowbound hush,
when the frozen peewit lands on the laundromat

and the bluetit dies in the lace panties,
you may drag your bones home again

through the dark wood beneath the violent hawk
to the long peace that will fold you.

Passing Through

I

Above the reservoir, my friend and I
picnic from a hamper like two provincials
in a French print. We watch
cherry sails on small boats
with little figures in them –
distant specks on calm water.

A solitary fishes from a skiff at the rim,
oblivious to the racers waiting for a breeze
on a June day of tropic heat,
of lemon light when the sun
warms us like some kind reward,
doing its duty at last.

Below on a wooded slope
a couple flick cakecrumbs to the birds
hopping close, domestic for a moment,
sharing this hour with us.
They almost come to the hand
competing for scraps in a free restaurant.

II

I absorb the scene, a fragment of harmony,
squinting through glasses at those far dots,
knowing it will never be repeated
exactly as it is today.
We try to preserve the cherished
but the sift of time dissolves it.

My friend, the endearment I feel for her
(especially now in her Venetian boater with a blue strip),
those red sails and small figures, the sun
spoiling us, the young couple
and the birds blend together
for a while, then pass ...

It is not simply drift
But a severance too sudden, unlooked-for –
a thin wire of love soon snapped.
Even these images will crumble

as a poor reminder of this day –
transient, heartbreaking, gone ...

Let me linger here above the reservoir
to keep something only for a minute,
to hold what passes like quicksilver,
I have an instinct to preserve
which seems to rely on loss.
It is the loss that is insupportable.

Connection in Bridgend

In the bus café, drinking tea, I watch
nothing happening in Bridgend.
I mean, there is rain, some shoppers
under canopies, tyres sloshing them
from the gutters. Otherwise not much.

(Do those Pakistanis feel the cold?
What are they doing in Bridgend?
How did they land here, and those lost
Sikhs and Chinamen?
I am sorry for them, they look bereft.)

In the café a young mother is being given
stick by her two boys. They want Coke
and her baby cries for no reason
unless he's seen enough of Bridgend.
I feel an odd kinship with him.

At last my bacon sandwich is done;
it was something to look forward to,
slicing a minute's delight into the murk.
Balancing the plate, I hold the sad babe
while his mother fetches the Coke.

Then a one-armed paperseller comes in
with a strip of frayed ribbons on his coat.
He wants to tell me his story,
so I listen while the baby sobs
and his brothers suck straws.

An hour ago I was alone; now
there are six. Even the café-owner
squeezes out a smile. We are in it
together, until the last buses go out.
One by one they leave the bays.

At the Rainbow's End

A selection of Prose Contributions to Magazines

At the Rainbow's End

John Tripp in Tenby

'Tenby ... a holiday resort with a difference ... a difference that is pleasing, restful, enjoyable, because its beauty and natural charm remain unimpaired'.

Thus runs the official blurb. It is true that there are no factories within the ancient borough to pollute the air, and its hotels and guesthouses offer comfortable accommodation to suit the tastes and pockets of all visitors. But something has happened to Tenby, and what has happened is the mid-twentieth-century, with its telly and muzak and fish fingers. The juke-box has come here, the squadrons of motorcars, hippies, skinheads, and Australian claret which is guaranteed to put any Frenchman off his stroke. The new wave of spenders have discovered Tenby, and most of the inhabitants, although they take their money, are unhappy about what the summer hordes are doing to their town.

It is a small township with five thousand residents, situated at the heel of Pembrokeshire's southern peninsula and separated from the northern parts of the country by the estuary of Milford Haven, where the oil tankers berth. The resort is built on a promontory which culminates in its own miniature peninsula, capped by the meagre remains of the castle. It is soaked in history, and the Flemish, Norman and Saxon settlers resisted Welsh efforts to take the province, which even today remains stubbornly un-Welsh, still 'Little England beyond Wales'. It is good to look at, and there are sands and sea and boats. But most of the people who come here now are from the midland and northern industrial belts, where the aim is to get as much loot as you can for the baubles and gadgets of life, and these have left their peculiar mark on Tenby, in recent years. The quaint gift shops are full of junk, the cafés serve minced concoctions with two veg., and the pubs have lost their character to the regulars of Coronation Street. At dusk, youths roam the narrow streets and alleys in packs, and police wait outside the rougher taverns at stop-tap. There is an undercurrent of hostility and violence in the place at night, the smell of dangerous boredom in the air. Expected at Southend and the other gimcrack resorts of the English coasts, it is something one never thought to feel in respectable, genteel Tenby.

Cash, of course, pours into it. There are few poverty-stricken landladies and hotel-keepers, and the restaurants are heaving. A landlady running one of the hundreds of small guest-houses bitterly complained to one of the 'drop in quality'. She wouldn't give her name because she didn't want her neighbours to think she'd 'let Tenby down' (there is a rapid closing-of-ranks between the cash-takers), but she left me in no doubt as to her waspish opinion of the present generation of visitors.

'They've no courtesy,' she said. 'And they stay in these caravans. Caravan people they are.'

What were they really like?

'Not gay, you know what I mean? No fun in them like the old crowd, the old class of people we used to get. A higher class came here then, with their nannies and dogs and children. But these today, I don't know what to make of them. They're quite depressing, they never seem to smile or enjoy themselves. And they watch the television half the time, wet or fine. You'd think they'd get enough of that at home. They're clean enough, but they're sort of dead.'

The landlady painted a dismal picture as she chain-smoked her Embassy cigarettes and looked worried to death at the unlikely prospect of any chop in her seasonal profits. She had a face like a quiet grave and jangled her arm-bangles while she offered me an eclair, Welshcakes and lemon tea. 'These gangs from Llanelli and thereabouts come down and cause trouble. And their girls! Like scarecrows. They burned about 800 deckchairs one night – stacked them against the sea wall and set fire to them. There's no shape to their girls at all. My friend next door was burgled, they took all her late husband's medals and cups and things – he was a golfer. And there's the coloured too. Except for a few diplomats and people like that, there are too

183

many of them coming here now. I can't take them, but some in the business say the diplomats are quite clean and well-behaved and they've got nice cars.'

As she talked of cleanliness being next to godliness in her ornament-overloaded front room, I could visualise the Tenby she wanted back. She and some of the other ladies I met belonged to a lost platoon of empire loyalists clinging to the pathetic shreds of the wreck of Victorian values – the lace-and-gingham world of yesterday before everything blew up in the trenches. A world in which everything was ordered, people knew their exact station, and the morning breakfast gong preceded the kidneys and bacon under silver covers.

'It's not the same now,' she said to me at the door. 'Nothing's the same now, is it?'

Down on the front, in the sun, the scene was more in keeping with the conventional delights of holiday. There is something rather beautiful about young healthy families enjoying themselves on a beach, and men quietly fishing off the shore. They had all come away for a break from bosses and bills, and the dark Monday mornings of winter would soon be greeting them in the cities. This was the way all people should live, capering in permanent sunshine on a bit of coast, without quarrels and bicker and stress. Yet when the sun went down over the top of this cluster of faded buildings, this little walled town set like a coronet on its history, you could walk up to a public house that looked about as charming as the inside of a 1905 tram and see the same people fallen into silence and staring at the ubiquitous box. It was as if their own sitting-room had followed them on holiday and trapped them in habit.

To cheer myself up, I searched for a serious dinner in elegant surroundings and discovered a mock-Tudor cellar above the South beach. Here the poker-faced landlady's vanished society made a welcome and fleeting re-appearance in the form of snails, French onion soup, roast Lincolnshire duckling in orange sauce flavoured with Cointreau, crème caramel and fresh farm cream, Turkish coffee and good Burgundy. I was almost skint when the bill was paid, but it was worth it.

Outside in the dark the young savages were strutting the streets and making a noise, looking for trouble or girls, or perhaps both. They appeared to be wilful spoilers, and I thought, God knows what this place will be like another generation from now.

It is the same in the village of Saundersfoot, along a pleasant coastal footpath from Tenby. It has fine beaches, good swimming, rock-pools, a harbour and long walks, but again it is given over to the junk shops and the supermarket. Back of the wide sands there is a dreadful seediness about the place. No lush hotel or opulent residence on the cliffs can disguise the new drabness which the free-spenders have brought. Within a decade it could be only a prosperous shanty town perched on a strip of sand.

There is more beauty in the ruins of Carew, Manorbier and Pembroke castles, which compared with the resorts are like home-made bread next to a sliced loaf. And further along the coast, in the other direction, comes the big bonus of Laugharne, where the poet lived. A weird, shuttered village, but peaceful after the racket of the resorts. You cannot see much of the old boathouse from above, on Dylan's Walk, and there is an obscene TV mast sticking out of the roof (who looks at the screen now, in that room where the poems were chiselled?) But the view of the estuary, where he watched the herons and curlews, snatches your breath away, even when a power-boat is buzzing round in circles. The marvellous quiet and the long sweep of the low green hills and the water is a picture for memory's album.

It is far from the new, tainted Tenby at the fag-end of summer. There, despite its natural beauty and superb light, one fears the slow modern rot has begun. Where the pot of gold is found to be made of plastic, the rainbow ends.

Living on the Strip

'Have you got a copy of *Barn* please?' the visitor from Bala asked the girl in the shop in Cardiff.

'What's that – a farming magazine?'

True story. Cardiff is an odd place. It is supposed to be the capital of Wales, but it is very un-Welsh indeed. A stranger coming here could be forgiven for thinking he had arrived in an English town by mistake. Except for some of the names on bus routes outside the station, from which frequent Inter-City 125s run to Paddington within two hours, there are not many clues to tell him where he is. I have seen more than one visitor look bewildered as he waited for a cab – perhaps he thought he was in Newcastle. There was a Frenchman who came for a rugby international and believed he had been dumped in Bristol. The clichés never fail: he probably expected to see pit-wheels everywhere and short stocky men with black faces coming up out of the pavement, wearing leeks and nattering in a strange tongue.

The only problem with holding an Eisteddfod in Cardiff is that most Cardiffians are not interested in it. Those who speak the Welsh language will come to the capital from all over Wales, and tourists will pour into the Field, but for local citizens from Splott, Riverside, the wrong side of Canton and other deprived districts, it could be a non-event organised by unknown foreigners in an alien lingo. A strange affair indeed, a ritual of baffling capers, that brings some money into the city but has no relevance to their lives and no grip on the interest or imagination of the English-speaking populace. I have lived in this place long enough to know that space given to the Eisteddfod in the *Western Mail* is of less moment to them than the trivial titbits scattered through their favourite rag, the *South Wales Echo*.

On the theory that if you cannot get what you want, you had better learn to like what you get, I still find it difficult to explain the attraction of a particular place, why it grows on one. (Graham Sutherland, wondering why he loved a certain, muddy estuary in Pembrokeshire, said it was like trying to describe rice pudding.) In my case, the rice pudding is this: behind the respectable temples of local government and the warrens of bureaucracy, the smart stores, big hotels and flash restaurants, there is an element of the *seedy* about Cardiff, and where there is seediness there are usually 'characters' who can be raw material to a writer. For instance, at the top of St Mary Street we have the old Prince of Wales theatre, now a blue porn cinema sitting there like some monument to bad taste. The titles of the titillating films are in blood-red and they hit you from all sides: *I was a Frightened*

Virgin, *Bare-breasted Countess*, *Sex in Algiers*, *Kiss of the Whip*. Long ago, in more literate days, the theatre showed stage plays with real people, who actually spoke up there on the stage. Now it is offering lust from Scandinavia and tatty bedroom sequences shot in Bermondsey tenements. Seedy ripeness is all. I have never seen men in dirty mackintoshes enter or leave, but somebody must go there week after week; perhaps they hold season tickets. The last play I saw there was *Journey's End*, about 1958 – an apt title indeed.

Another corner of squalor is Hayes Bridge, up the street from the Prince of Wales, where vagrants gather outside the Greyhound scrumpy-cider pub. This is a brotherhood of the leaky boot and meths bottle, the defeated look in the eye, unable and unwilling to communicate with their fellow-men. But sometimes you can catch a fragment of good dialogue:

'People give me clothes.'

'It looks like they're glad to get rid of 'em.'

'I'm wearing dead men's clothes now.'

'He di'nt need 'em any more, did he?'

This is the stench of failure at the fag-end of a prosperous city. I have spent many hours in the company of humorous tramps caught on the hook of life, and old mariners washed up on the beach, listening to their yarns and laughing at their bawdy memories of Rio and Havana. At the other end of the town, I like to walk in the sun in St Andrew's

Crescent, under the trees, and then eat hamburgers and chips at the Lexington. From there you can stroll along the car-free pedestrian precinct of Queen Street, which now has almost a continental look, and walk from the Angel Hotel through Bute Park and green fields all the way up to Llandaff Cathedral. It takes about an hour, and there at the end is snobbish but quiet Llandaff village, with a choice of five pubs. What more could anyone ask?

Up there on the height, where the choirboys rehearse Byrd and Tallis unaware of Anglican history, among the villas and neat gardens of people who like to call themselves middle-class, we begin to draw away from the notorious 'Care-diff' accent of the lowlands – a deadly ear-insulting sound which is being preserved by the so-called 'Cardiff Language Society' founded some years ago by a group of philistines in the bar of the BBC Club in Newport Road. I was there at the time, and nearly vomited. Even the Cardiff accent is not Welsh, but more like the dialect of an obscure colony. There is not another one like it anywhere – it is as unique and recognisable as the Brummy's or Scouse's twang. But it is about as Welsh-sounding as a Pakistani's racy sing-song; in fact, the Pakistani's probably comes closer. This peculiar local accent is at its most excruciating in the inner districts of Grangetown, Splott, Adamsdown and the Docks, and it ends approximately at Whitchurch to the north of the city, near the Hollybush Inn at the foot of Coryton Hill; then beyond that line the accent starts becoming a little more authentic, from Tongwynlais onwards into the Valleys. In the other direction, to the east, it blurs into Newport and disappears somewhere in the countryside before Chepstow.

The village where I live – Whitchurch, or Eglwys Newydd (nobody calls it that except the one Welsh-speaking Post Office sorter) – is depressing in its loss of identity. It is really nothing much, a sad coffin of the Tory-Macmillan culture of meretricious hollowness. Life is dull there, the doomsville of conversation, the inhabitants having little interest in Wales except the rugby fortunes. Devolution is a word that would send them to a dictionary, if they felt like making the effort. If I met an extremist of any persuasion in Eglwys Newydd, the shock might be too much for me. They have been educated on the simple brevity of the *Reader's Digest*; apocalyptic visions embarrass them. In Whitchurch, life is too banal and humdrum to accommodate thoughts of calamity of any shape or form – and Welsh independence, or even mild devolution, is one of them. I believe that even the use of words like love or God in conversation, and the plea for colour tolerance, are considered extreme, sufficient to disperse the company completely. The unfortunate user, no matter how sincere he or she may be, is henceforth avoided like a bad smell.

191

It makes me feel sad rather than angry. That's the trouble with buffer-zones like Eglwys Newydd – a sorrowful irritation is the prevailing feeling among the few residents who want more of life than telly, bingo, the betting shop, and the Thatcher-Powell philosophies of the rat's nest.

Cardiff, like other ports and centres of commerce with their hotels full of carpet baggers, has always been fairly cosmopolitan since the opening of the docks around 1840 and their extension by the second Marquess of Bute and his ambitious trustees. To the shipowners, money was there for the taking; you can still see vestiges of all that wealth in the big houses and squares of Canton and Roath. Over the years, people poured into the busy port from all over the place, looking for jobs and a spot to settle down. Yet there is a touch of rootlessness about Cardiff – with its coastal strip including Penarth and Barry – as in most cities. In this respect it is unlike another declining port, Swansea, which somehow appears more stable and community-minded, or certain inland agricultural towns such as Brecon or Carmarthen, though there is no comparison in size. One has the feeling that most of the population are in transit, on their way to somewhere else. They are just here between trains. You have to go a few miles further out to feel a sense of people being settled, and even then their values are not steeped in any sort of tradition.

In places like Rhiwbina or Pentyrch there are Plaid Cymru pockets, loyally raising funds with barbecues and barn dances, though some of them are salon nationalists doing the fashionable thing at cocktail parties, then following the hunt the next morning. In Radyr, Lisvane and Cyncoed there are the snooty skimmed milk of the south Welsh bourgeoisie, the indomitable *crachach* – about as far from the Dyfed or Gwynedd countrymen as the middle-class of Esher. Most people, especially students, from other and older parts of Wales cannot stand living in Caerdydd for very long, and find the first opportunity to go home. The only things they miss are the choice of pubs and chip shops, and Arms Park. Dylan Thomas once referred to London as 'the capital punishment' and Cardiff has the same effect on other Welshmen.

Few Cardiffians speak Welsh, and most of those who do seem to work for the BBC or HTV. Many, in fact, are openly hostile to the language, seeing it as a vague threat to their well-being like Fidel Castro's menace to the American home, associating it with militant nationalism, anarchist sabotage, and a weird kind of 'foreignness'. This is rather like a primitive, irrational fear of the unknown. Welsh history, language and culture mean nothing to them and they tend to look on patriots as some lost tribe out of the northern bogs. They are anglicised and well-conditioned through generations of English influence, though I am still surprised at the number of royal-blue Tories and archaic monarchists among them.

The spearhead of loyal kow-towers came out in force during the Silver Jubilee celebrations last year, making good republicans shake their heads in sorrow. (I think it is this feeling of being surrounded by alien anti-Welsh Anglos which makes the English-speaking nationalist in the south harsher and more aggressive, conscious of his roots and ancestry, overreacting but supplying his own definition of Welshness.) When the Queen visited us, she looked suitably baffled as she listened to the clergy speaking Welsh in Llandaff Cathedral, and was probably relieved to get away with her husband to review her fleet at Spithead. The proceedings seemed like some 19th-century charade played out as in a dream. In fact, when I saw pictures from Llandaff of the assorted Anglos, long embedded in south Glamorgan, wearing their fruit salads in company with businessmen in frock-coats and anonymous hangers-on who have been foisted upon us for centuries to perform their odd functions, I was reminded of something that Ned Thomas wrote about unattractive local establishments: 'One cannot avoid the conclusion that the English are at their most destructive when they are in an enclave, at a social and economic level that is high compared to that of the local population, and where they see themselves as integrated into a British and professional class.'* It is worse here than in West, North and Mid-Wales because the moneyed ones still have fake patrician attitudes to the working-class and do not consider themselves answerable to the community – something which the English in other parts have had to learn to understand in the last 15 years.

But undermining does not come only from these moneyed quarters. Not long ago I was with some English-speaking Welsh artisans in the well-known Conway bar off Cathedral Road. These men didn't like Wales; they thought the Red Dragon was the name of a pub. This is nothing new, of course. These churls complained about everything from the people and the language to nepotism and the lack of opportunity. The undiscovered geniuses among them still thought they had to go to London for recognition. 'There's the station,' I said, 'there's the train.' Listening to them, I was surprised they weren't wearing bowlers and carrying union jacks. But it has always been so: this reduction process, belittling ourselves. As long as we believed we were inferior, we would remain inferior. In the inter-war years, when my uncles and cousins emigrated to the Slough trading estates and the Midland factories, they were saying that it would take generations to sort out things here, that there was no enterprise or initiative in Wales – it was dead, narrow,

* 'The English in Wales', *New Edinburgh Review* 37.

provincial and deacon-ridden. Some of them are still saying it today, particularly in Cardiff and the south-east.

Anyway, Cardiff is not Wales and never has been. A phoney castle, a big museum, an expensive civic centre and a sprawling university will not make it more Welsh. You have to go further afield – west and north – to find the real country. Most Welsh-speakers look on Aberystwyth, Bangor or Caernarfon as the genuine capital, the real thing. This is as it should be.

In my more optimistic moments I like to maintain that we are all Welsh even if we speak English and our great-grandfathers came from Naples or Somerset. It is hard going to convince oneself of that. It would be better if we had all spoken the language at our mothers' knees – though who knows, that day may come again, even in Cardiff. It is not such a bad town to live in when the sun shines or when you have a good night out with friends. (One of the better evenings the visitor can spend in Cardiff is to drink real ale (Bass) or sherry-from-the-wood at the Newmarket Tavern next to the back entrance of the Central Market, and then go on to the Welsh Room in Whitchurch road, opposite the military barracks. This is a good restaurant which looks like a Habitat canteen, run by a serious Welsh-Italian or Italian-Welshman who knows how to cook, and his bubbling wife who winces with you when she brings the bill. They do a very nice dinner/supper, including

196

mysteries like 'Steak Lloyd George' which is a hunk of prime beef with laverbread wrapped in pastry, and 'Chicken Snowdonia' which is anyone's guess, followed by orange slices in Cointreau. They haven't yet come up with 'Lamb Nye Bevan' or 'Duck Cader Idris' but I expect they will.)

I have an old love-hate relationship with Cardiff – mostly a grudging love, I think, a prickly affection despite the occasional feeling that one is a bit of a displaced person in a neutral belt waiting for one's own troops to arrive, and the fact that the philistinism has not been checked by the insertion of a subsidised arts centre and the costly Sherman Theatre (named after its angel, a millionaire bookie). For some, the worrying analysis of what it is to be an English-speaking-and-writing Welshman at this point in time, the constant tinkering with the problem and its underlay of self-contempt, will continue on the southern strip for some time to come. Sadness and dismay at the sorry sight of the sediment of a colonial mess are somewhat offset by signs here and there of people coming out of a long sleep.

Alliances

I am reading a chapter
on the Easter Rising in Dublin
when the telephone rings: Dinner at 8,
could I come? It will be elegant
in a house on Rhiwbina Hill
with patriots in their green enclave.

(We met on the blue diesel
between Didcot and Swansea
over high tea, their politics locking
into my own. It is simple
to clinch to your opposites
in the warmth of a shared creed.)

What shall I wear tonight?
Appear decent, not to enter
like some troublemaker in denim
or worn cords. I choose my biscuit
linen suit and Louis Philippe shirt.
It has come to this.

Hypocrisy smirks at me
in the glass as I knot my tie;
spaghetti and wine by candlelight
and the conversation of unrest.
Our rifles have turned to rust
in the Post Office in Westgate Street.

The English at the Eisteddfod

Planet's new literary editor begins a regular personal column.

In his book of essays, *What Became of Jane Austen?*, Mr Kingsley Amis the well-known humorous novelist, former jovial left-winger and present pessimistic right-winger who seems to believe that only a cheerful benevolent despotism can cure England's ills, wrote a piece about the Eisteddfod called 'Where Tawe Flows' – which I shall come to in a moment.

I must confess a liking for Mr Amis. He taught English literature at Swansea University for a while and got to know the Welsh as well as any visiting Englishman can (he even wrote a novel about them). What I find rather impressive about him is that he backs off panaceas, he propounds no single philosophy and takes nothing for gospel – but he assumes that any creed in which people believe is bound to fade eventually and that the epitaph should be inscribed not in 'sombre respectful sepia', as the mandarin poet Roy Fuller put it, but with a certain gaiety. Let us hope that when Wales eventually comes jolting and complaining to her full stature, the loyal nationalists who rebuilt her will go out with gaiety and not with melancholy, once the job has been done and her position made safe. That day will come, I have no doubt. It is only then, I feel, that Welshmen can afford

200

the luxury of practising a morality of moderation – learning, painfully and uncharacteristically, to view the temperate not merely as a tactical negative but as a crucial positive.

Anyway, just a few years before Kingsley Amis had a press button fixed to his lapel with *Y Wasg* on it, at the 1964 Ystradgynlais Eisteddfod, he thought in cobwebbed cliché of Wales as a vast rugby ground with Cader Idris on one side and a slag-heap on the other, populated by pit-caked miners who only stopped singing 'All Through the Night' to bawl 'Look you to goodness whateffer' at one another, and subjected to continuous rainfall. In his essay, after doing his habitual smarty-pants bit and taking the customary unsubtle English piss out of the Welsh – an exercise which even the most intelligent can't seem to resist – Mr Amis is suddenly made aware of our remarkable 'difference' and 'foreignness' by noticing the passage of time when one has to listen to proceedings in an unknown tongue. Probably he would have felt more at home in Paris than in Ystradgynlais. Sweating in a stifling wooden box without a fag or Guinness, he is 'moved' considerably by the singing of our national anthem and 'Men of Harlech'. He is struck by the traditional Welsh respect for scholarship, and the fierce argument going on between a clerk and a shopkeeper in his bank as to whether a bardic adjudicator should or should not be a poet himself.

A discussion of this familiar point, at such an unfamiliar level, momentarily throws him. He reverts to quoting Matthew Arnold: 'When I see the enthusiasm the Eisteddfod can awaken in your whole people, and then think of the tastes, the literature, the amusements of our own lower middle classes, I am filled with admiration for the Welsh.' Mr Amis, slightly sheepish, quickly dismantles Arnold's starry-eyed view, but concedes that 'despite all that clever London stuff' he is a bit starry-eyed himself. Even after relinquishing his 'adopted semi-Welsh citizenship', he never wants to have the Eisteddfod ridiculed.

At least the man is honest, unlike others who slip across the border like thieves in the night to report the supreme event in the Welsh calendar. Year after year, the correspondents of English newspapers write in overblown prose about this institution, laying emphasis on its 'quaintness', its seemingly archaic and obsolete rituals, and its general air of parochial solemnity, with a touch of flamboyance, as if the participants and visitors formed the last remnant of some peripheral province of Rome, before the barbarians came. At Llanelli, Llandudno, Newtown, Aberavon, Bala, Fflint, Ammanford and Bangor, reporters from glossy magazines have wallowed in purple descriptions of the chaired bard, honoured by his literary establishment, striding in his robe through a huge wood-and-corrugated-iron pavilion between

202

cheering thousands to the strains of a patriotic march, passing beneath heraldic banners and escorted by sagacious pillars of the Gorsedd, as the great assembly rises and the music thunders around him. Etcetera. I remember a headline in an English women's rag that ran: 'CROWNED BIRD IS A PARSON'.

Once, long ago (on the Ebbw Vale field, I think it was), I met an apprenticed lady reporter from one of those posh county periodicals with names like *Hound & Horn* or *Trout & Stream*. She was looking at the London Welsh Association's portrait gallery of eminent hucksters and exiles, and was carrying an empty notebook about as thick as the Shorter Oxford. Her sadistic editor had sent her from the calm of Berkshire to Ebbw Vale to do a piece on the Eisteddfod, and she couldn't have looked more lost if she had been dumped in the middle of Outer Mongolia. I felt sorry for her and bought her a cup of tea. She was surprised to learn that the pavilion was a moveable structure and did heavy duty anywhere from Chester to Penarth. I don't know if she ever finished her piece for *Hound & Trout* or whatever it was, but she should never have been sent to an Eisteddfod in darkest Monmouthshire on her first assignment without someone to hold her hand.

Our own reputation for flooding rhetoric and our gift for histrionics are often given a good run for their money by some of the boys from the London journals and the odd 'observer' from the Central Office of

Information (I have a private theory that a sprinkling of these pale, chain-smoking Saxons are really lost, romantic Celts in disguise). Phrases like 'voluptuous splendour,' 'oratorical glory', and 'blazing pageantry' have been known to run amok through columns of the stuff, or else they wax mock-lyrical about the 'hardy, tweedy country folk' in paragraphs of treacly slush, as if Iago Prytherch had never existed. God knows what their weary sub-editors, surrounded by tapes of disaster and mayhem, mutter to themselves at the other end.

This is the sort of surface copy they file to their home base, but I have heard them later in a bar when they loosen off their cynicism at such sentimental, medieval goings-on. They wear about five hats. The best among them, of course, like those from the *Times*, *Guardian*, and *Observer*, realise that we couldn't care less what they think, that we convince ourselves, if nobody else, that our culture is worth preserving. We leave the sly digs, the thinly veiled envy and the often-bitter criticism to the anglicised cosmopolitans who want the Eisteddfod riddled with English. These shrieks from various quarters for 'fringe events' in English do not come from Dr Bobi Jones's 'colonial' Anglo-Welsh literati. They are more likely to emanate from uncultivated aldermen, councillors and business-men sipping Scotch in the Park Hotel in Cardiff, waiting to kiss the hem of a former secretary-of-state or a property millionaire, and blissfully unconcerned about the English-speaking Welshman's vacuum of cultural disinheritance. If they do see an image of separation, it is doubtful whether they look beyond the possibility of making a combined take-over bid for the modern Welsh spirit.

Even among the Welsh-speakers there are churlish and curmudgeonly fellows who cavil at the Eisteddfod, their prescriptive misgivings over the years amounting to a programme of action. One whiskered faction would like it shoved well back into the nonconformist heyday, dragging its black stove-pipe hats and boots behind it; the other, pink-cheeked lot would have it streamlined and updated out of all recognition, a sort of mobile Dafydd Iwan-Lolfa Show (and I am all for gaiety), with Cymdeithas loudspeakers and Plaid Cymru klaxons drowning out the attempts at art. There are places for the publicity of the Welsh truth anywhere throughout Europe, but the Eisteddfod field, where only the converted would be preached at, is not one of them. The answer, as usual, probably lies somewhere in the middle, where the Eisteddfod is trying to remain, zealously guarded and unique.

And how unique it can be. At the Barry National in 1968, I met an American of Merioneth stock from Pennsylvania who was festooned with cameras and exposure meters. He was in the company of a Breton, a Basque, a Taff farmer from Patagonia, a Dubliner who knew O'Casey, and a Cornishman who spoke fractured Welsh and Spanish (he and the Patagonian got on like a bomb). Both the Breton and the Basque were interested in *cynghanedd* and the history of Calvinistic Methodism. I gave them copies of Williams Parry and Euros Bowen, and showed them a couple of good chapels.

In the evening, we all went over to respectable Cold Knap and sat on the sea wall, drinking cheap plonk from bottles and gabbling like fishwives as we watched the orange sun go down across the water. It was the last day of the Eisteddfod. Later we had fish and chips in Barry town and then went our ways. It was a small, lovely gathering of Celts and their allies, brought together by an event where the very essence of a nation was concentrated for a week – an accidental meeting which might happen only once in a lifetime. Someone like Gwyn Thomas, with his warmth and appetite for such unusual occasions, would have enjoyed it hugely.

Also at Barry that year was the editor of a technical journal who gave me the chance to do a well-paid colour piece on the Eisteddfod. He had the expression of a man on his way to the block. I asked him the reason. Apparently someone or something had upset him, and he felt crushed. He was a knowing political animal, with a nice, home-grown line in irony and sardonic wit that does not appeal to all tastes, as well as long, chastening experience of his more corkscrew compatriots. He confided in me that he thought the Welsh possessed almost every virtue except magnanimity. This saddened him. He felt a new, fresh, warm wind when it blew through his country, but he also fully comprehended that the only thing which could ruin our renaissance was ourselves, with our singular talent for cutting each other up, while the smug Anglo-Saxon continued to grin through the window.

That day I learned a valuable lesson from my friend, though I had long suspected it was the correct one. It is this: the only enormity that the complacent, pontificating, Englishman cannot cope with is utter, articulate rudeness from his apparent inferiors who do not know, or have inconveniently forgotten, their station. If an abusive tirade doesn't work, we may have to resort to a deviousness – which should come naturally to us – that would make his Machiavellian ancestors look like dim children. If this fails, too, the final alternative is a swift kick in the groin, without observing the Queensberry rules.

The other type of Englishman to beware of (and there are many lurking about in this present decade) is the wishy-washy, fence-sitting, do-gooder liberal, as personified in countless TV chat-programmes, who has the best interests of all struggling and suffering minorities, everywhere, at heart, from the Angolans to the Basques. He worries so much about us, it's a wonder he finds time for sleep. But when the crunch comes, like the white 'friends' of the American blacks, he is usually out of sight, on his mentally pure, idealistic way to shattered Biafra or underground Greece. (I recall what my old Fusilier sergeant used to tell us: 'You know who your mates are when you're in a foxhole.')

Another species of liberal to watch are those tough, sophisticated TV political anchor-men, a fairly recent breed of death's-head box performers who put the wind up me. They'll have the shirt off your back and your trousers down in five minutes. They have been in the lucrative game of overpaid objectivity for so long that they think a cause or an ideal is something you purchase in a supermarket. I doubt whether Wales, even now, means much more to them than the cradle of Lloyd George, the Depression, Nye Bevan, Cliff Morgan, Richard Burton, and a film-clip of Dylan Thomas in his boathouse – not necessarily in that order. You should take a very long spoon if you sup with one of them.

Such 'experts' spawned by our peculiar time never come to an Eisteddfod, of course. It might unbalance their sense of urgent priorities, of what they consider to be immediately significant, like the drearier aspects of domestic current affairs. Doubtless they are a portent of even worse to come. Last year, for instance, in the churning mud and squelching duckboards of Haverfordwest, several scribes leapt with glee on the storm-in-teacup friction over flags and grants. They must have blessed the people who originally triggered off the fuss. This year, when parsimonious Glamorgan and other bilingual counties jibbed at their contributions to the Eisteddfod, our own English-language press were among the first to send out their ferrets to open up the sore. Most newspapers hook on to bad news and trouble like ghouls at a traffic accident. Grubby, ephemeral sensation captures the attention before any noble celebration of art.

Sometimes, all too humanly, things go dismally wrong for the organisers. The skies open like the wrath of God, the tents and booths collapse, the vehicles are jammed for miles in every direction. All those visitors look so cold and hungry, in the drizzle, with good Welsh muck clinging to their boots, wanting not so much a definition of a *pryddest* or *arweinydd*, or even a sermon on the mechanics of language, as a thick steak and a big mug of tea. But old friends meet here again, leaking affection, perhaps once in the year; old enemies avoid the shifty eye or patch up a trivial scar. The squabbles about dwindling funds and the fluttering Jack having to partner the Dragon are soon forgotten (why not take the 'Royal' out of the National Eisteddfod first?). Some fainthearts drive home from the saturated field swearing never, never to return, and ask 'Where's it going next year?' on the way out.

Truly, how far would we have to travel to find a land that honours its language and its bards so magnificently? Where else does a people insist on such exclusion? Let those English scriveners, with nothing much left to believe in, snidely chuckle as we give them a show of quality, sensitivity and intellect, laced with a contemporary gaiety, panache, arrogance and strut. Let their kinder, wiser brothers be made welcome in the taverns and hotels bursting with a confident goodwill. And let our nostalgic exiles and the open-mouthed, wide-eyes citizens from abroad go away with amazing snapshots for their family albums in Surrey, Nantes, Stockholm and Kiev, with a memory of a people who live with style, wear their ancient pride lightly, and keep their simmering patriotism like a revolver in the cupboard – no longer some obscure enclave overshadowed on England's western flank. They will never see another festival quite like this one. Behind it are generations of effort, decency, artistry, love, and high accomplishment. May time and our own dignity preserve it.

Aimez-vous Solzhenitsyn?

I was at one of those cocktail-parties given by a hostess who 'collected' local writers and liked to show them off to her friends. She lived in a plush house in a smart district of Swansea, and ran a 'literary club' that met once a month in a posh hotel with guest-speakers like a best-selling chain-library lady novelist, a flower-arranger, or the editor of a gardening weekly with very green fingers. She was a busy queen-bee, and after assembling her chosen scribes she'd let them loose on each other and then bring out the AfterEights. It isn't easy to entertain writers, local or otherwise, unless you try to keep them happy with some kind of pencil-and-paper word-game or fill them with enough booze to stop them growling about royalties. Even then, they nearly always end up talking about writing and themselves. (Some of my best friends are writers, and I often wonder why we have to spoil the nice relationship we have in correspondence by meeting one another at boring parties.)

Anyway, a woman at this particular party asked me, out of the blue: 'Do you like Solzhenitsyn?' A few years back it was 'Do you like *Dr Zhivago*?' or, if you actually knew who wrote it, 'Do you like Pasternak?' At least this lady could pronounce Solzhenitsyn, which can be a bit of a jaw-breaker, like the names of most of the Russian literati.

It turned out that she'd just read *August 1914*, written by this man who's become the conscience of the political opposition in his country. Like most of his other major works, it's been banned by the Russian authorities. According to Solzhenitsyn, it's the first part of a principal project analysing the 1917 revolution, and its place in Russian history. The core of the novel is the crushing defeat suffered by the Tsar's forces at Tannenberg, in East Prussia, a few weeks after the outbreak of the First World War, when an entire Russian army was surrounded and wiped out. Its commander, General Samsonov, shot himself. Solzhenitsyn seems to imply the controversial view that the Russian revolution would probably never have taken place if the country had kept out of the war, and its strength not been sapped by a disastrous series of pulverising defeats. (Does he think that blanketing social change would have come about peacefully, without upheavals, in that racked land, where the rulers wouldn't have budged an inch?) He argues that Russia's war effort never recovered from this catastrophe. But one might just as well say that if the allies had captured Gallipoli from the Turks in 1915 to let their grain-ships through the Dardanelles to help feed the Russian army, or that if Lenin had not been smuggled into Russia from Switzerland in 1917, the revolution would never have happened. Given the jingoist reasoning and the multi-pacts and alliances of that time, Russia *had* to go to war, anyway, under the Triple Entente with Britain and France, and also because of her desire to dominate the Balkans as an outlet to the Mediterranean. There are so many 'ifs' in history.

A number of the dramatis personae in *August 1914* are real historical characters. The main fictional one is Colonel Vorotyntsev, an honest and efficient General Staff officer, who witnesses the Tannenberg calamity. He's a patriotic Russian who despises the remote, ramshackle and corrupt Tsarist regime. Solzhenitsyn contrasts the drive and murderous efficiency of the Germans with the simple, slogging courage of the Russian soldiers, who mostly fought on hard tack while their high-ranking officers lived in a very different style on wine and caviare. Unlike Tolstoy, who in *War and Peace* takes a negative view of the influence of leaders in the course of history, Solzhenitsyn largely – and rightly, I believe – blames the incompetence and cowardice of the generals for the disaster in East Prussia. Yet apparently he has no time for the men who eventually flung out the blimps and their masters, the Romanovs. His hero Vorotyntsev represents the progressive and skilful elements of the officer class, though ultimately the Tsarist army has no use for him. (In the Civil War, Trotsky recruited thousands of disillusioned ex-Tsarist officers of this type to fight for the Red Army.) But Solzhenitsyn has no sympathy with the revolutionaries, who are presented as naive, narrowly fanatical, and totally lacking in human warmth. (What, *all* of them?) From his novel, one would gather Solzhenitsyn is a very moderate socialist indeed, like Kerensky, and none too sure about being that. He's the eternal man in the middle.

This makes me wonder if he really thinks the Tsarists were better – those cold, aloof aristocrats who kept the people in serfdom for centuries. Surely, if he'd been around then, he would have fought on the side of the Red Army? I mean, a just, honest, kind, compassionate human being like him? It almost amounts to heresy now in the west to criticise Solzhenitsyn, but sometimes I think there is a slightly fishy smell hanging around him. In his fame and isolation he is veering perilously close to a fake-'liberal' rhetoric. Certainly the amount of greasy praise and flattery lavished on him by sycophants, the Hampstead liberal intellectuals and their like, should be embarrassing to a man of such confessed humility. One day I wouldn't be surprised if they erected a monument to him in Fleet Street, because of all the copy he's given them.

Recently, a lonely critic or two – and *not* in the Soviet Union – has suggested that the Russians should have considered publishing Solzhenitsyn's emotional

Nobel Prize speech, in all its shoddy thought and mental confusion, in the humorous magazine *Krokodil*. Evidently it was a very accurate translation for western consumption, and left out no subtleties of thought that were present in the original. If the author inserted close, rational argument, presumably this would have been safely transferred by experts to the English, French and German texts.

Reading that throbbing address, I see what his critics mean. Solzhenitsyn refers to 'the timeless essence of human nature' – a phrase which would make any philosopher blush but at which we're supposed to nod sagely in heartfelt agreement. This 'timeless essence of human nature', trotted out as a piece of universal wisdom that is unanswerable, apparently makes us all brothers. I know what he means, but Hitler's and Stalin's ideas about human nature differed considerably from those of Spinoza or Marx, as Solzhenitsyn knows to his own cost. Yet he seems to draw no distinction between groups that use the same means but have different ends. This, I submit, is a grave error in his thought, which stems from a rejection of any analysis based on the concept of class. Real, continuing divisions between the haves and have-nots in the world, and the lengths to which both will go to survive, don't appear to exist in his mind. Consequently, he attacks the element of violence in human conduct without ever referring to the very different situations which can provoke that violence. For instance, on this view he would make no distinction between the Greek and Spanish regimes cracking down on democrats and republicans, and the people fighting back; between the armed hijacking of airliners for personal greed, and to bring attention to the plight of the Palestinians; or between the long Portuguese oppression of their colonies, and the struggle of the Angolans to throw it off. And I doubt very much whether he'd draw a line between the power-backed police manhandling Welsh language demonstrators, and the sporadic violent protests of those demonstrators to preserve their own language.

It follows, then, from Solzhenitsyn's line, that power, envy and greed can swamp both the workers who, in his own term, 'grab', and the capitalists – whom he conveniently fails to mention – who continue to exploit them. To him it is all ruinous for what he calls, in typically woolly fashion, 'society', as if the millennium is already in sight. But whether the particular societies affected by random oppression, hijackings, rebellion, social problems or industrial disputes support the right of a rich, powerful minority to monopolise the majority, or are committed to building an equal society, appears to be wholly irrelevant. Surprisingly, I detect here and there a touch of ultra-conservatism in Solzhenitsyn, which leaks out in his frequent pronouncements. After his experiences, perhaps it's inevitable that he occasionally appears to occupy a position at the other extreme to communism. But when I contemplate the almost-religious sense of mission in his recent statements, I'm reminded of what Eliot wrote about D. H. Lawrence: that the notorious 'Inner Light' is one of the most untrustworthy guides that ever offered itself to wandering humanity.

To come back to the lady at that party, who asked: 'Do you like Solzhenitsyn?' My reply was: 'Yes, as a writer, though he's a bit lumpy. No, as a thinker.' She didn't pursue the matter any further, and I must say I was rather relieved.

Postscript: Since this piece was written, Solzhenitsyn has been exiled to the west by the Russian authorities. He was arrested and bundled out at top speed, as if the hard men were determined at all costs to avoid the embarrassment of having a dead martyr on their hands. When he arrived in Zurich, his reaction to the tumult of cursing police, jostling cameramen and screaming women – as if he were some pop-idol or movie-star – passed from amusement through annoyance to some horror. It was the worst sort of circus that we undignified westerners can stage, and poor Solzhenitsyn's bewilderment must have been total.

Like Pasternak before him, he is the kind of writer who drew his creativity from deep national roots, now severed, though he seems to have the notes and research for at least two more huge books up his sleeve. He is not much at ease in West European countries, and his sudden upheaval must be rather like going from a cottage you've built yourself to live in some flashy four-star hotel. No doubt he will soon be approached by an assortment of anti-communist émigrés, those floaters who belong to a lost, footloose world but who would be overjoyed to take Solzhenitsyn up as a prize catch. There is something very sad and rootless about such communities – no matter how 'broad' and 'sophisticated' they may consider their thought and life-style to be – that would not appeal to a man like Solzhenitsyn who, despite his bitter criticism of the Soviet political system, needs the creative nourishment of his own roots, and gravely misses this when it has gone.

Oddly, one feels more compassion for him now than when he was in Russia. He is really a loner, whose main resources were provided by his own land, and his exile – once the excitement is over, the hubbub dies down, and the international Press drops him – will probably be a very difficult and unhappy period for him.

Spirit of a Union

The long car journey from Cardiff to distant Harlech becomes a real drag after Aberystwyth, even though the scenery takes your breath away. 'I don't believe there's such a place as Harlech,' said my companion, longing for sustenance and the prospect of a short kip. 'I was there eight years ago,' I replied. 'We saw an orange sunset over the Lleyn Peninsula.' 'Oh yes,' she said.

We were going to the first full annual conference of the Welsh Union of Writers, sponsored by the Mid-Wales Development Board and by HTV, which filmed the proceedings on the Saturday and screened an edited (or severely chopped-up) version a week later. (Apparently the huge HTV complex at Culverhouse Cross outside Cardiff is called the Taf Mahal – mercifully free, one hopes, of the Cosa Nosda.) This conference, indeed, was a milestone, an event long overdue in the sorry saga of monopoly by the Welsh arts machine in which individual writers and independent groups were regularly minced up and spewed out.

The college itself, in a lovely setting of sea and dune, is a complicated old structure, its foundations sunk so low on a slope that the accommodation is below ground level and the reception area is on the seventh floor, making for much confusion with the single lift and outside stairs. The refectory is on the sixth floor, where on Friday between 70 and 80 members had a delicious cold buffet, and plenty of it.

Later at the St David's Hotel next door, our chairman, John Morgan, welcomed the flock before the start of what he called a 'social evening' – a sort of pre-60s disco without the shattering amplifiers. John, who is still something of a public swell in the best sense, a man of parts, oozes confidence after his long run in journalism with experience of the *New Statesman*, BBC current affairs, the boardroom of Harlech TV and similar battlegrounds. His has been the world of E. M. Forster's 'telegrams and anger' with whisky and humour thrown in. He thought it was high time that the Union came to north Wales after an 'absence of eternity' and outlined the programme for the weekend. A witty speaker, he put us in the right mood for the skirmishes and fun to come. He was concerned to give us accurate directions to a secret room in the theatre where, tomorrow, a 'remarkable gift' of extraordinary hospitality would await us in the form of free booze provided by the executive committee. We licked our lips in anticipation. Then we had lively tavern-and-busker-pitch music from the folk group Bonclust (roughly translated, 'a bang on the ear') whose sounds a few people couldn't fully appreciate; but they are a talented trio and the girl singer, a buxom Breton named Brigitte Kloareg who's mastered Welsh, has a rich voice accompanied by her male-mates on the fiddle, fife and cittern. The prices at the downstairs bar were on the astronomical side, but we were able to take refreshments back to the college for our nocturnal chat.

Here, in the lounge, the survivors of the social evening looked out across the dark sea towards the peninsula where the Rev. R. S. Thomas composed much of his terse verse, and between swigs of Guinness and lager some of us made up a composite, spontaneous poem in the manner of a drunken pseudo-Dylan or sober surrealist:

We see the pompous ones full of Maltesers
surging through plastic blooms
undone like ruptured crows
loving only ice, cobwebs, wine gums,
cod-liver oil and Weetabix.
They vanish with the deadly mandarins
down the crusted tunnels of Time.

And so on. At conferences, the best moments often occur late at night or in the early hours among cronies who are fond of a jar. One fraternal brother, Dick Edwards, a young playwright, passionate left-winger and lover of Scotch, said that establishments of all kinds – political, economic, cultural – couldn't organise a piss-up in a brewery, but we, the put-upon, were so disorganised that they exploited the chaos and got away with it. Tory divide-and-rule etcetera. Dick's not the only *one* to believe in the conspiracy theory of history, or at least the cock-up theory.

Next morning the survivors among the survivors felt frazzled and far from debonair, but the bacon at breakfast was nice and crispy and the coffee black.

We trooped to the theatre, a large audience to hear, first, a short puff from a representative of the Mid-Wales Development Board – our generous joint-sponsor – for what they were developing in the region: factories, workshops, education and sports facilities, all manner of enterprises against the odds in a deep depression, to prevent further depopulation and the drift of the young away from this desolate territory. The Board attempts to do good work in the rural areas, and the gentleman asked writers to spread the word whenever they could.

Then we had a debate on 'The future of the word' (a different kind of word from the Development Board's, or the Biblical Word), to see if it had any future at all. The three guest-speakers were not particularly optimistic. There was a powerful playwright who's a legend in his lunch-time, an Englishman living in Ireland (John Arden); a critic and historian who's an Irishman with a Welsh name living in Scotland (Owen Dudley Edwards); and a Welshman

222

who's an MP and man-of-letters and has to spend a lot of time in England (Dafydd Elis Thomas). John, looking rather careworn, still wrestling with entrenched and irrational literary and theatrical cliques in his own impressive way, attacked the mumbo-jumbo jargon of closed elites and the subordination of the word to image in television. In fact, he pulverised the priority which TV gives to the visual over the language, reducing literate viewers, most of the time, to the role of spectators at a comic-strip lantern-slide show. Intelligence, perception, sensitivity had gone out of the window. He also gave examples of the sinister pressures against logic, common sense and the free spirit in newspapers such as the *Irish Independent* – though it could just as easily have been the *Western Mail* or *The Scotsman* – from which he quoted at length in a sheaf of cuttings he'd brought with him. It all sounded like very bad news for serious, and even humorous, writers: apart from the general abuse of language, there was more than a hint of fascism in the opinions and reports which John selected. One had the impression of a combination of old panzer and U-boat commanders controlling our collective destiny.

Then came Owen, dapper with a knotted dark-blue cravat, who looked and dressed like a late-Victorian romantic artist, a friend of Oscar Wilde perhaps. He'd apparently abandoned his original paper in order to take issue with some of John Arden's remarks, but he seemed to more-or-less agree with him, firing of his intellectual squibs with Celtic panache and taking, all in all, as pessimistic a view of the scene as the famous playwright. There was wit and eloquence here, but also a slight lack of coherence, I thought, in the cascade of rapid concepts he put forward which made up his literary philosophy. It was a brilliant academic performance, off-the-cuff, and ample evidence of the professional lecturer's utter confidence in his own ideas.

Dafydd, our dazzling Plaid Cymru star, had more than a touch of the Meirionnydd peacock with his canary-yellow slacks and green loafers. Dressed like that, one would think that here was a fellow who was about as sincere as an Italian waiter just before the restaurant is due to close. But he is a structuralist as well as a politician, and between his in-jokes with the HTV film crew and ourselves, his close analysis of the relationship between the Welsh and English languages was enlightening – as is his committed interest in black cultural affairs and the approach of the so-called 'multi-culture' (God forbid). He has more imagination than most politicians, and it shows, but a mufti-culture like multi-nationals and everything else 'multi' is something that swallows people up. Dafydd's socialist interests now are much wider than they used to be, and rightly so, but I hope they don't become so broad that he has to travel too far from his old parish-pump.

This glittering debate left us wondering once again whether advanced literary studies – as interpreted in their different ways by the three speakers – will ever stop being frightened of feeling, let alone metaphysics. The examples given of the modern assault on comprehension and clear language were a stark warning, and made one shudder. Behind it all is something bleak and terrible, like an end to meaningful communication. On a more frivolous level, I was reminded of the time I sent a poem to an American editor which contained the words 'he had a gay red pluck'. This editor returned it, asking me if I was referring to a homosexual communist, a Marxist faggot, and could I change the words to 'brave new'.

We broke for lunch – pork, with separate crackling (a treat). The pudding was good too. But before lunch we had been guided in a conga-line by the chairman to his promised 'remarkable gift' of extraordinary hospitality in the secret room, where we were greeted by the lovely sight of bottles of Bell's and Teachers' whisky, red and white plonk, ale, Harvey's amontillado sherry and Dry Fly. We toasted the providers with happy smiles.

The awful prospect of a lack of meaningful communication within Wales itself was amply illustrated by the title of the afternoon debate: 'State patronage of the arts and the procedures of the Welsh Arts Council' – procedures which still remain a mystery and a source of woe. The Union's chairman had already made our position clear to the Press, explaining that for the past two years, relations with the Welsh Arts Council had been 'bewildering and unpleasant'. An invitation to the conference had gone out to its Literature Committee chairman, the old composer Walford Davies, or a suitable replacement, but they couldn't – or wouldn't – attend for one reason or another, the main excuse being that no 'full' invitation had been received (by 'full' they probably meant a gilt-edged card and return petrol expenses to Harlech). The council's literature boss, Meic Stephens, had been in Moscow on holiday, but came home three days before the conference. It was all nonsense, of course: there were at least three deputies who could have attended, but the committee is biased against the WUW because of its democratic membership and its ability to receive good media coverage. This was plain for all to see.

Our chairman, perspiring under the TV lamps, was furious, but laced his fury with humour as droplets slid down his nose, pointing to an empty chair upon which a WAC bum should have been. 'They are not faceless bureaucrats but invisible ones,' he said, shifting his glasses to his bridge as the sweat still dripped. (I thought, sadly, of the famous empty black chair at an old Eisteddfod for the dead soldier and bard, Hedd Wyn.) The chairman said that if Union representatives were invited to the WAC in Museum Place, Cardiff, for another meeting, they'd probably find ten empty chairs. He banished such 'unworthy thoughts' but the whole shambles was a typically Welsh situation. 'That's why I understand it.' He chronicled the battles with the WAC over a new magazine and the need for WUW representation on the Lit. Committee. If a Martian landed, he said, it would be baffled by a situation in which people who hold money for writers won't give it to them. 'Please can I have some money to launch this intelligent magazine?' 'No, we're keeping it for ourselves and the chosen few.' The WAC were the guardians of the public purse, custodians of mediocrity, solid citizens protecting the poor readers against indiscriminate scribblers who only wished to make a fast buck. His use of irony was commendable, since irony and paradox are the best, perhaps the only, weapons against conventional mediocrity.

So it goes. It's pure Monty Python, and sometimes I think that only a battery of satirists could adequately expose these unbelievable fish in their culture tanks. During the debate, contributions from the floor only served to stress some depressing truths familiar to most of us by now: the secrecy and seemingly dark motives of bureaucratic establishments, cold as charity, sinking anything in sight that made waves or rocked boats, always playing safe and hostile to change. It was scoundrel time, all right. At one point I thought the bitter criticism was being overstated, giving us a picture of people who were good husbands and fathers (or wives and mothers) but had a touch of evil when they got to the office. Could this happen in *Cardiff*? I always saw them as a row of Toby jugs, each trying to play Captain Bligh, or occasionally Maggie Thatcher.

John Osmond, ex-editor of *Arcade* and a writer who has good cause to be cynical about the ways of the WAC, said that literature, unlike music or painting or the other arts, was the only really controversial art because it could shift opinion and disturb the status quo, or words to that effect. As members commented on this eternal dilemma of individuals versus the state, I almost felt the threads of my own ideals coming apart at the seams. This is what makes skilful subversion so attractive, to do what one can to prevent the smothering processes of the insensitive and unimaginative.

Before tea, gossip in the corridors revolved around the bland leading the bland inside the Welsh arts system, and how a sniff of power corrupts even more than Lord Acton said it could.

The last session was on the re-launch of *Planet*, its content, editorial staffing, and fees to contributors. As is known, our 200-strong Union opposed the WAC decision to give £50,000 a year to re-jig this literary and current affairs journal, edited by Ned Thomas and closed in 1979, and of which I was literary editor for nine years. The Union put forward its plan for a *New Wales* magazine, produced a full first issue at very short notice in about two days and waited for the verdict. It was rejected. One of our members thought it resembled a poor man's *Encounter* or the sort of bumf one is handed at the entry to some provincial arts festival; another called it 'the longest suicide note ever written'. This latter utterance was an overstatement to which our chairman replied in an interview: 'We encourage our members to be witty and sardonic.' He also said, after he knew *Planet* II was on the way: 'We are being treated to a *Planet* of the past. The in-built weaknesses of old are still there. How will it be sold, from where will it get advertising?'

There is no doubt that John Morgan would like to edit a reputable magazine, with the talented executive committee behind or around him, comfortably ensconced. This ambition must have been in their sights, and I only wish they'd had the opportunity; it may yet come, one way or another. But now Ned Thomas, a keen WUW member, came bravely to Harlech without flanking support from Museum Place, to tell us that *Planet* II would be set up in Aberystwyth in May 1985 with a part-time managing editor (himself), a full-time deputy editor plus assistant, and £50 per thousand words for contributors, which is fair bread, better than the thin crust of Barclay's we used to receive. Ned summarised plans for distribution and advertising, and said it wouldn't be a *Planet* of the past but of the present. As for content, historians and sociologists would be particularly welcome, and journalists, short-story writers and poets too, of course. The plan already has a suspicious academic rattle about it, another mandarin excursion for the arid school of thought into more over-analysis of the 'Welsh predicament' so beloved of their kind. Such material goes on and on, like an endless funeral.

Ned himself should remember that many of the younger writers in English see the advent of *Planet* II as a repeat performance of an exercise in safety, protected by the WAC, with a tidy bias towards a Welsh-language core. (To be fair, I don't remember any Arts Council editorial interference on the old *Planet*, though there may have been mutterings in the background, as was the case with *Arcade*.) Ned should take account of this disenchantment and unease if he wishes to freshen the present drab scene, to rid it of sickening blandness and the dry-as-dust.

This *Planet* business hasn't split the Union, but there are those who say they'll 'boycott' the mag and those who say they won't. Divide-and-rule again, perhaps. The debate didn't generate as much heat as I thought it would, which was rather disappointing. Janet Dubé rebelled, as expected, being an admirable woman of strong opinions and a bonny fighter, but there may be no magazine in the Western world radical enough for her. She's on to a loser, for there isn't a bourgeois arts apparatus in existence which would fund what she represents: a once-and-for-all finish to the hypocrisy and conformity that stifles us, the dispiriting pragmatism of politics in our day. The other members of the executive committee, sound men all, seem like SDP moderates compared with Janet in full flight. Maybe she and I, plus a handful of others, should have lived in the middle of the French or Russian Revolutions. Certainly nothing about this present society will ever satisfy us.

A parting note on Ned Thomas: I know him to be a splendid editor, and excellent on the printed page, but in speech he was mildly criticised by certain members for seeming to take his arguments into a tunnel from which he couldn't extricate himself. He does ramble somewhat, unaware of the marshalling process when he's particularly excited, but this is simply because the sheer speed of his intellect is too far ahead of his mouth which is trying, about a minute behind, to deliver his thoughts. Sort that one out.

Now it was time for dinner and passable legs, breasts and wings of chicken (union drumsticks) with scrambled eggs and limp lettuce with rice for the vegetarians. Another fine pudding. Then to the hotel for more sounds from Bonclust and readings from members, bits of the performances shot by the cameras for future transmission. Rob Minhinnick 'coordinated' the evening which included a moving elegy on the Welsh military dead on the Falklands by Anthony Conran, poems by veteran (in the poetic sense) Peter Gruffydd, ex-miner Terry Hetherington, and that careful craftsman Steve Griffiths. Duncan Bush, who also read, collected £100 for the south Wales miners. Even the HTV film crew, not exactly renowned for aesthetic pursuits, stayed on to savour the poetry. And a lecturer in philosophy at Swansea, Hugh Price, quoted two of Wittgenstein's fragments of wisdom: 'Everything that can be said can be said clearly.' 'Whereof one cannot speak, thereof one must be silent.'

There was a slight verbal tussle upstairs at the hotel when an elderly barmaid tried to sweep our fraternal group out with the fag-ends. She was brusque and abrupt, squawking at us like a Gwynedd hen, and chairman and friends resented it, especially after spending a small ransom on drinks. 'Patience, dear lady,' we said. 'It doesn't really matter.' However, peace was made and we shuffled off to the college lounge for a nightcap. There Janet Dubé made it up with Ned Thomas – on the surface anyway – and both were last seen arguing amiably about *Planet* II, or the word or whatever. Then the dregs of a Stewart's Finest Scotch bottle donated by Emyr Daniel of HTV. And so to kip.

One mystery of the weekend was that while the members were doing something else, the chairman and guests were being interviewed by Emyr the hot-shot in various parts of the interior and grounds, but I never saw them at it. Of course, as they helped to give us a free conference, the boxmen had every right to structure their own programme, but they could have asked some of the members what they thought of their own Union. The glamour of 'names' continually seduces TV presenters.

We had a Sabbath breakfast of pale sausages. I wanted to inspect a pub called the Rum Hole down the hill from the college but it was a Sunday and nothing was open. My friend Jean went for a walk on the dunes and saw a green streak pass her. It was Dafydd Elis Thomas, MP, jogging in his emerald track-suit, keeping fit for the sedentary House of Commons and dreaming in daylight of the total collapse of the British State.

The rump of the conference, about 35 souls, attended the AGM. Our chairman, looking as if he possessed the remarkable gift himself of never suffering from hangovers, appeared sprucer than some of us felt. We were coming to the end of the long weekend, not as spry as we were on Friday and blurred around the edges. Dick Edwards looked pale and interesting sipping water, shepherded by his mate Duncan Bush who had to look after his Volkswagen driver for the twisting journey back to the south. The lovely hospitality, and our struggle against official art, were taking their toll.

The chairman said that the committee had sent condolences to the next-of-kin of two members, Walter Haydn Davies and Richard Burton. (Mr Burton had generously given a sum of money to the Union.) Nigel Jenkins, who had done such a fine job in helping to organise the week-end and so many other things, was resigning as secretary and Janet Dubé would take his place. We thanked Nigel and welcomed Janet. Cliff James had resigned as editor of the Newsletter and his replacement would be Dick Edwards. We all agreed that it was a good idea to fill these jobs on a regular rotating basis. The treasurer, Robin Reeves, said we were in the black and with the latest subs coming in, the coffers weren't exactly full to overflowing but the position was fairly healthy.

We passed three motions, after some tinkering with semantics: that we deplored the way the WAC's magazine decision was taken, and its Literature Committee's craven acceptance of the cuts in WAG funding; that we write to the WAG about the present uncomfortable relationship between the WUW, WAG and its Lit. Committee, and ask the council to direct its committee to meet the Union EC; that the EC publish the proceedings of this conference, thus initiating an annual presentation and account of the

Union and its members' work.

Small Jaci Stephen, a bright dark babe and budding fiction-writer, suggested we meet with the WAC 'with a view to their surrender' (laughter). Robin thought we should negotiate for a ceasefire, pending armistice talks. More and more in this long-running dispute, one is tempted to use the jargon of military communiqués, as if we were securing an Anzio beach-head of the imagination against our old conventional foe.

There followed some very Byzantine and labyrinthian discussion of the Theatre Writers' Union and its problems between its metropolitan (London) and provincial (meaning Wales) branches, most of which eluded me – and others too, I suspect. By this time a few members were yawning and wanted more coffee. There were sensible proposals from younger members for the WUW to help widen the WAC 'writers on tour' list, but the latter's reply to this would doubtless be that certain people had to finish their apprenticeship first, to learn to walk before they could run. Several members rightly boil with indignation and resentment at the chronic shortage of literary and journalistic outlets in Wales and are already involved in their own DIY versions with *Spectrum* (Chris Bendon) in Lampeter and *Maximum Load* (Brian Phillips, David Fellows) in Penarth. I was wishing that the treasurer had enough loot to hire a helicopter for our poets, as Rob Minhinnick told me that Faber the publishers were sending out Seamus Heaney and the spoilt Craig Raine in a chopper to do a reading tour through England. What publicity for the WUW if we could do this – perhaps HTV would lend us theirs.

Duncan Bush then invented a new term, 'point of rumour' (much laughter), when conveying the hush-hush information about the threatened import of 'big names' from England into Wales to give poetry and prose readings. If this is so, let it be a two-way traffic and Duncan can control it on behalf of the Union this side of the border. Big names from elsewhere, especially London, usually mean visits from the Metaphor Men and assorted, well-heeled academics of fashionable reputation.

The chairman wound up, pronounced the conference a success, and promised another goodie for next year, probably on censorship and held in the south, with a 'distinguished' speaker and open to the public for any key debate. He said we were packing up at Harlech feeling more cheerful and buoyant than ever. This was true. There would be no official Union 'boycott' of *Planet* II and he wished it well, a gesture which brought a smile to the face of Ned Thomas, who didn't need any bandages, though he knew that the whole affair was much more than a storm in a pint-pot. A couple of us only hoped that the Union wouldn't lose its focus without a magazine, and that we would become more than a lobbying body.

On the way to lunch, a platoon of us were led like the Pied Piper of Harlech up and down those bloody stairs and out of the lift on the wrong floor until we eventually found the food-trough. Sunday lunch was roast beef, of course, with Yorkshire pudding; you could have two Yorkshire puddings if you didn't have soup. Then the rains came and the sky dripped like wet cement. Through the refectory windows we could see the white horses out in Cardigan Bay and water, water everywhere. At the table I wondered if two of the guest-speakers, Arden and Edwards, had been bewildered by the twists and turns of our parochial literary affairs. They had left, as had the HTV crew with their equipment and ourselves trapped inside their reels of film. We said so-long to fellow-member and deputy warden of Harlech, Graham Allen, who's one of our favourites. It was about the best weekend I've spent in over 20 years of such junkets. Conspicuously absent were the petty cordial hatreds of the literary coteries. I liked the laughter, goodwill, intelligence, care, drinking, and *spirit* of our Union.

The last sight was of a patient member still waiting for a missing member (there's always one) in the car park. She had offered to give him a lift and he had said he would meet her after he'd eaten his orange. He was still adrift when we left – locked in his room or in one of those lavatories that look like part of the wooden wall. Perhaps he's still there.

Fringe Diversions

A selection of Literary Criticisms and Reviews

Richard Burton: A Biography
by John Cottrell and Fergus Cashin (Arthur Barker, £2.50)

This is called an 'intimate' biography of Richard
Burton, and, presumably, will have to satisfy enthus-
iasts until the definitive one is written as he passes
into thespian venerability. The authors interviewed
almost everyone who has known him well during forty-
five years; relations, teachers, actors, producers,
directors, girl friends, miners and rugby players.
According to the smothering blurb, 'they have
plumbed the depths of a still, brimming pond, running
disturbingly deep'. From this one may rightly gather
that the portrait is rather a fulsome one, as if commis-
sioned by the subject himself, and one receives the
impression that the authors were in keen competition
with others to throw in the first bid. Much of it is also
written in the depressingly ephemeral prose of show-
biz journalism, leaking with sentiment. Parts of it fail
to ring true. There is a good deal of exaggeration, the
padding so dear to the hearts of cinema publicists, and
tedious repetition of facets of Mr Burton's character
and personality. Inevitably, his Rolls Royce and a
number of other objects are 'bible-black', and the
hometown survivors who remember him sound like
fugitives from *How Green Was My Valley*.

Richard Jenkins was the twelfth son of thirteen children, born in 1925 to a bright miner and a former barmaid in Pontrhydyfen, Glamorgan. He arrived into bleak poverty, and was brought up during the Depression, then removed from grammar school in Port Talbot, because of hardship at home, to work in the local Co-op, as a haberdasher's apprentice on thirty shillings a week. His early mentor, an eloquent teacher named Meredith Jones, saw his potential and helped to get him re-admitted to school, where he came under the wing of Philip Burton, who steered him into acting and became his guardian. He went into *The Druid's Rest* by Emlyn Williams, and then to Exeter College, Oxford, for a six-month course under a Service recruit system, reading English Literature and Italian. After that came the RAF, the London stage years, marriage, Stratford, Hollywood and Broadway, where he was idolised by the bobbysoxers and praised by the mandarin critics. The next part of the book, headed 'Richard and Elizabeth', sounds like a chapter from medieval English history; certainly they and their retinue have seemed like a court without a country. There was the scandal in Rome during the making of the disastrous *Cleopatra* when he and Miss Taylor capered in the sun. *Hamlet* in New York, the string of mediocre films they made together, then the winning streak and the boom period. The rest of the saga, unless you are a hermit or have been cut off from

Western society for the last ten years, is familiar to all.

Mr Burton and his beautiful wife are two of the most golden people of our time, with everything money can buy. Like royalty, they travel by private jet and yacht, and maintain households in Mexico and Switzerland. They claim to outspend the shipowner, Onassis, and estimate their annual treasure in millions. Their movements across continents are reported in the popular press with a loving detail which would do credit to Samuel Pepys. Here described are the parties at the Dorchester and elsewhere, the scribes, the cameramen, hangers-on and free-loaders – all the dismally peripheral and shallow, pin-headed, brittle figures who clutter in their wake for a brush with glamour.

The Burtons are well-off, but apparently their overheads are enormous. If they stopped working tomorrow and sacked everyone in what they call 'the family', their combined income would be about three hundred thousand dollars a year, but to keep their present entourage it costs a million a year, including the yacht, jewellery, paintings, and insurance on the jewellery and paintings.

Mr Burton is revealed as a very straightforward person, and also a masterly teller of tales, a Welsh cock of conversation, his anecdotes enriched with choice bits of verse or maliciously precise mimicry. He likes cannelloni and vodka-and-tonic, and is a prince among drinkers. He is boosted as having been a great one with the ladies before falling heavily into love and loyalty with Elizabeth Taylor. I saw him once when I was a very junior clerk at the BBC in Cardiff. He was on leave from the RAF, and came into the canteen looking for a dark, pretty secretary he liked from Aberdare. I think he asked her to accompany him on a boat trip to Weston-super-Mare, but she declined. Years later, when he became famous, she was said to have regretted her refusal, but young Burton would probably have slipped away from her, anyway.

He doesn't understand actors, or what they think or talk about when they discuss acting. He thinks Gielgud, Olivier, Schofield and Redgrave are good, but he doesn't know why they do it. He says he does it for money and sheer enjoyment, which is probably why the others do it, too – but 'when the bug gets into your blood it stays all your life'. His part as the narrator in the film version of *Under Milk Wood*, through which he wandered like a lost sheep, was the first Welsh role he played since *The Last Days of Dolwen* in 1949. In his entire career he thinks he has given only one good performance, and that was *Coriolanus* at the Old Vic. He still hopes to devote time to writing when he retires. His Dylanesque piece of prose, 'A Christmas Story', was published by Heinemann, but he says he writes with painful slowness and will have to be out of screen action if he hopes to produce more. He thinks the greatest poem in the English, French or Welsh languages is the present tense of the verb 'to be', but with a taste for poetry as austere as that, one imagines he might have severe reservations about some of the passages in *Under Milk Wood*. (Burton knew Thomas, but not well: 'His moods were tidal, they came and went', he once said.)

Handsome, rugged yet sensitive, and with a superb voice, Richard Burton has come a long way from Taibach and was obviously destined for a fat slice of the cake. A number of people consider that he might be better employed developing his fine talent in good plays rather than squandering it in poor films (his own view of the shambles of the artistic side of his career was once described by Gwyn Thomas as 'embarrassment sliding into horror'). But there is no doubt that he is a splendid, brooding actor, and he generally emerges from this cloying tribute as a kind, warm, honest, generous, intelligent and articulate human being.

Killhope Wheel

by Jon Silkin (Mid Northumberland Arts Group, College Road, Ashington, Northumberland, 30p)

Jon Silkin has been one of the few authentic, independent expressionists in English poetry of the past two decades, keeping well apart from The Movement, The Group, and Post-Movement Drab, and only marring his record by some involvement in the poetry-and-jazz business. His work has followed a trajectory of its own, developing away from a style of heavy rhetoric – which stemmed from his admiration for Isaac Rosenberg – towards something sparer and bonier. There is a good deal of density and enjambment in his poetry, an opacity which he finds difficult to avoid in his tenacious pursuit of truth. Jon Silkin is much given to reports on cemeteries, burial mounds, skulls and bones, clamping mud, and the battlefield that is underground – all done with a knotted and tortuous compression that I personally find impressive, but which can also border on the incomprehensible.

In this rather emaciated, well-produced booklet, he writes of an abandoned mining district in Northumberland. The title-poem is to do with the military crushing of a miners' strike in 1860 at

Killhope Wheel in Durham, and there is a lot of blood on the sheep runs and soaked into the turf by the actions of the brute soldiery:

> Why have
> I to see red coat soldiers prick
> between washed stones, and bayonets
> tugged from the seeping flesh?

The poet feels real pain at visiting the scene of a day's horror that occurred a century ago, and turns in other poems to a monologue by a platelayer or to descriptions of the stilled wheels and rusted scrap of old workings.

Jon Silkin, like Basil Bunting, has a faithful following in the north and elsewhere because of the genuine seriousness of his attempts to speak of public matters and bad moments in history in an urgent, personal way. He gives the impression of being one of the few poets writing whose work really costs him something. It is full of rawness and torment. Unfortunately, he is often tardy in allowing images and situations sufficient freedom from his own worried probing, and much of the visual impact is blurred by his drilling, over-intent gaze. He seeks a harsh clarity, but a tortuous and winding syntax occasionally bogs him down.

Still, there are some strong passages in this book, as

247

in his recent collection Amana Grass. Mr Silkin is to be recommended as a poet whose struggle with language to convey his brittle vision, coupled with the size of his particular undertaking, contributes weightily to the general sense of naked effort in his work.

Mercian Hymns

by Geoffrey Hill (Andre Deutsch, £1.75, paperback, £1)

Geoffrey Hill's third volume is a sequence of thirty brief prose-poems, coming three years after *King Log*, which in turn followed *For the Unfallen* after a long gap of nine years. He is a poet with a profound historical sense who has been called 'one of the great enigmas of his poetical generation', and one feels it is his cold, austere reticence, his cerebral restraint, which appeals to many of his more rational contemporaries who are sick of undisciplined emotion and posturing. Many find him a welcome relief from the current wave of minor Black Mountain Americans who have climbed on the Olson-Creeley wagon; he could be called an intelligent poet's poet, continually striving for 'formality under duress' (his own words) – a phrase which reminds one of Hemingway's 'grace under pressure'. Many of his pieces are unyielding, and resist even several readings.

Today there are several English poets who are jettisoning direct personal experience and going back into folk-tale, myth and legend. One thinks of Jon Silkin's gnarled reflections on a nineteenth century Durham mining settlement, George Mackay Brown's Orkney sagas, Jeremy Hooker's nostalgic explorations of agrarian Wessex, Thom Gunn's recent *Moly*, Bunting's *Briggflatts* – and now Geoffrey Hill's Mercian legends. Mr Hooker himself has pointed out that both Geoffrey Hill and R. S. Thomas bring to traditional forms a world larger than the 'ego-system'. The only danger, it seems to me, is that poets on this course may end on the far reaches of a polar ice-cap, with the historian or archaeologist pitching his tent and the poet left miles behind. There is probably a good case to be made against the poem as straight narrative, as documentary, or as an explosion of egotism such as those dreadful domestic dirges of the fifties. But fragmentary and too-knotted excursions into the distant past, with their shying-away from personal experience, could put modern English poetry on a very cold and monotonous track indeed.

Mercian Hymns are canticles in honour of the historical – but also legendary – Mercian king, Offa, who established the supremacy of the west midlands in eighth century England. They reconstruct his career from his naming and crowning, through his striking of coins, law-making, dealings with the church and conquests, to his death. They are diggings not only into history but also into the lost childhood of the poet. Some of the poems are spoken by Offa, and in others he is the hero of a short narrative or cameo. Mr Hill sees him as a creature of legend, the 'presiding genius of the West Midlands', whose dominion stretches into the twentieth century, as a power maniac at any time in any place. Ancient and modern interlock:

> Cohorts of charabancs fanfared Offa's province and his concern, negotiating the by-ways from Teme to Trent. Their windshields dripped butterflies. Stranded on hilltops they signalled with plumes of steam. Twilight menaced the land. The young women wept and surrendered.

(This is very neat: the windscreens *drip* butterflies because the butterflies too have blood.) Here is the opening Hymn, with a sardonic-comment on power and pride at the end, 'X' being Offa:

> King of the perennial holly groves, the riven sandstone: overlord of the M5: architect of the historic rampart and ditch, the citadel at Tamworth, the summer hermitage in Holy Cross: guardian of the Welsh Bridge and the Iron Bridge: contractor to the desirable new estates: salt-master: moneychanger: commissioner for oaths: martyrologist: the friend of Charlemagne.
> 'I liked that,' said X, 'sing it again.'

Offa was 'architect of the historic rampart and ditch' but is also 'overlord of the M5', a description which

251

carries the intellectual's disdain for the way we live now, and the lack of colour, ritual and pageantry in our cramped lives.

By shifting Offa from his historical frame and letting him move about the centuries, Mr Hill is cheating, and asking us to accept too much fantasy in the chronicle. But, when he digs deep into the past, the poems are little excavations in themselves, an act of archaeology which accumulates images of coins, metals, stones, plants and dead animals:

> Their spades grafted through the variably-resistant soil. They clove to the hoard. They ransacked epiphanies, vertebrae of the chimera, armour of wild bees' larvae. They struck the fire-dragon's faceted skin...
>
> It is autumn. Chestnut-boughs clash their inflamed leaves. The gardens fester for attention: telluric cultures enriched with shards, corms, nodules, the sunk solids of gravity. I have accrued a golden and stinking blaze.

The main activities of Mercia were coining, hammering, carving, and these are the qualities of Mr Hill's poetic technique – rigorously compressed verbal structures that match the theme. Here is the excavating of Offa's coins:

Trim the lamp; polish the lens; draw, one by one,
rare coins to the light. Ringed by its own lustre,
the masterful head emerges, kempt and jutting,
out of England's well. Far from his underkingdom
of crinoid and crayfish, the runestone's province.
Rex Totius Anglorum Patriae, coiffured and
ageless, portrays the self-possession of his
possession, cushioned on a legend.

Geoffrey Hill was born and brought up in Offa's
territory, and some of the king's memories of
childhood – schoolboy rivalries, wartime air-raid
shelters, and the like – are obviously the poet's own
(this is what I mean by fantasy). The despotic king's
blinding splendour is also associated with a boy's
dream of majesty, or what he thinks is majesty, so that
Offa becomes both child-substitute and respected,
awe-inspiring father-figure, who frightens 'malefactors
with ash from his noon cigar'. In a way, Mr Hill's
sequence is an original version of a personal saga, like
Hughes's *Crow*, Lowell's *Notebook*, or Berryman's
Dream Songs, with the plodding reader following his
clever but rather baffling guide through bits of broken
pottery and historical remains which have recently
been unearthed, while the guide uses formal, elliptical
English to describe his own childhood or to pay
affectionate tribute to long-dead soldiers. (For some
odd reason, I kept thinking of myself being taken over

253

the peripheral ruins of the Old Priory on Caldey Island by a particularly articulate and erudite monk.)

Still, it is all quite impressive, even if the dominating Offa-figure is slightly too grandiose to carry the small puffs of the poet's autobiographical fragments. There is also a poker-faced, frugal economy of means that would make R. S. Thomas seem verbose, that recoils from anything resembling an emotional spurt. It is certainly austere *grandeur* that Mr Hill is after, with skulls lying on velvet in tunnels propped with bone while a piece of ceremonial magnificence is taking place outside. He has always wanted us to remember the armies of the outnumbering dead, the glory that was England, and to hold requiems for the Plantagenet kings. He is besotted by a sense of loss when contemplating history, but what he is actually *saying* about it, or what lessons he thinks it can teach us, is anyone's guess. He promises in certain lines and chopped fragments that he is on the brink of something remarkable, but they seldom come to much. Given this limitation of brave ambition – of which Mr Hill is probably only too aware – then one wishes he could face the perfectly ordinary with less horror and settle for more of the satisfying pinpoint accuracy contained in this particular prose-poem:

When the sky cleared above Malvern, he lingered in his orchard: by the quiet hammer-pond. Troutfry simmered there, translucent, as though forming the water's under-skin. He had a care for natural minutiae. What his gaze touched was his tenderness. Woodlice sat pellet-like in the cracked bark and a snail sugared its new stone.

A strong clue to what prompted *Mercian Hymns* has been given elsewhere. In 1969, Geoffrey Hill published a piece on *Cymbeline*, in *The Morality of Art*, edited by D. W. Jefferson: 'A British king is seen for what he is: uxorious, irrational, violent when prodded, indulgent, of absolute status and ultimately invulnerable. This might be taken as a disinterested view of the "law" of Prerogative.' To reinforce his claim, he also quoted from Bacon's *Advancement of Learning* where that Prerogative is seen as 'drenched in flesh and blood, civil history, morality, policy, about the which men's affections, praises, fortunes do turn and are conversant'.

As a poet Geoffrey Hill is different, bizarre, very eloquent and out on a high path of his own. One accepts his seeming obsession with the divine right of monarchs, the trappings of cynical, often tyrannical kingship, and reads on with relish.

Another World
by James Hanley (Andre Deutsch, £1.75)

It is nearly ten years since James Hanley last published
a novel. This was *Say Nothing*, which was based on
one of his plays. He has had a long stint in the theatre
and television, where he sharpened his talent for irony
and wit. In an interview with Philip Oakes of *The
Sunday Times*, he said, modestly enough: 'For eight
years I lived under the delusion that I was a dramatist.
Now I know that I'm not. and I'd better get back to
the job.' His welcome return to novel-writing reveals
the same complete authority and control over his
material that we remember. His reputation has rested
mainly on his novels of the sea – V. S. Pritchett once
said, 'he is the only living English writer who knows
how to write about the sea' – but he has also tackled
other themes. This new book is about Wales, a country
which he likes to call 'the place of kingdoms' – a
romantic description which reaches rather far back
into history – and he has explored these 'kingdoms'
before in *The Welsh Sonata* and *Don Quixote Drowned*.

The conflict of *personal* ideas of what life is all
about is central to Mr Hanley's vision, and has
increasingly attracted him. The characters themselves
seem to build the narrative structure, and the
situations that arise from their own conduct and

desires keep their tensions squabbles and pettinesses on the boil and their continual misfortunes stoked-up. Whether on board ship or in a closed community, they thrive on discord and inhabit a deprived, tight, limited and mean world, often looking for happiness under very odd and eccentric conditions which appear dead-set against its achievement. In this separate, rigidly shut and self-supporting society, James Hanley seems eventually to have chosen personal conflict as the one piece of evidence that human life exists in a state of freedom. It is an idea that may attract a younger generation more than the clinical concepts of blatantly-optimistic purveyors of impersonal revolution. His very isolation and integrity, his anti-utopian position as he grubs among the stoic moaners and sufferers, comes as a relief from the rhetorical wanderers in dreamland.

In the aptly-titled *Another World*, the society remains as closed and stuffy as that of Mauriac, though funnier, and there are plenty of echoes from the past. It is full of touches of individual, eccentric, almost-Edwardian behaviour. When Miss Vaughan, a recluse, arrives in the small Welsh coastal town of Garthmeilo and the porter, reaching for her suitcase, says 'Allow me', she replies 'I will not allow you', and picks up the case and walks away. She is equally disconcerting when the splendid and ebullient Mrs Gandell, gin-swigging proprietress of the 'Decent' Hotel where Miss

Vaughan lodges, asks her a few civil questions while welcoming her, though Mrs Gandell and her henchman handyman-assistant, Jones (who does his duty in both dining-room and bedroom), are too glad of a guest in the dead of winter, however weird, to betray disapproval. Miss Vaughan takes a job in an office – quietly efficient, she gives no sign of strangeness unless someone tries to invade her privacy, whereupon she shuts the door in his face so firmly that he can catch no glimpse of what is on the other side. The person who most wants to overcome Miss Vaughan's icy reserve is Mervyn Thomas, the minister at Penuel chapel, who is in determined pursuit. He is so violently drawn to her that his fury of a sister, Margiad, who leans all her nagging weight on her brother to save him from disgrace, fears he has completely lost his wits. He follows Miss Vaughan, or stands, single-minded, a dark shadowy shape outside the hotel where she lies on her bed in her room talking to an imaginary friend. The novel reveals the growth of his obsession until it compels him to trespass on territory which Miss Vaughan is bound to keep inviolate.

The story of Mervyn Thomas's passion develops in counterpoint to that of Mrs Gandell and Jones, who receive a delightful surprise which will enable them to maintain their scandalous relationship. Looking on both the tragic and comic with the same combination of intensity and detachment, Mr Hanley makes the conventional distinction between them seem unreal. He shows the reader experience rather than inviting him to mourn or laugh over it. Everything is almost-acceptable in this world.

One hopes that this new novel marks the end of James Hanley's long silence among the drama scripts. Facing the title page – in place of the long customary list of previous books which make up the entire Hanley canon – is the simple notice: *In preparation – A Woman in the Sky*. Last year he celebrated his seventieth birthday and the fortieth anniversary of the publication of his first novel, which is a rare achievement in English literature. E. M. Forster called him a novelist of distinction and originality; Henry Green thought him superior even to Conrad; Herbert Read described him as one of the most vigorous and impressive of contemporary writers; John Cowper Powys unequivocally used the word 'genius' (Powys is much admired by Hanley, who wrote a book on him called *The Man in the Corner*); and C. P. Snow has gone on record with an opinion of him as one of the most important of living authors, unsurpassed in qualities of humanity, compassion and sheer power – words which people like Snow and Priestley usually reserve for Dickens or Balzac. This is indeed heady praise for any writer, no matter how long he has been at the job. James Hanley, with his fine gifts displayed in this latest offering, fully deserves it.

Round the Poets

Any responsible editor will tell you that his spirits sink a little when he receives parcels of poetry for review. All he can do is to try to sift the good from the fair, and the fair from the rubbish, and then send them on to chosen reviewers, who are waiting in their attics for the postman's dreaded knock. Any reviewer will tell you that his spirits sink even lower as he contemplates the bundle of books, containing perhaps a couple of artists, and the rest nowhere, skimpy volumes written and privately printed by self-regarding doggerel men in Camden Town or elderly ladies in Melton Mowbray. Now the reviewer must attempt a further sorting-out, and temper his urge to make a sweeping indictment of most contemporary verse with justice and a constructive honesty that his old professor told him was essential.

I have to hand Raymond Garlick's latest offering, *A Sense of Time* (Gwasg Gomer, 75p). I had already read a number of the poems in magazines, and re-read this volume with pleasure. It includes his customary mixture of praise and lament for Wales, with a tart-apple of bitterness creeping in here and there, and an extract from his long, dazzling radio poem 'Acclamation', about the Catholic martyrs. Mr Garlick has been in the field for a long time, and his work has become more elegant each passing year. It is like watching the progress of a master in calligraphy. Seeing the classical measure of his verse, sensing the almost-perfect rhythm and stress in his lines, one would expect Mr Garlick to agree with Robert Frost that he would as soon write free verse as play tennis with the net down. His technical accomplishment is considerable, his structures worked out as if on a metrical slide-rule. Thus, in the poem 'Agincourt':

> I live in Llansteffan
> and I know Agincourt –
> the bonemeal verdant meadows
> over which they fought:
>
> green places, both of them now,
> but then, in 1415,
> at Agincourt the blood
> clotted the buttercups' sheen
> and the earth was disembowelled
> where stakes and hooves had been.

How splendid is that 'bonemeal verdant meadows' and 'clotted the buttercups' sheen'! His work is full of such chiselled perfections. The economy of his imagery, and those marvellous phrases punching out from the page, convince me that one day Raymond

Garlick will complete a masterpiece. He is too formal for some tastes, giving the false impression of a pedant, his very preciseness acting like a red rag to the sloppy barbarians. But the craft, the peculiar excellence of Raymond Garlick remains. In danger of seeming fulsome, I consider him to be one of the delights of Anglo-Welsh poetry, showing the cocky apprentices, upstarts, hustlers and nine-day wonders how it should be done. No one achieves the effects he does without long experience and a supreme control over his material.

Just now and again I feel that his continual effort to squeeze Wales into a wider European context is rather forced and slightly overdone, but there is no doubt that he genuinely thinks of himself as a European. Perhaps his allegiance to Rome and his sojourn in Holland have something to do with this. He operates a two-way telescope, so to speak – the political lens on Wales, and the religious one on the centre of his ancient faith. Out of the apparent incompatibility of embracing the ornate religion of pre-Reformation Wales, and standing up like a true nationalist-Calvinist, a ramrod of severity, for Welsh independence, his poetic status has been achieved. Unfortunately, the slow patriotic struggle in the Welsh backyard must, sadly and inevitably, cut off many of us from real integration with Europe for perhaps another generation. Sometimes it is necessary to remain separate to put one's house in order before joining the neighbouring community.

A collection I have been awaiting with interest is Jeremy Hooker's *The Elements* (Christopher Davies, 25p) in the Triskel series. It is a somewhat emaciated booklet, thin as a Giacometti, giving us only eleven poems, although the sequence 'Elegy for the Labouring Poor' is a long one. Most of the poems are correspondingly austere, a few almost crumbling at the touch. But I like Jeremy Hooker's work, very much. He has come to Wales to spend a few seasons among us, and his attitude is one of curiosity expressed in eloquent terms combined with the utmost respect for our history and traditions, realising we have a mind of our own, and doing his best to comprehend our foibles and whims (would that there were more Jeremy Hookers crossing our battered border, with sensitivity, intelligence and goodwill to offer).

The stark countryside of mid-Wales with its own associations finds a place in his recent work, and, as Sam Adams points out in an introduction, he seems to have gained from his Welsh experience a desire to establish connections with the past. The clear sense of history in his work, and his intense pre-occupation with a search for personal roots, elicits considerable sympathy from some of his Anglo-Welsh colleagues, who have listened to his perceptive strictures on their own output and have found these worth acting upon.

One might go so far as to say that this compassionate young man from Hardy's Wessex has helped certain Welsh practitioners to develop a little further, scrabbling out of the difficult impasse of rhetoric and discursiveness in which they were bogged clown. He understands, completely, a poet's love of his land and his desperate need to relate to his own people. Thus, his own integrity has been a quiet, steady example to others, and those poets he particularly admires – Edward Thomas, David Jones, R. S. Thomas and Roland Mathias – all contain lessons of restraint that heated Celts could usefully absorb.

It is Jeremy Hooker's dignified reticence that appeals, each word and line fully scrutinised for its allotment of truth and accuracy before being committed to the page; his refusal to embroider, to gloss, or to shout noisily. He reminds me of some patient, skilful sculptor working very slowly to chip away the best pieces from a slab of recalcitrant granite. Such work has the cleanliness of a skeleton, picked clean of fat:

He moves like timber on a swell,
In mud gaiters and clay-coloured cord.
Bent to it, sculpting a furrow.
Mould's his name: James Mould
With shoots in Hants and Wiltshire.
His blunt boot-prints, fugitive

As the cloud at his rear,
Are unseen by the camera that exhumes
Celtic patterns from suave downland.
But the tread's purposeful.

('Elegy for the Labouring Poor')

Of this collection, I especially liked 'Wasps', which deserves to be quoted in full:

Mad for nectar still,
Dying wasps crept everywhere.

They blundered against the windows
And spun on invisible pins,
Stunned by coldness we did not feel
Though the sun shone whiter
At a different angle.

I remember the beginning of its peace,
Blue autumn's blood-drowse cooling,
Agitated by the pitiful anger of wasps.

(I would guess that this poem was written after the summer of '71, the time of the Great Wasp Invasion of the western seaboard, when a swarm of the deadly things buzzed me while I was eating cake in the centre of Aberystwyth.) And here is a Hooker love poem, called 'There':

As sent to badger dark in the warm soil;
As moist places to the secret mole;
As essential darkness to earth itself:
Love, the night surrounds us.
We are the confluence of underground streams.
We grow together and in daylight
Flow out apart, now each in each, remade.

Jeremy Hooker leaves most of his fellow-Englishmen in the metropolis looking like spitters of microscopic cherrystones and stunted purveyors of scurrilous crap. His grave and impressive 'Elegy' is a brave, imaginative and moving sequence which wrestles with the heartbreaking problem of trying to pierce the darkness of the botched lives of his rural ancestors in Hampshire and Dorset, in the days of harsh poverty, cottage slums, dawn-to-dusk grafting in the fields, burning thatch and 'Captain Swing'. The melancholy tread of his poetry ('Nothing lasts / But the mortal nature of all that's unique'), the grapple to make some sense of the shaping landscape and the earth's continuity, fuse to make his undertaking a serious, coherent and ambitious one. Jeremy Hooker is already an important poet, having pushed on from his first selection in the Faber anthology *Introduction One* in 1969, and he may yet become a major one. Whether he chooses to be published in Wales or England (and he will always find a welcome here), it will be interesting to watch his future development. A man who can write like this has my small vote:

> For this is purgation: to scour men
> By divorcing them from all they know.
> But the things they love go with them,
> Untouchable, at times ferociously clear.

In the summer of 1970, Gillian Clarke submitted four poems to *Poetry Wales* that slightly shook the editorship, and so a poet who formerly wrote only unsuccessful prose and is supposed to have been 'overawed' by reading English poets, finally surfaced into a well-deserved place under the dappled Anglo-Welsh sun. She is one of the most interesting poets to emerge in Wales through recent years, and in another Triskel pamphlet, *Snow on the Mountain* (Christopher Davies, 25p), she lays before us the best of her work up to last summer. To be fair, I should state that part of Gillian Clarke is not really my kind of poet. I approach her touch of earth-motherhood, her sub-Lawrentian union of love and blood in family relationships, with a shiver of misgiving. One winces at the flooding celebration of the instinctual and physical life, 'The moving stream, the swelling bud nothing can halt' etcetera. Instead of nodding my head sagely and murmuring that all will be well in the worst of all possible worlds as I sit at the feet of the

Universal Mother, I find myself longing for a streak of good old sensible Greek masculine pessimism, and simply smile a trifle cynically at fecund, burgeoning, proliferating Woman as portrayed in Epstein's 'Genesis'. Gillian Clarke is fulfilled as wife and mother, writing about love, pregnancy, birth and infants. Or is she? Behind the young woman who shows 'concern for the man or child / Who pulls forward a chair and eats', I detect something deeper and darker, a questioner tugged by her share of unhappiness and frustration when 'All day we felt and watched the sun / Caged in its white diurnal heat, / pointing at us with its black stick' (I may be reading too much into this, but it's that 'black stick' which intrigues me). The poem 'Death of a Young Woman' contrasts brutally with all the commendable sanity and optimism of domestic certainty:

> The difference was that in her house
> The people were broken by her loss.
> He wept for her and the hard tasks
> He had lovingly done, for the short,
> Fierce life she had lived in the white bed,
> For the burden he had put down for good.
> As we sat huddled in pubs supporting
> Him with beer and words' warm breath,
> We felt the hollowness of his release.
> Our own ungrateful health prowled, young,

Gauche about her death. He was polite,
Isolated. Free. No point in going home.

Gillian Clarke is almost second to none at describing
the small incidents of family life, and the fond
'burnished' friendship that can exist within marriage:

In the little house at night
We can hear each other breathe.
Turning in our beds, and things
Moving in the grass, and the leaves
Of the laburnum trees combing
The roof all night.

Her observation, her thrush's eye for detail, is evident
in 'Blaen Cwrt', where she buttonholes you in the first
line:

You ask how it is. I will tell you.

Then:

There are no brochure blues or boiled sweet
Reds. All is ochre and earth and cloud-green
Nettles tasting sour and the smells of moist
Earth and sheep's wool. The wattle and daub
Chimney hood has decayed away, slowly
Creeping to dust, chalking the slate

Floor with stones. It has all the first
Necessities for a high standard
Of civilised living: silence inside
A circle of sound, water and fire,
Light on uncountable miles of mountain
From a big, unpredictable sky,
Two rooms, waking and sleeping,
Two languages, two centuries of past
To ponder on, and the basic need
To work hard in order to survive.

Gillian Clarke possesses discipline, clarity, precision, delicacy, tact, subtle insights and an original, reflectively conversational manner as she weaves her private story. She has been highly praised in some quarters. Many of the poems are touching and effective, and a warm, attractive personality shines through. She is often splendidly descriptive about nature, beautiful or hostile. But, as I said, that section of her subject-matter to do with birth pangs, the breeding-cycle and fertility-parallels, tends to be laboured, if you'll excuse the pun. What I would like to see her do is to plot the darker, tragic side of life (her 'black crow' of mortality), which, as she grows older, I am sure she is quite capable of doing.

Glyn Hughes lives in Yorkshire and won a Welsh Arts Council prize for his collection *Neighbours*, which caused a short ripple among the London critics. He writes about animals, farm people, his wife, and derelict mills. His latest, *Rest the Poor Struggler* (Macmillan, £2.00 – compared with Gomer's 75p for Garlick!), derives its title from the name of a now-demolished pub kept by a retired hangman, Albert Pierpoint, at Strangeways, Manchester, who later was rumoured to have hanged himself, which seems a nice piece of poetic justice. His language is exact, in the manner of the Irish agrarian Seamus Heaney, another educated country poet who has become rather sophisticated and suitably detached from the land he describes. Mr Hughes' method is full of cramped stress for his eternal struggle with the elements, which is as good a theme as any, I suppose. His stuff is packed with nostalgia, he has a lively eye and does not abandon himself to the superficial bucolic that characterises the outpourings of more fashionable nature poets, who may be secretly looking for God in the bare landscape. He has a definite flavour all his own, and after saying that, there is really not much more I want to say. Mr Hughes is aware of his immediate environment and does not prescribe for it, but if he hopes that his poems are open and un-claustrophobic, he may at least be disappointed by my own reaction. He believes that the resonance of an image has increased 'for the time being', and that an interest in narrative has diminished. It's that 'time being' which bothers me, as if he were climbing onto somebody else's bandwagon, before 'narrative' makes its timeless, interrupted come-back.

B. S. Johnson's *Poems Two* (Trigram Press, £1.75, cloth; £1.00, paper) has a naked-breasted lady on its cover, presumably for sensational purposes, as it has little or nothing to do with the contents, which carry one section-heading called 'Rotting'. I have enjoyed Mr Johnson's prose so much in the past that I was disappointed in this collection. It is a well-produced job, elegantly designed and printed with nice green end-papers. Mr Johnson was Gregynog Arts Fellow in Montgomeryshire for a year, and is remembered here with affection. These poems were written between 1964–71, created between his prolific bouts of novel-writing. Here is a sampler, called 'The Poet Holds His Future in His Hand':

Tonight I looked at it: I don't often

it performs its two functions well enough
in return I keep it reasonably clean

but quite by chance I looked at it tonight
and there were several dirty marks on it

I of course looked harder: and they were veins
underneath the skin, bloody great black veins.

they weren't there last time I happened to look
certainly the light was bad in that place

but there's no doubt that the pressure is on

Recently Mr Johnson criticised the Anglo-Welsh
because he thinks that the forms they employ are
almost without exception traditional, 'to sometimes
deadening effect'. All I can say is that some of the
poems in this volume certainly had a deadening,
stultifying effect upon me. These seem hardly worked-
on, they transmit a feeling of having been caught in
mid-air on their way to the waste-bin. He includes one
'found' fragment chopped-up into lines of varying
length which is actually the transcription of a dead
man's will. His diction is mostly urban-colloquial, the
man of parts, the cosmopolitan mixer not wanting to
seem bogus or parochial. Much of the work is pretty
thin, and a touch over-smart, which is hardly ever
apparent in his prose. Somehow, B. S. Johnson loses
much of his essence in his poetry. It is as if he requires
a wider area to move in, to gain space to comment
with honesty, pity and wit on both the beauty and
ugliness of life.

A few poems convey the impression of being the
products of a tired mind at the end of a long day's
novel-writing, the burning of the prose-craftsman's
candle, which after all is Mr Johnson's first concern.

In a sense, his sporadic poetry output is marginal to his central priority – that of sustained, carefully-sculpted fiction. The novel of highly-articulate experiment is at the centre of his activity, and verse strolls on the periphery, occasionally offering itself as a convenient deposit for the nagging worry, the logical thought, the witty aside, the condensed anecdote, and the haunting memory. One only wishes that the 'traditional' forms he criticises the Welsh for using were more regularly employed to rescue his own subject-matter.

Ruth Bidgood's *The Given Time* (Christopher Davies, £1.05) is her first collection, packing in more than sixty poems. The blurb says that her fondness for, and her 'involvement with mid-Wales' (how can you be involved with a geographical territory, unless there are people in it?) have deepened over the years. Some of her work owes a debt to Edward Thomas and lesser observers of landscape. She loves the Welsh countryside and its history, and her poems arc perfectly rational, sensitive, and tranquil. Together they make a pleasant picture of a region she is obviously wedded to. Otherwise, she tends to be a victim of dusty cliché, and the indolent phrase. She is exceptionally gentle without being genteel, and makes no pretensions at aiming for adventurous, unlimited objectives.

Among my pile of books, Peter Finch provides his edited version of *Typewriter Poems* (Second Aeon, 35p) and his own *Blats* (Second Aeon, 75p) which is a collection of what he calls 'non-poems' involving 'chance', the arbitrary finding of data in magazines and overheard conversation, etcetera. In other words, mostly 'found' pieces, and very funny some of them are. The residue of puritan finger-waggers will be out to lick a trickle of Mr Finch's blood if they read some of this naughtiness. The *Typewriter Poems* are something else, a fun-purchase for the ingenious designs alone, displaying the incredible versatility of the typewriting machine and the patience of the crossword puzzle minds behind a few contributors, including Dom Sylvester Houedard who is a monk at Prinknash Abbey and a leading 'concrete' poet on his portable Olivetti between attending Matins and Vespers. Peter Finch himself has persevered against the odds to keep his small press turning in a suburb of Cardiff. Through the years he has churned out booklets, pamphlets and broadsheets by various hands, and has recently maintained a very respectable list of contributors for his magazine *Second Aeon*.

Lives by Derek Mahon (Oxford, 90p) comes after his first book *Night Crossing*, dubiously heralded by the *Times Literary Supplement*, which is quite capable of consigning him to oblivion next year. Mr Mahon moves away from the romanticism of his earlier volume towards a confrontation with personal and historical forces at work in his native, benighted

Ulster. He tries to push it a bit further, implying that the Ulster shambles is the world at large, but he is hard put to it to make his shattered province appear universal. Many of the poems are sombre, but Mr Mahon is equipped with sufficient wit and lyricism to give him an individual style.

The prolific Scot, Iain Crichton Smith, brings us his *Love Poems and Elegies* (Gollancz, £1.50), which is split into two parts – poems on his mother's death, leading to general reflections on mortality and on the dying Highlands; and a sequence of love poems addressed to some mysterious X. Iain Crichton Smith has always seemed to me to be a poet who never quite knows where he is going. He laments the decay of the Highlands and of Scotland generally – symbolised by American tourists buying up all the tartan in sight in Edinburgh, but he constantly falls back on mawkish private regret and the odd series of weary love-poems. At his best, his pre-occupations expose the 'average-ness' of much that happens in Scotland and its present threadbare culture (*From Bourgeois Land* was one of his better collections). His particular contribution has been to bear in mind certain wild, extravagant and glorious excellences of will and vision, and he has presented them to those of his compatriots sheltered by a royalist and middle-class history, as completely unattainable, unenviable, and largely ludicrous. He is analytic, questioning, loves exactness, dislikes sentimentality – a Calvinist without theological allegiance who accuses himself of a lack of warmth and humanity. He tends to write verse which is rather intellectual, being suspicious of the 'heart' in poetry, his best barbs reserved for the Scottish 'bourgeois' element which he thinks has prevented the Scots from getting anywhere – apart from producing MacDiarmid's poetry and the Celtic Football Club – in the past thirty years. He certainly doesn't like the idea of the Highlander, with his proud history, becoming a servant to anyone, particularly tourists.

Finally, *Poems '72* (Gomer, 75p), a collection representative of the best in Anglo-Welsh poetry and edited by John Ackerman, is well up to standard. Mr Ackerman has plumped much more for the social and political 'Welsh element' in the recent best than did Jeremy Hooker as the previous year's editor, though Mr Hooker made it clear that the exploration of nature and the problems of personal relationships dominated his selection. Mr Ackerman has gone wholesale against derivative, descriptive nature pieces, the poetry of recollection and simple nostalgia, and the paralysis of domestic dirges. He has declared his bias towards more 'public' poems for inclusion. I for one am glad to see an anthology-editor moving towards such acceptance, which is overdue. An easy pastoral lyricism has bedevilled a lot of our talent, and it is good to see in this book a few poems that recall the wounds Wales has suffered, both social and political – wounds that remain and, as wise Glyn Jones has written, 'must not be comforted'. Mr Ackerman in his preface refers to 'radical rock', the voice of dissent against unemployment, official disregard of the Welsh language, and soulless technology – a very Welsh voice which one hopes will never be stilled. He is well aware, like most of the poets represented, of the ultimate truths of the human condition, but he sees a place for those poets who find in Wales and its history a fit and proper theme, who have not rejected urban and industrial imagery, and who simply continue, clasped to an *idea*, while the thin anglicised pipes squeak that debased word 'parochial'. (All they have to learn is to 'bowl slow left-arm spin, instead of bumpers', as John Ormond once put it.)

To close on a personal note: the writing of poetry is as important today as it ever was, perhaps more so in a brittle, materialistic, fish-finger time. The audiences for public readings are substantial, and the paperback has put good verse within the reach of thousands. Unfortunately, the writing of it does not become any easier, and there has never existed a lady called the Instant Muse. What saddens me is the spectacle of an increasing number of charlatans committing mayhem in the name of poetry, and being backed to the hilt by irresponsible, philistine publishing houses which have a Shylock eye for quick profit and precious little else.

I believe that in Wales our hands are fairly clean, we are not too enmeshed in the money-nexus, and a good deal of work of real quality drops through the rigorous sieve of the Welsh Arts Council readers, and the editors and publishers – later to be scanned by a range of fairly astringent and responsible critics in the leading journals in both languages. It is a pity that we still have to be subsidised to such an extent, but through the system – and it is the only practicable one at present – the charlatan, the poseur and the carpetbagger cannot surface. It is something to be thankful for, something in which to take a quiet pride, without complacency, as others elsewhere wallow in a bad period of pap, pulp, and the disappearance of notions of excellence.

Gleeman by Gavin Bantock (second aeon, 18p)

Eve by Alison Bielski (Aquila, 25p)

Behind Heslington Hall by Cal Clothier (York Poetry,

unpriced)

Prayers by George MacBeth (Aquila, 20p)

Mabon Six (North Wales Association for the Arts, 20p)

Here Be Dragons by Elizabeth Saxon (Outposts, 20p)

from alphabet to logos by J. P. Ward (second aeon, 25p)

Scores of packets of pamphlets, booklets and little magazines ('Our intellectual marines, landing in Little Magazines', as Auden put it) arrive through the year on editors' doorsteps. These are then passed on to hapless reviewers, hiding in attics and basements, who shelve them for a while before drumming up a mood to face them. Sometimes I think there are more small collections of poetry printed today than anything else. Everyone is trying to get a piece of the action. What one does is to weed out and jettison those offerings where the poetry is sunk without trace, of which the American critic, John W. Aldridge, once said: 'It is all a matter of soul speaking to soul, lovers passionately sweating skin to skin, blown minds exchanging psychedelic mash notes – non-thoughts floating in non-words between nonentities.' There's no particular trick or talent to this sort of stuff. It's as easy as taking your clothes off. It only lacks all those qualities that make poetry worthwhile: privacy, originality, discrimination, insight, and the conviction that the poet is more aware and better able to express himself than others. For scribblers of 'non-thoughts', intelligence is equated with sterility, stupidity is mistaken for innocence, and the tritest, most banal free-association for inspiration. It makes no demands, and cocoons these would-be poets from the rough world outside.

Gavin Bantock defines his 'Gleemen' as those who 'turn through many a land with their ways of singing, uttering what they need to, and speaking their thanks, forever north and south'. (So that's what gleemen are? Dafydd ap Gwilym and the troubadours were doing this around the taverns centuries ago.) Bantock has plenty of energy to spare, crashing about here and there rather in the manner of Peter Redgrove – a bit of an arrogant 'visionary', fond of journeys and sea-images, slamming it all down until he's out of breath. I think he's after big themes, but he doesn't seem to me to possess – yet – sufficient equipment for the job. Much of it comes pouring out like lava, and just as unshaped. There is already a note of authority, though, and he's not scared to write bluntly and boldly about man's fragile vanity.

Alison Bielski is ubiquitous these days. She's churning out the pamphlets. On the cover of this one there is a drawing of a skinny nude combing her long hair, sitting on a rock in front of a red-hot poker or thistle. Here is Eve's (or Woman's) progress, charted rather like Crow's, but much less shattering – poems of innocence, violence, mysticism, birth, love, death. I particularly liked 'Eve at the Supermarket' where her innocence is 'trapped in that snapping metal till'. Alison Bielski has long been a slight bafflement to me, and others. Her work is uneven and inconsistent (whose isn't?), tending to spray out her prevalent enthusiasms. But occasionally the mind behind it, when it gets to grips with the purgatory it has evidently been through, is capable of switching on some power and making poems of surprising force and beauty.

Behind Heslington Hall – which is at York University – is a plain, blue, nicely-produced pamphlet from enterprising York Poetry. Cal Clothier is a cool poet who is good on landscape ('skyline of the Angus coast dissolves / terrace after terrace to sand'); creatures ('the hedgehog snuffling through bread ... a molehill in process'); and his own asthma –

My crimson towel
suppurating
over the radiator

>opens woundedly
>the day's grey lung.

An excellent small collection, this, with interesting things in it, though if I have to read lines like 'pedantic men designed to dwell in prose / grind down poets for their eyes' much more often, I think I may scream. (Ezra Pound thought that before attempting verse, apprentices should try to master the 'unspeakably difficult art of prose'; and Flaubert, who could eat most poets before breakfast, took a week over two pages of a novel.)

Years ago I saw the humorous George MacBeth at an international poetry junket in Cardiff when the first wave of Hairy Beats took over, and he was dressed in his best fawn gaberdine BBC executive suit, with short hair and looking more than ever like Dr Crippen. Years later I saw him at a similar event and he had gone hip almost overnight. The distance between his sartorial contrasts is the distance between his poetic modes. *Prayers* form a parallel group to some poems in a book called *Shrapnel*, which is an apt title for George's habit of writing poems from which the blood spurts all over the place. His great violence in earlier work – even sicker than parts of Hughes – is almost laughable at times, and perhaps he intended it to be. He's a certified quality-joker in contemporary literary circles, and good value if you're in the mood. Here in this present sheaf are fragments to the Lords Squirrel and Owl, Lady Mouse, the Flea Combed from My Cat's Back, and My Daily Love, Who Is the Meat of Desire, etcetera. All are as extraordinary as his sequences of kitchen-vegetable and 'Orlando' non-poems, which he performs at readings with obvious relish and high delight in the Running Con. There's some lovely language here, as expected from a veteran hand who's spent most of his life with words, and we know him to be intelligent, erudite, articulate and witty. But he's a rum customer, is MacBeth. I confess that much of his output – and no one is more prolific – continues to bewilder me.

Mabon is a tidy magazine at twenty pence, well-produced and often containing very readable essays and poems. Unfortunately, it doesn't seem to have found a personality yet. One doesn't go out of one's way to buy it. The clever, perceptive Anthony Conran guest-edits this one and contributes a long 'attempt at assessment' of Idris Davies, which is a nerve-racking task, as no two people appear to agree where to place Idris in the canon, even if he was once admired by Eliot and Faber. There are also poems by Philip Pacey and Peter Gruffydd, and an attractive collage-type drawing by Alan Perry, who fires on two cylinders and is as good an artist as he is a poet. His vivid brush-strokes are always apparent even in his weakest poems.

Here Be Dragons (Welsh and Chinese) is the work of

a young woman who is an education officer in the female branch of the military and is much-travelled from Aberystwyth to Singapore and back again. She is sharp in her observation, and can pin down a scene accurately, whether in Paris or Swansea. In a poem called 'Love, Fifteen' she says 'Soon I will be thirty', looks back on the years the locust ate, sees time still whipping by,

> But now
> I must hurry to be wise, successful,
> smoothly beautiful, even naughty
> for soon I will be forty.

(I hope Miss Saxon doesn't mean it.)

J. P. Ward gives us an experimental folder of loose sheets with a drawing on the title-page that makes him look like a young prefect at Greyfriars. His work is another baffler, taking off in all directions at the drop of a notion. It's been scattered all over the map recently, and very varied and impressive some of it is, too, especially when he opts for more conventional forms and stays still for five minutes in the traditional trench without going over the top towards the rattle of experimental machine-guns. For the reader's possible elucidation, I will quote Ward's explanation that the Logos is the 'highest achievement that arrangements of the 26-letter alphabet forms can produce. A society's logos is usually imperfect; a society may not have this logos at all. In English, it is perhaps the works of Shakespeare and the authorised version of the Bible that most nearly qualify for the title, or have done so; yet they, too, are physically no more than myriads of permutations and combinations of these same 26 letters.' (So now we know.) What follows is a dozen sheets of incredible 'permutations and combinations' and amazing evidence of semi-linguistic donkey-work that must have burned up his typewriter, and certainly made my eyes ache. It proves – what? Nothing, as far as I can see, unless there's an esoteric key, a private code I can't find or decipher. Wittgenstein would either have been intrigued or flabbergasted, and he was fairly way-out. Still, the author probably had fun doing it. 'Come home, come home, John Ward, to the good old-fashioned stanza! Language and poetry need you!'

Brief Encounters

by Goronwy Rees (Chatto & Windus, £3.00)

For some years now, the former Principal of the University College of Wales, Aberystwyth, Goronwy Rees, has been deeply engaged in English life – as a Fellow of All Souls, Oxford, in the engineering industry, at *The Guardian*, *The Spectator*, and *Encounter* – but has preserved a degree of detachment from it. Certainly his distinguished career has been rather mixed – writer, academic, soldier, businessman – as if working out a pattern as he's gone along, letting next year take care of itself. (Besides a translation of *Conversations with Kafka*, he's written a book called *St. Michael: A History of Marks and Spencer*.) He has travelled a long way from Aberystwyth, both mentally and physically. On the one hand he has been imbued with European, especially French and German, culture, and on the other he has never quite lost the Welsh identity, although sometimes seeming to come close to losing it. This selection of long articles from the journal *Encounter*, under the heading 'Column', follows on from his book of autobiographical sketches, *A Bundle of Sensations* (1970), and his controversial, extremely honest, and highly successful auto-biography, *A Chapter of Accidents* (1972), with its

287

gripping portrait of the unfortunate defector, Guy Burgess. These articles range, from 1966 to '72, over a number of political, social and literary subjects: permissiveness and censorship, conditions in the universities, science and the environment, Grub Street, the Eichmann trial, the world of Lytton Strachey, Stalinist Russia, Solzhenitsyn, the Moors murders, and many others.

Mr Rees concedes that this selection, even as a mirror of the age, or of his own reactions to it, is necessarily inadequate. On a monthly magazine, many subjects are pre-empted as deserving of more serious and lengthy treatment than a columnist can give them. Writing at least six weeks ahead of publication, the subject he has chosen may by then be as dead as mutton. But he has not fallen into the columnist's fatal trap of exploiting the vagaries of his own personality, which is something of an accomplishment for one who has always been presented with the particular difficulties of the problem of personal identity. In these pieces he sometimes emerges as an intelligent spectator of world events, and at others, as he says himself, 'like a bit player in one of those epic theatrical productions in which no one really knows what it is all about'. He thinks it would be quite reasonable to state that there has probably been no period in history in which the world has changed faster than during the last seven years. He is talking here about the continuing influence, at the time of writing, of the war in Vietnam, which gave a 'certain tragic unity' and direction to the events of the period, like the ripples in a pool when a stone is flung into it. But wouldn't it be equally reasonable to say that the world changed just as fast in a few years after 1917, when the Russian Revolution exploded and about five empires collapsed – not to mention the effect on a whole generation of Verdun, the Somme and Passchendaele? (One has only to re-read Remarque, Graves, Hemingway, Fitzgerald and Aldington to realise that possibility.) Or the years after 1945, when the two bombs were dropped on Hiroshima and Nagasaki, and the Cold War made arch-enemies of former allies, almost bringing another calamity? In both these periods, events moved at a fast clip and turned many an institution upside down.

If there is a loose, connecting theme running through the book, it is this: that the mess of Vietnam, and the divisions it caused, triggered a spirit of revolt in apparently unrelated fields against the accepted conventions and entrenchments which, these rebels believe, originally created the shambles of Vietnam. This was the time of student revolt, negro and youth and sexual revolt, the revolt of women and revolt in the arts. A serial and cultural upheaval throughout the west. From all this, Mr Rees goes on to analyse what he thinks are the pros and cons, rights and wrongs, of current fundamental issues – coming out strongly for reason and rationality, but not completely out of sympathy with occasional folly and excess, or the eccentricities and aberrations of human thought and conduct.

In his modesty, and reluctance to rush to judgment, he is often rather on the fence, though we know he is *for* Solzhenitsyn (who isn't these days, except possibly his own countrymen?) and his 'hope and faith in the dignity of man' as compared with the almost unrelieved pessimism of writers who enjoy the liberties of the west. Still, I suppose Solzhenitsyn, against whom the mildest whiff of criticism is taken as heresy in western liberal circles, looms like a universal saint when one considers the English parochialism of Kingsley Amis and similar domestics, who keep their boundaries and sympathies limited. Mr Rees takes a nice sideswipe at Kenneth Tynan and Brigid Brophy, too, for their irresponsible pro-permissiveness within coteries of mutual admiration, believing that they and all the other promiscuity-pornography-supporters will one day sound like twittering bats hanging in a dark yet still habitable cave. He even spends a few pages diagnosing 'the English disease', which is that of a man unable to see that there is anything wrong with him. Once Turkey was the sick man of Europe – now it is England. Indeed, it is not hard to see that, as a benevolent rationalist, Mr Rees is an advocate of some sort of order in the midst of chaos, violence, and idiocy, of which the most recent past has been so singularly productive. The problem is, how to create it. Since he wrote these pieces, the present cannot have made him feel particularly optimistic.

Over the years, there has been a good deal of waspish criticism of Goronwy Rees from some of his compatriots, who either turn pale or go berserk at mention of his name, depending on their own temperaments. They do not care for the man, for his anglicised sophistication as a darling of the London-Oxford literary-journalistic establishment, with friends in high places, or his apparent disdain for certain things Welsh. To a few, he is the black sheep who strayed from the fold, the too-clever independent who was banished from Salem. We can be very good at hating when we want to be, and Goronwy Rees has come in for his share of malevolence. But that is a separate argument, to be taken up elsewhere by other hands who may have more information about his ways and dealings. Live and let live is my attitude at the moment. As a reviewer, who should try to keep his mind on what he is supposed to be reviewing and then report what he thinks about it, I must say that I liked this volume very much. Together these articles – though it's a pity the title is almost a cliché – form an interesting contribution to contemporary history, and they are also a pleasure to read as literature, for they possess the qualities of sensitivity, acuteness in analysis, elegant style, and a freedom from egotism, sensation or resentment. It is also a rare treat to see such a fine intellect at work,

Wide-Eyed in Babylon
by Ray Milland (The Bodley Head, £2.95)

Nine times out of ten, life stories of film stars written by themselves or by some fawning hack are sheer rubbish, spilling over with narcissism or massive ego. This one is an exception. It is an autobiography by a well-known Hollywood actor whose best performance was as a dipsomaniac in 'The Lost Weekend', for which he won an Oscar. Altogether he has appeared in over two hundred films, some of which were monumentally dreadful, where the 'stars' outdid one another in hamming up their lines of duff dialogue. For years he was on a highly-paid treadmill at Paramount studios, which turned out film after indifferent film, with stilted scripts and predictable plots.

Ray Milland was born on a mountain called Cymla above Neath and was given the posh-sounding name of Reginald Alfred John Truscott-Jones. Much of his youth was spent on his aunt's stud farm, and his experiences with horses led him into the Household Cavalry, where his career, to say the least, was chequered: once, after drinking a glass of champagne too many, his mount bolted with him down The Mall and into the courtyard of Buckingham Palace. He drifted into acting by chance, like several young men in America who were former waiters or truck-drivers, with no idea that he had any talent, and spent some time on the tattier English stage before going to Hollywood in 1930. He was often a debonair romantic lead in a very light vein, playing opposite spoilt alluring actresses and, at his first exposure to drama with the formidable Charles Laughton in 'Payment Deferred', he says it was obvious that serious acting came as a surprise to him by the expression of puzzlement on his face. He is good at sending himself up in this way, as when he writes that as a result of a misspent life he was given the role of the bald-headed father in the tear-jerker, 'Love Story', in 1971. He has grown older realistically, with no regrets for lost glamour.

He knows and writes about almost everybody in Hollywood – peppering his pages with anecdotes – from Hitchcock and the marvellous humorist Robert Benchley to the 'sarong girl' Dorothy Lamour and the clever, cynical director Billy Wilder. He also met a few of the unspeakable characters in the dream factory who were only safely neutralised when they were asleep. The booze-ups and parties masked the sadness and inner torments of many people living within Hollywood's shallow boundaries. He is an entertaining storyteller – by turns gracious and sardonic, witty and charming, always sensitive and intelligent. Including as it does a thick sheaf of nostalgic photographs, this book is one of the best un-ghost-written works I have read on movie-making, by an actor who is blunt, honest and earthy about his profession, his glamorous and often shoddy milieu, and himself. Certainly his fine performance as the compulsive alcoholic in 'The Lost Weekend' will give him a paragraph in film annals.

Come Out, Wherever You Are
by Herbert Williams (Quartet, 65p)

In March 1945, sixty-seven German officers escaped from Camp 198 (Island Farm) near Bridgend in Glamorgan. It was the biggest break-out by prisoners-of-war from a British camp in the Second World War. From this distance, there is almost a sadness in reading about an obscure peripheral event of World War II, a forgotten footnote to military history. Today horses graze among the derelict huts, and people pass the barracks without knowing that it was once a scene of frantic commotion.

Herbert Williams, who has spent many years in journalism and radio, does a remarkable ferreting job in drawing on contemporary press reports and documents as well as reminiscences of hunters and hunted to describe how the escape was made in that eventful week during which all sixty-seven men were captured. It was a time of excitement, panic, embarrassment and fear – together with unexpected moments of *bonhomie* and even humour – involving troops, police, farmers, housewives, schoolboys, ex-U-boat commanders, Luftwaffe pilots, SS men and spotter planes. Even at that late date in the European war, many of the Germans shut away in the compound hoped that Hitler would still win; others looked on the escape as an adventure to bring relief from the boredom of captivity.

The break-out was planned down to the last detail, though Island Farm was not exactly a Colditz. The Germans' exit was through a sixty-foot tunnel which had been dug under the wire. They risked death because the guards had orders to shoot if their warning was ignored. Apparently the tunnel was a piece of typical German efficiency, a masterpiece of its kind, being shored in mining fashion with uprights and cross-sections of timber, and having an air-line constructed from scores of condensed milk tins strung end-to-end after their tops and bottoms have been removed. This was wedged into a bucket and air forced through by means of a primitive four-blade fan made out of tin and operated by hand. The unarmed escapers took with them bully-beef, cigarettes, makeshift compasses with magnetised razor-blades serving as arrows (the compass-base was obtained by stuffing an empty Vaseline tin with chewed-up bread which dried hard), and maps showing railway lines and ports drawn on handkerchiefs, scarves and even a shirt-tail. Such ingenuity makes one wonder, not for the first time, how these people ever lost the War, even allowing for the numbers and the fire-power against them. The practical cleverness of the Germans was so stunning that I shudder to think what would have happened to us if they had not made the fatal error of attacking Russia in 1941 and had not had a leader who was raving mad. Herbert Williams reminds us of their boring arrogance when he writes that these Nazi officers arrived in Bridgend more like swaggering, insolent conquerors than a defeated remnant of a losing army. (They were in sharp contrast to the Italian POWs I saw at that time, working in the potato fields of Pembrokeshire; these noble Romans were glad to be out of it and only wanted to go home.)

While the Bridgend pursuit was on, there were some odd incidents, such as when two respectable school-teachers chatting to each other in Welsh in a Cardiff hotel were mistaken for Germans on the run; and two sisters living on a lonely farm on Margam Mountain put out food at night for the POWs they knew were hiding in the bracken to dissuade them from breaking into their farmhouse. One German, in jackboots and a Luftwaffe greatcoat, had the nerve to knock on the door of a terraced house to ask for food; the terrified woman who answered the door assumed he had been shot down on the mountains and slammed the door in his face, but he was soon captured.

After the escape, eleven men had been recaptured just outside the wire. Most of the others were gradually rounded up in the hills and valleys. Some were glad enough to surrender after a couple of nights sleeping rough with rations running low and the chances of getting clean away looking increasingly remote, though three of the fugitives who went to earth on Mynydd Margam high above Port Talbot seemed to be made of tougher stuff until they weakened and gave themselves up. Four enterprising prisoners posed as Norwegian engineers and strolled about the countryside for some days in civilian clothes with haversacks slung over their shoulders before they had had enough. They hid in a train wagon and, without knowing where it was going, actually got as far as the outskirts of Birmingham airport. These had gone further than any of the other groups, apart from two men recaptured near Southampton, making for the docks. Only eight managed to get out of Glamorgan, including two who were caught between the Severn Tunnel and Magor in Monmouth. A combination of tiredness, hunger, cold nights and the harsh terrain brought most of them to heel, and the road blocks and search parties did the rest. Later, because of the holes in the security at Island Farm, the prisoners were transferred elsewhere: not just the escapers, but all sixteen hundred officers.

Herbert Williams is a good writer; he handles his difficult narrative expertly, and must have done an enormous amount of research in interviewing all those who remembered the events and in tying up the complicated sequences. The twists and turns of the pursuit would have defeated a less enthusiastic burrower. He also has the discipline and economy of the professional reporter, and tells his story well. It is an interesting and little-known story which needed to he told (it was made into a BBC TV documentary), throwing light on the bravery, stupidity, cunning – and humanity – on both sides; the press furore, the anxiety of those living on isolated hill farms, and the extremes of bravado and desperation experienced by the Germans. There are thirteen photographs in the book, including one of Rundstedt, the marshal who planned the shock Ardennes offensive in the winter of 1944 in a last bid to break through to the Belgian coast, and who ended up at Bridgend in the summer of 1945. He was there with Brauchitsch (C-in-C of the German army until 1941), Manstein (commander on the South Russian front), Manteuffel, Kleist and others among the military fallen who started out in a blaze of Prussian glory and eventually landed in a compound for losers in South Wales. Of course, most of them denied that they were still Nazis. Some generals suffered from 'hypertension' which turned out to he high blood pressure due to the intake of strong drink consisting of Camp coffee drunk neat with a little sugar.

Repatriation was slow. The last man to quit Island Farm in 1948 was a German NCO who married a Welsh girl, now lives happily in the Vale of Glamorgan and considers himself as British as the next man. He probably has his British counterparts in West Germany. These men were once trained to shoot at one another, to kill each other on sight if possible, and they end up marrying the daughters and sisters of the enemy. A nice irony, that.

The Loved Ones

Since the air hostess was invented, there has been only one job possibly more glamorous and that is a TV presenter or front-person. They are also known as announcers, newscasters, celebrities and personalities. Why, I don't know. They only have to sit there and read off an autocue, while shuffling papers to give the impression that they've written the stuff themselves.

But there are some faces we almost learn to love, to grow old with, whose owners continue to steal our attention from the more important business of living. One of these is Vincent Kane, the poor Welshman's Robin Day. I've kept a certain amount of respect for Vince ever since I saw him enjoying himself in the old Spanish Club in Cardiff, run by Barcelona John who decanted cheap plonk and Double Diamond.

Kane is sharp, as a hawk is sharp. He sits up there in the trees at Llandaff and rarely lets his victim off the hook, unless they manage to slide away under their own grease. If he weakens in any way, I begin to wonder what's wrong with him, because when V.K. becomes a softie it will be time to bring in Alan Taylor of the terrible *Mr and Mrs* from the other side to do his job. He appears to be left of centre, though one can never be sure, because in the struggle for objectivity an inquisitor can often end up sounding the opposite of what he really believes in. Besides, the good money and general bourgeois atmosphere of television must play havoc with even the vestiges of a person's radicalism.

It is not an easy brief to know when to make people shut up without actually putting a bag over their heads or to prick the pomposity of politicians and the egotism of actors and show-biz narcissists who think the sun shines out of their backsides. Trying to keep self-centred twits on a rational level is uphill work. After all, nobody has heard of them in Peru, and front-men like Kane are there to remind them of this fact. He seems to sense, instinctively, when some of his interviewees are about to go over the top, and does his best to keep prattling bores and sentimental exhibitionists at bay.

Like all hard-nosed people who have a touch of brilliance, he has been accused of being a mean machine with a certain lack of warmth, but I much prefer him when he is tenacious and unrelenting with evasive bureaucrats than when he is carrying on a friendly chat, as he does occasionally, with some glittering thespian or similar mediocrity. All that sticky self-congratulation is not for The Hawk.

Also, Kane's current affairs programme, *Week In, Week Out*, is nearly always worth watching in case he digs some dirt up, even if the man himself is not exactly your cup of char. The editor, Jeff Iverson, is nobody's fool, and in his company one feels the right amount of intelligent scepticism; the researcher, Beata Lipman, obviously takes her work home with her; and a fairly recent investigative reporter, Bob Humphrys, is a very efficient ferret indeed.

The handsomest fellow on the Welsh box is David Parry-Jones, charm itself in immaculate clothes. He wears exotic light suits even in winter, hopelessly unfitted to the Cardiff weather, as if he is on a visit to the tropics; plus remarkable loud shirts and reckless ties that belong on London Weekend, perhaps to disguise the fact that he is getting older like the rest of us or to convince himself that nothing changes.

David is very attractive to the ladies, with his distinguished grey sideboards – to which are added a few more silver hairs every time Wales loses at rugby, which isn't often. His total dedication to the game, his knowledge of it, and his well-known double act with Carwyn James on Sunday afternoons in *Sports Line-up* are three of the smaller wonders of our time. Both of them know who played hooker for Llansamlet in 1905 and how many tries were scored by Penarth in 1927.

Fair dues, David is a fine commentator, exact while describing at high speed and with the ability to lift viewers to his own pitch of excitement without damaging their eardrums. As a studio lounge-lizard he doesn't try too hard to be nice to everyone. I suspect

304

he has moments when he imagines he's quite important, if not indispensable, like most darlings on television, which is a notorious destroyer of authenticity and a puffer-up of frail talents.

What he is, apart from a rugby fanatic, is a pleasant, well-paid newsreader and sports presenter. Others, from Colwyn Bay to Mumbles, insist that they could do it, but such techniques are not learned overnight. Good luck to David Parry-Jones and may his silver hairs not increase in 1981.

His colleague, the solicitor John Darran, reminds me of a benevolent army officer; he would still be unflappable if the Russians were bombing Barry Island. I like the way he smiles warmly and makes a mild joke before signing off to pass us over to the leggy Sue Lawley and *Nationwide* in London. He has been in that seat for so long that he is now everybody's favourite brother, or uncle, and makes us remember that one of the best things which ever happened in BBC Wales was not just a free ticket for a symphony concert, or the subsidised beer in their club. Darran is a rock.

Like D. Parry-Jones, there are too many men in TV who have three names with or without a hyphen, depending on how posh or anglicised they want to be; it becomes confusing to separate the Gareths from the Geraints from the Gwilyms (why don't they have two names like the rest of us mundane mortals?)

There may be other loved ones in HTV, but they are not household names and faces, except perhaps for Gwyn Erfyl among the Welsh-speakers: he has a memorable face like a cross between Magwitch in *Great Expectations* and his friend Annigoni the Italian painter, on whom he once made a rather beautiful film. The reason for this comparative obscurity may be that we never get a chance to know the men of Harlech, since they are too busy keeping one eye on the studio clock in order to clear off the screen before the adverts come on. (Michael Lloyd Williams, another three-namer who wears a sequined suit at Christmas, speaks faster than a cattle auctioneer and hardly has time to say goodnight before he's switched off.)

They seem to be in a permanent state of panic, which is understandable considering the number of times they have to open their mouths only to find the pictures missing. There is an old pro on the commercial side, John Morgan, who never appeared to be fighting the clock as he went about his topical business. The nervy younger ones could take a leaf out of his manual.

HTV is flushed with profits, but after all these years it still has no real personality of its own and is slowly sinking under the combined weight of the big English companies; it is like a fat little sardine swimming far behind the sharks of ATV, Granada, Yorkshire and Thames. A fortune has been coined, but the pathetic bilge remains on the so-called 'people's channel'.

To close on a brighter note, their prettiest and sexiest announcer is Eiry Palfrey, who relieves the others when they go to Mallorca or are off having babies. She looks as if she'd like to ask you in to see her etchings. We should view her more often, in both English and Welsh.

Fringe Diversions

Even contact at one remove, as it were, with television and its people can provide moments of near-lunacy and delight. Like those in the acting profession, they know how to enjoy themselves, though in such a circus of talents and hangers-on there are bound to be intervals of testiness, if not turbulence. 'Creative' temperaments have been known to chew scripts when their whims are not satisfied.

One of the more depressing little experiences for an outside contributor is to be rehearsing while the carpenters and scene-shifters are hanging around watching the performance and passing muttered comments among themselves. Of course they might have much to grouse about, but they should do it in the corridors of the canteen. Perhaps this practice has now been corrected at Pontcanna and elsewhere, and they take the programme into the canteen instead of the studio.

I didn't want to complain in case I caused a wildcat strike, but the equivalent experience for the chippies and scene-shifters would be for a performer to stand over them criticising their work as they planed a piece of wood or humped a piano about. It is very off-putting indeed, especially when you are trying to read a love poem for an old flame in Tredegar.

Still, HTV are good on hospitality, or at least they were. When a recording was finished, they'd go to some secret cabinet and pour out the liquid refreshment, generously. I remember once being ushered into the office of Aled Vaughan, then controller of programmes, to discuss 'close-down poems' or something equally impossible, and the first thing he did was to open his drinks cupboard and offer me a brandy. Good old Aled, he always had the right order of priorities. May he never have a single nightmare about his days at Harlech. You could talk to that man and share a laugh with him, unlike so many plastic ramrods and humourless deacons who have reached the top in his business.

In my limited experience, the BBC are a bit more parsimonious, but this may have something to do with the streak of puritanism that still runs through the Welsh wing of the noble Corp, dating back to the time of the old wireless in Park Place, Cardiff, where many of the men and women in control were children of the rural vicarage. Perhaps they still are. Like the Moslem teetotallers I knew among the diplomats at the Indonesian Embassy in London, they probably kept a flask in a locked drawer or mixed gin with the orange juice. However, the few free spirits in the Beeb make up for this dead hand of the chapel when they are let loose in their jolly club.

I've pressed my nose more than once against the windows of the pricey Gibson's and Harvesters restaurants in Cardiff and watched the fat cats of Welsh TV (both channels) gorging themselves on snails, pigeon pie and apricot sponge, washed down with Portuguese rosé, Cordon Bleu cognac and Cointreau. Maybe that very day they have produced more telly garbage for the people, and they know it, but any sliver of conscience or responsibility ends the moment their mouths close on the flavour of succulent woodpigeon. By the time they've reached the brandy, who cares?

If you're not careful, you can bump into TV people even in weekend country retreats. At a writers' conference at Dyffryn House, near Cardiff, I saw an HTV film crew shooting scenes for a thriller in Welsh which included a writers' conference. A lot of extras were playing the writers. What a coincidence, I thought: life was imitating art again, or the other way around. The ensuing tangle of actual writers and fictional ones among the snaking power-cables, cameras, lamps and microphones would have made an hilarious half-hour in itself:

('Are you a writer?' 'No, I'm an extra playing a writer. Who are you?' 'I'm a writer playing a writer.' 'Who's he, then?' 'He's a writer playing an extra.' Etcetera.)

That day in Dyffryn I also saw a few familiar faces

from the permanent Welsh-language TV Repertory Company, which numbers about six, I think, all rotating at intervals between Llandaff and Pontcanna. We see them time and again in every bit of Welsh drama that goes on, in disguise and out of it, playing three roles apiece. They must be among the most privileged actors and actresses in West Europe, hardly ever out of work. Good luck to them, and may they continue to play multiple parts in every play –especially Sharon Morgan whose varied talents I'm delighted to plug.

After a talk on humour I once gave to the pensioners of Llantwit Major, they asked who were my favourite TV comedians. I listed Dave Allen, Billy Connolly, Monty Python's Flying Circus, Stanley Baxter, Rowan Atkinson, Pamela Stephenson (a mimic), Kenny Everett, and Barker and Corbett. Among the Welsh, the late Ryan Davies could be original and very funny, as can Max Boyce, sometimes, when he doesn't shout. But I'd swap most so-called Welsh 'comics', especially Stan Stennett, for the scenes between Hugh Griffith, Windsor Davies, Dewi Morris, Dillwyn Owen and Sion Probert in *Grand Slam* (BBC Wales), that classic Paris weekend rugby romp from Gwenlyn Parry and John Hefin which could be repeated every year for the next 10, plus the sensational Sharon M. as a French bird. It was a masterpiece of editing as well as having a terrific script and an excellent director.

There is also a lively card named Wyn Calvin who does radio shows for the BBC. He once made a disastrous excursion into television with his own chat-shambles. It was like watching amateur night in Abergorki. But on the wireless he comes across well with a slight spluttering lisp, and I imagine he prefers it to the box. Any fading stars who happen to be at the New Theatre, Cardiff, that week, like Margaret Lockwood or Anna Neagle, are soon grabbed and whisked up to Llandaff to face Wyn, who always has a guaranteed studio audience of 'senior citizens' and enthusiastic ladies who form his unofficial fan club. He is an old trouper of the seaside promenade and panto school; he has a bigger following than the Lord Mayor.

Incidentally, *ARCADE*'s Raspberry Awards go to *Mr and Mrs* (HTV, Border etc.) and *This Is Your* (Boring) *Life* (Thames), which are both unbearable. Its much-coveted Super Leek Award has been won by last year's *A Touch of Glory* (BBC Wales), celebrating 100 years of Welsh rugby, written by Alun Richards and narrated by Richard Burton. The BBC can be proud of it.

Richards's script was a bit purple and overblown in parts, bringing in words like 'categorical imperative' (Kant) and 'sin' (Calvinistic Methodist), but it was also witty and majestic: 'Barry John – slight, royal, with a coronation every year.' What he wrote about Gareth Edwards is usually reserved for a god at least. Writers on rugby bust their typing keys with large words like 'tragedy' and 'glory' when describing a game, as if it were a turning-point in history like Waterloo or Stalingrad.

A Turn-Up in a Million (Westward) was how Ernest Bevin described himself, and it was justified. This documentary showed him to be tough, crafty, pugnacious, determined and ruthless, with a sense of humour. He also became bitterly anti-Communist after Joe Stalin snubbed him over an extension of the Anglo-Russian Friendship Treaty. When George VI asked him where he'd been educated, he replied: 'In the 'edgerows of experience.' And when a colleague suggested that Herbert Morrison was his own worst enemy, Ernie growled: 'Not while I'm alive, 'e ain't.'

The Shrewd Goat Recaptured

The Life and Times of David Lloyd George (BBC2) is a mouthful and sounds more like a series of lectures by a professor of history. Written by Elaine Morgan and produced by John Hefin, it is the most ambitious chronicle ever offered by BBC Wales.

We've seen LG get a woman with child early on, elected to old Caernarvon Boroughs as a Liberal, become a fiery radical and 'Welsh nationalist' ('The others always get the jam; we get the empty jar'), a prominent pro-Boer during the South African war (little did he know then what the awful consequences would be of a Boer ascendancy).

Then the battles over Disestablishment, social security, Irish Home Rule, and women's suffrage, his acquisition of a private secretary-cum-mistress, the Marconi shares scandal, the Great War and his hassles with Kitchener and later Haig; Minister of Munitions when he shut the pubs in the afternoons so that factory workers could make more shells instead of boozing, cutting through the red tape to get the ammunition to Flanders; and then the crown of thorns as Prime Minister after Asquith lost his grip. From here we'll see him continue his spicey and dicey progress, with both men and women still under the wand of the magician towards the inevitable decline and fall.

He was a strange mixture: in the background one could almost hear Welsh hymns colliding with Elgar's *Pomp and Circumstance*, not to mention the French Can-Can.

As Lloyd George, Philip Madoc is excellent. It's good to see this fine actor in a solid part after so many secondary roles as a German officer (even in *Dad's Army*, once), detective-inspector, crooked tycoon or whatever; he's popped up in too many silly things, just for the bread. On screen he's usually a suave gent, smooth as silk and wearing at least three rings on his fingers, but in this series he really grinds his molars into the Goat-meat. Somebody has performed miracles of make-up on his face: as LG in old age he looks like King Lear with his white locks streaming in the wind.

Lisabeth Miles as his long-suffering wife, Margaret, looked suitably disgusted at his loose ways. Kika Markham, as his paramour, Frances Stevenson, doesn't seem to possess enough sex in the part, but perhaps the charms of Frances weren't supposed to be obvious and she was gifted with what Alfred Hitchcock called 'quiet passion'. Rachel Thomas, who has been in every Welsh drama since Paul Robeson came here, played LG's mother-in-law and still looks a handsome matriarch, while Meredith Edwards as his ancient uncle is superb.

I'm waiting for the versatile Ray Smith to make an appearance later as Nye Bevan: he certainly looks the part, and may sound it too, even to the stammer and lisp. Ray seems capable of playing almost any sort of character over 40.

As for the two main architects of this series, the sensitivity, perception, and skill of Elaine Morgan were evident in her adaptation of Vera Brittain's *Testament of Youth*, where emotional understatement was raised to an art; and the creative talent, civilised good taste, and historical sense of John Hefin have given him an enviable track record – he's one of the best programme-makers in Britain, let alone Wales.

How encouraging it is to see two people at the top of their crafts, producing work of this quality from Wales to rivet a few million viewers. Together, they're a formidable team, and the historical advice of A. J. P. Taylor on this production probably helped, too. What will they tackle next, if this saga hasn't exhausted them and if they can find the budget to cover all those locations and to pay all those extras in the crowd scenes?

The blurb accompanying the series refers to 'Lloyd George's sexual dalliances. Women fascinated him and they were fascinated by him. It is almost miraculous that he was able to conduct the highest affairs of state with his many affairs of the heart simultaneously.'

You can say that again. He seemed more philanderer

than philosopher, a force of nature father than a patient pragmatist, and the rumours – which later became facts – of his constant randiness shocked the straitlaced. With that cape and long mane like a retired fencing master, he stood on farm wagons during the hustings and made eloquent speeches, but the thoughts of this dazzler were probably on the lady he would have tomorrow in one of the discreet Cabinet rooms. I suppose he needed his relaxation, and sex was his favourite one; even a tussle in a taxi seemed worth a mild scandal.

Still, he knew the splendours and miseries of power and, like Clemenceau and Woodrow Wilson, became a 'man of destiny' – whatever that means. Churchill was considered to be a man of destiny, too. I think journalists invented the term long ago to describe somebody who happened to be in the right place at the right time, like Wellington and Napoleon, though in the latter's case it was the wrong time and it didn't do him much good. Responsible historians, who have reservations about almost everything, seldom use the term because they don't know what it means either.

Fortunately, LG had a sense of humour as well as a sense of the ridiculous and seemed to stop short at thinking that he was a political version of the Second Coming. He said that Neville Chamberlain saw foreign policy through the wrong end of a municipal drainpipe, and Sir John Simon had sat so long on the fence that the iron had entered his soul. In 1933 he belatedly discovered a cardinal truth: 'The world is becoming like a lunatic asylum run by lunatics.'

But it was his first-rate political brain that impressed others. Keynes the economist noted Lloyd George's mental speed, and he seemed to Keynes to be very intuitive with a strong feminine component in his character. But at the Paris Peace Conference in 1919, LG was not his own master; he listened to the national sentiment that had put him in power and showed the primitive passion that called for revenge and punishment rather than reconstruction. He said he had to pay the 'butcher's bill' in the First World War by explaining the terrible losses on the Western Front to the people.

His courage in standing up to the blinkered, bloodthirsty generals and holding them accountable was one of the best things he ever did. He had a clear, compassionate picture of all the bereaved who were suffering.

Yet the wizard-as-ruthless-manipulator keeps breaking in. There was a touch of the shrewd Welsh-exile Tudor about LG: he would have made a good plotter in the court of Henry VIII, having Wolsey and Thomas Cromwell as his mates, or fellow-corkscrews. A love of conspiracy for its own sake was part of his nature, as it was for several of his contemporaries, including Churchill and Beaverbrook. They got away

318

with it most of the time, too, since the odious Beaver and Northcliffe and the other barons controlled the popular press and there was no television to keep a beady eye on them or to expose their patent insincerity before the cameras.

Many Welsh people think there is a slight stink at the core of the Lloyd George story: Taff-on-the-make, brilliant cottage-bred boy without resistance to glamour, even untrammelled power-mania after being at the summit for so long. You need a sense of proportion at that altitude, they say. But perhaps most shocking of all, to them, was his hypocrisy, his lip-service to respectability mingling with his continuous randy pursuits. It was like something out of Caradoc Evans – the cloak of convention covering the morality of a hot tomcat. As he grew older he looked like an Old Testament prophet in *Life of Brian*.

Present-day patriots prefer the martyr's example of Saunders Lewis, the aloof Catholic nationalist who is now an aged recluse living in Penarth, to that of the slippery LG, who soon forgot about the modest aspirations of his own country when he was called upon to save the British Empire. My grandfather said he didn't trust him even if he did speak good Welsh, because he was a 'King's man', a servant of imperialism; another reason may have been that he was a North Walian. What Lloyd George loved even more than women was the climb to the top of the greasy pole of politics. He was in his element there.

Elaine Morgan herself thinks that he had 'a certain combativeness, a kind of optimism always convinced when everyone else was in despair'. Well, now he has the posthumous accolade of a definitive television series in nine parts. I shall long remember that last, frozen shot of Madoc-LG as a very old man walking by the river at Criccieth – and that haunting theme music.

No Peace for Dando

Uncollected Fiction

Apricot Sponge with a Sage

I was down in West Wales doing a travel piece for a magazine when I decided to call on the Sage (a well-known philosopher-poet who had retired to the back of beyond) to find out something about the meaning of life. Usually I had been disappointed when I called on philosopher-poets to ask them this question. They invariably looked embarrassed, shifted about uneasily, and never looked me straight in the eye. They were stoics, unwilling to entertain such questions.

I needed to get an answer that day because my luck and post office savings were running out. I was having practical problems with my woman friend, and the landscape was particularly depressing. If forty-nine others had been down there with me, feeling as I did, the Samaritans would have had a field-day.

It was the end of summer, and along this bit of coast there were the usual tatty ice-cream shacks and junk stalls, a clutter of caravan sites and frail, ramshackle chalets that looked as if they had been made out of packing cases and old tea chests. Paper chip-bags and the odd used Durex littered the grass. Small herds of flea-bitten ponies were strung out on the dunes, trotting up cliff paths or wandering about in gardens, like the mangy sheep back in the valleys. The wind blew like a cutlass and penetrated my thin coat. It howled dramatically on the high ground.

I looked at the seaside mess around me: it was nearer to what George Orwell described before the war than to the jolly childhood excursions of Dylan Thomas. People had brought their dung here, and it stuck. I couldn't help envying the Cistercian monks across the water in their chosen isolation in a monastery on Caldey, away from the thump and crunch. Somebody told me they lived only on potatoes, parsnips, swedes and cabbage while they meditated and made their perfume. But a local grocer who supplied them denied this and said the brothers lived well on red meat and plenty of fruit. Anyway, Caldey looked tempting in the afternoon lemon light, the cold sun sitting flat on the roofs of the long, white house. You could have written the Great Welsh Novel there in perfect peace.

I had to hoof it inland to the Sage's place, and should have brought a compass because it was at the end of nowhere. After an hour's trudge through drab coastal country, with not a soul in sight, I came to the silent, shuttered hamlet – like something out of Mauriac – where the great man lived. I bought a box of chocolates for his wife in a smelly little shop, and a cigar for him. The woman in the shop had a twitch, and her scruffy Welsh terrier kept scratching himself.

When I knocked on the door of the Sage's wooden

cottage, he appeared in a sagging corduroy suit and beckoned me in. He looked like King Lear gone to seed. I gave him the cigar. In the small front room there were those three awful china flying ducks on one wall, and the Mona Lisa, Chinese Horse and Laughing Cavalier on the others. Some poor philistine woman's touch was everywhere, but the Sage didn't seem to mind. He was sucking a Polo mint, bringing it to the point of his tongue from time to time, and didn't say anything. There were only three books in the room – a Bible, Spinoza, and a cookery book.

The wife came in, or rather crept in. The old man must have led her a cat's life, she was so scrawny, nervous and subdued. She nearly vanished into the carpet. She had scraped in his long shadow for fifty years and had not experienced much kissing, by the look of it. When I put the chocolates on a table, she gave a little cry, scuttled almost sideways across the room without looking up, and snatched the box. 'Thank you, oh thank you,' she whispered. 'Diolch yn fawr.' Then she retreated to wherever she had come from.

This was my moment. I didn't hesitate. 'What's the meaning of life?' I asked the Sage, suddenly, like a dagger.

But he had already switched on an obsolete television set and was watching a Western. 'I remember this one,' he said. 'They're just getting to the bit where the Indians come in.'

'No, they're not,' I said, trying to put him off. 'This is one of those intellectual Westerns where they just talk.'

'The Indians were the finest light cavalry in the world,' he said.

We both stared at the tiny screen for an hour until my eyes ached. Later the wife padded in with food and we sat down to eat. We had oxtail soup, a big mixed grill with kidneys and mushrooms, an excellent apricot sponge soaked in sherry, followed by Gaelic coffee stiff with whisky and cream, and two bottles of cheap but potent Portuguese rosé. No one spoke. I was full as a frog at the end of the feast and collapsed in a shattered armchair. They might be a pretty crummy pair, I thought, but they knew how to eat and drink.

Exhausted, I fell asleep, and when I woke up about two hours later the Sage was still watching the box, and the wife had disappeared again.

He switched off with a sigh. 'No Tom and Jerry tonight,' he said. 'Time to go. I'm going to bed now.' It was about eight in the evening.

'All right,' I said.

I was closing the front door and wondering how I would get back to civilisation when I heard the great man shout:

'What's the meaning of apricot sponge?'

Last Day in England

York stepped off the train at the end of the line. It had arrived dead on the stroke of noon. The town station in Weymouth was built by Victorian engineers with a thought for the convenience of visitors: they had situated it at the entry to the esplanade. Lazy holiday-makers and day-trippers who didn't like to walk very far appreciated this piece of foresight. Weymouth was a popular resort in summer but York had not been there since he was a little boy, when his parents were still alive.

About a dozen people got off the train. York was travelling light with only a Gladstone bag. In the middle of the platform, between the chocolate machine and an advertisement for Bournville Cocoa, stood the beaming station-master, very aware of his position in life as controller of a terminus, proud of himself, his staff and the Southern Railway, in that order – the passengers were merely his bread and butter. He had a crimson face and mutton-chop whiskers under his tight skull-fitting black cap with a knob of black braid on the crown and a strip of gold braid on the peak; his immaculate black frockcoat, with frogging on the lower sleeves, and his many-buttoned waistcoat denoted a methodical man who wore both braces and belt, and who would keep the expresses and goods of southern England running efficiently for king and country, as he checked the arrivals and departures by his large magnificent pocket-watch. York envied such men their simple everyday certainties, but not their eagerness to become petty uniformed officials in a domestic railway system. He gave up his single ticket from Waterloo at the barrier and walked out into the street.

It was a dull Sunday in autumn, the sort of day that would lie forgotten on the calendar despite romantic descriptions of russet tints and falling leaves. York could hear church bells in the distance, somewhere far out in the country. The first thing he wanted to do was to find a quiet pub. Along King Street he stopped at a conspicuous green-and-gold frontage, went inside and asked the barman for a pint of Devenish. There was no one else in the place. He sat on a stool at the bar and drank the good ale. It was so good, in fact, that York decided to have another. This was the life, he thought, if you could only wangle it, if you could just arrange your affairs satisfactorily – doing nothing but sitting in silent pubs drinking ale and watching through the windows a busy, peaceful world going by. But life offered such delights only to artful dodgers, successful punters, and the inheritors of legacies, among whom York could not be counted.

He took his cryptic instructions out of the inside

pocket of his jacket: 'Proceed Weymouth Quay – board S.S. *Palma* for Barcelona': then followed details of dates and times of departures and arrivals, the names of the captain and the few other Brigade volunteers who would also be on the ship, and the locations of the Loyalist assembly points in Barcelona. That's straightforward enough, he thought, clear orders and no red tape. He liked the brevity of the headquarters instructions after the long-winded paperwork that had been involved in his former occupation at Holborn. He checked his pass and the money in his wallet: one big white fiver and a pound note, the last pay-packet from his clerk's job at Crawford's Import and Export. Good luck, Yorkie, he whispered to himself, the very best to you mate, as he downed his second Devenish. Somebody was cooking a roast in the back, and the appetising smell made him feel peckish. He looked at a brown, crusty Marsh & Baxter pork pie that lay alone in its wrapper on a dish under a glass lid on the bar.

– Is that fresh? he asked the barman, pointing to the pie.

– Yesterday's.

– I'll have it. And ten Woodbines, please.

– Mustard?

– No thanks.

York tore off the wrapper and bit into the pie hungrily, almost ravenously, the flaky crumbs dropping on to his trousers; he had eaten no breakfast at his Pimlico lodgings before catching the train, and had forgotten the sandwiches his kind landlady had packed for him. He munched the excellent pie, as tasty as a Saxby's. His next move was to have a look at the ship that was taking him to Spain the following morning. He finished chewing, lit a Woodbine, and picked up his bag from the floor.

– Cheerio. Thanks, he said to the barman who was mopping the top of his shiny bar with the same pride in his responsibilities as the mutton-chopped station-master had shown. (The houses of Devenish in the west and south-west were well-known for their obsession with cleanliness; York had once seen, in an alley in Bath, a peculiar sign over one of their wine-bars: 'No Vagrants, Beggars, Street Singers, Confidence Tricksters, or Animals Allowed.)

– All the best, the barman said.

York could already feel the ale going through him, so he called in the outside Gents before walking to the end of King Street and into the long esplanade. It was nearly deserted in the cold of an autumn Sunday, and all the shops and cafés were shut. But it was a famous, splendid promenade, one of the best in England, and much frequented by the rich, the genteel, and the retired Indian military who filled its elegant hotels in season, and sometimes out of season. They came here, and to Lyme Regis along the coast to the west and Bournemouth to the east, in first-class train compartments or by motorcar with rugs over their laps, a thermos of coffee and a flask of cognac. It seemed both odd and ironic to York that he should be travelling from a sumptuous English resort like this, on an obscure ship to a battered Spanish port in the middle of a civil war. Oh to be privileged, he thought, your day may soon be done if we win in Spain. If we can win there, we can win anywhere.

At one end of the esplanade, Queen Victoria stood on a stone block, looking eternally south towards a gaudy replica of George III at the other end, with a pink-icing Jubilee clock in the middle. A few motor-cars went by. Two old ladies sat in a glass shelter, and dogs scampered free on the sands. The whole place whiffed of high imperial days, the ascendancy of the British Empire and its blotches of red on the maps. A grand place really, York thought, as he faced the sea and sucked in the clean cold air, which was more bracing than the air of Pimlico. He walked south towards the quay station, and then on to the harbour wall. There were several foreign freighters tied up, and one of them was the S.S. *Palma*, flying the Spanish flag. Even from where he was standing, York didn't need binoculars to see that it was not so much a ship as a boat, an insult to self-respecting mariners – and not so much a boat as a scow-bucket. He remembered the last time, about a year before, when he had seen another ancient hulk like this one – filthy, stinking, and caked with soot, belonging to an Italian line. It was in dock in Swansea and he had to go from London to see the skipper, a greasy brute named Grout, about an import cargo irregularity which was being queried by his firm. It turned out that this Grout had been running guns to Franco's side in Spain and bringing back bananas. His name was linked with the notorious 'Spud' Evans, the Welshman who operated out of Barry, carrying cargoes of potatoes which were laid on top of rifles and Brens. York remembered the foul Grout had a rum breath that would have peeled off paint; his cigar-stump belched rotten cabbage, and he hadn't washed for about a month. The pong he gave off was unbelievable. He admitted openly to York, after he'd had a few strong jars in a docks pub, that he was not sentimental and he would run guns and ammunition to anyone, anywhere, to Stalin or the Pope, provided the price was right. Horror stories of treachery and slaughter poured from his mouth like a stream of dirty jokes. He showed York a wad of notes with a thick elastic band round them. York was both disgusted and unnerved by him, because he never expected to meet such a creature, only to read about him in the papers. Cynicism seeped out of Grout, his eyes were as cold as blue ice. York, frightened, drank up quickly and ran from that pub and from the authentic stench of evil.

Still, what did it matter that the *Palma* was a bad

tub? The voyage to Barcelona wouldn't take long, if the weather didn't act up in the Bay of Biscay. It could be very rough there. He only hoped he wouldn't be seasick.

He turned away from the harbour and walked back down the esplanade to the Royal Hotel to book a bed for the night. Between its twin domes a Union Jack fluttered in the sea breeze. It was a big, expensive place, but he thought he might as well spend most of his remaining cash on a small fling. He didn't expect he would need much where he was going – whether to the front or behind the lines – because his food, wine, cigarettes and accommodation would be paid for by the republican government (at least that's what it had said in the letter confirming his recruitment). In return he would be given a rifle, taught rapidly how to use it, and then sent out to shoot at fascist insurgents. It seemed like a fair arrangement to York, who believed that if you had a cause, an ideal, if you cared sufficiently about defending poor working people – even if far away in another land – you had to stand up to be counted. The breaking of poverty was the concern of all men of goodwill. His socialism was simple and basic, and probably unanswerable in its closed purity. Madrid was still holding out, he thought, and Catalonia hadn't yet been cut off from the main republican territory – but Bilbao, the second port of Spain, and most of the Basque country had been bombed into submission. He hoped that Barcelona wouldn't fall before he got there on the old scow-bucket. The sense of gladness in the anticipation of positive action put a spring into York's step.

At the reception desk inside the hotel, which was all gilt and plum velvet, he booked a room and signed the register 'J. York, Pimlico, London'; then he took the key and went upstairs to the second floor. It was a small, comfortable room, comprising a single bed with a sepia photograph of Victorian Weymouth above it, an armchair, wash-basin, cupboard and tallboy – anonymous and private, which was what he wanted. He put his bag in the cupboard, had a wash, and went downstairs to look for a cup of tea. The desk clerk said he would order it and directed him to a little covered courtyard at the rear, open to non-residents, a nook with three tables and chairs and a canopy of vines under a glass roof, rather like a miniature arcade. A plain-looking girl sat at one of the tables, sipping tea. York couldn't pretend she wasn't there.

– Good afternoon, he said politely.

– Good afternoon.

A waitress brought tea in a white china pot and two slices of madeira cake. York couldn't help wondering what he would be eating in a week's time in Spain – probably black-bean soup and bully beef. The contrast between this prospect and the delicate English tea before him brought a smile to his face. The girl was still sipping tea and nibbling a digestive biscuit. She was no beauty, but she was smartly dressed in a pale blue woollen cardigan with a sort of green silk cravat tucked into the neck, and a neatly-pressed buff linen skirt. Her wrist-watch looked gold and expensive, and her flat brown polished shoes were made of the thinnest soft leather. All this York observed in a series of furtive sidelong glances. The girl stopped sipping and nibbling and looked across at him. She had what novelists called a steady gaze.

– Do you come from around here? she asked.

Her voice was full of posh schooling, York thought. She didn't waste any time either. No preliminary nonsense about Weymouth or the weather. She must be one of these rich emancipated girls.

– No, I don't.

– What are you doing in Weymouth, then?

She reminded him of some forward little girl who was too advanced for her age.

– I'm catching a boat in the morning.

– Where to?

– Spain. Barcelona.

– Really? What are you going there for?

Despite her plain looks, she had the confidence of her class. York was an honest person, there was nothing devious about him, and so he told her the truth.

– To fight.

– Fight?

– Don't you know there's a civil war going on in Spain?

– Yes, of course. I've heard it on the wireless and seen it in *The Times*. But what's it got to do with you?

– It's a long story. Forget it.

– But I'd like to know. I would really.

York lit a Woodbine. He felt awkward, at a loss. Perhaps it was best to put a complex issue like Spain into the simplest terms.

– Well, very roughly speaking, the government and people are against the army and church, who started it to get back power for themselves at the people's expense. The Russians, the communists, are helping the people, and the Germans and Italians, the fascists, are helping the other side – led by a colonel named Franco. The government appealed for support from their sympathisers anywhere, and that's why I'm going.

– I see.

But York knew she didn't. The situation out there on that peninsula was too knotted for a clever person to unravel, so it would be clear as mud to a nice but indifferent girl like this one.

– Are they all Catholics in Spain? she asked.

– Most of them, I think. If they're not, they're probably atheists.

– I'm a Catholic, but not much of a devout one I'm

afraid. I thought the church was always good and on the side of the poor people.

– Not always, I'll tell you. In Spain the government put through some reforms and changes that were good for the people. The landlords didn't like this because it meant they'd lose land to the peasants, and the church didn't like it because the landlords gave them lots of money and besides they couldn't tolerate the prospect of peasants getting ideas above their station. So they backed the army to bring down the government, and one thing led to another. Etcetera. Does that answer you?

– It will do, I suppose. I'm sorry. I don't really understand politics, especially the messy foreign ones. These people Hitler and Mussolini and what's happening in Spain and other places is rather beyond me. I'm afraid. Foreign affairs... We're rather insular in England, aren't we – I like Anthony Eden, though.

You would, miss, York thought. You would.

– Don't you think, she asked, that it's none of your business really, what's going on abroad? Isn't it their own problem? I mean, they wouldn't help us, I'm sure, if we were in trouble. They never do.

What was she talking about? York didn't feel like explaining to her what to him was perfectly obvious. He wasn't sure that he could, anyway. He didn't consider he had to give his reasons to anyone, particularly a protected, upper-class girl who was so remote from any concept of chaos. He had no family to whom he was accountable, he was hurting nobody, and now all he looked forward to was meeting some comrades, companions, fellows of like mind and spirit on the boat and in the barracks in Barcelona. The recruiters of the Clement Attlee Battalion in London had told him that volunteers for the International Brigade came from countries all over the world, and from all walks of life. It would be an unforgettable experience, an experience that this pleasant girl and her shielded kin would never share, and could not even begin to comprehend. He couldn't communicate with her properly, where it really mattered; he was talking across the barrier of a common language.

– I can't answer your question, he said eventually. And I don't particularly want to. I don't mean to be rude, but it's very difficult, you see. All I can say is that a lot of good men have gone out there and a lot of them are dead already. I just feel a bit tired. I'm sorry.

She kept at him, like someone prodding him with a stick.

– But aren't there good dead men on the other side too, who died for what they believed in? Or are they all bad? Why is one side all white and the other side all black?

– Yes, yes, it's a big question, of course. It's a matter of opinion and where you stand in these things. I just don't like fascists and reactionaries and I think they persecute the common people. This is what I believe, you see. This is what I live by. Can we agree to disagree now?

– Of course. That's all right, I understand. I've enjoyed our little chat.

'Our little chat', York thought. His weary explanation and clarification, his almost-inarticulate groping towards the end to express what he felt about these matters of life and death for literally millions of people in southern Europe – all this to her was a 'little chat'.

– What are you doing here, anyway? he asked.

– I'm with my parents. They're on a late holiday, motoring around Dorset, seeing Thomas Hardy's cottage and that sort of thing. But we're based here at the Royal. Dorset's a lovely county, don't you think?

– Very nice.

She stood up. She was quite tall and York noted approvingly her shapely legs which curved from her knees to her ankles. That was something you often found with plain-faced girls, they had good figures. For a moment he felt an unaccustomed little shock of desire. He'd had so much on his mind lately that he had scarcely glanced at a girl. But this little prick of randiness did not happen to him very often: lust was something that occurred to other people or was read about in books. He thought there was more to life than rolling about with women between sheets, or on top of the blankets, or wherever one happened to be. Perhaps when he got to Spain, where wild things were possible, these reservations about sex might be modified or adjusted. It depended on events. He was still quite young, not bad-looking in a rather ordinary kind of way, and fairly susceptible to attractive women, especially older ones. Since the loss of his mother he realised that he might have been looking, unconsciously, for some sort of replacement. But it was never a matter of priority, especially not now when he was joining the Brigade.

– Are you feeling all right?

York jerked out of this train of irrelevant thoughts as suddenly as he had entered it.

– Goodbye then, the girl was saying. And good luck. I shall tell my friends I met a man who was going to Spain. Don't get shot or anything like that, will you?

– I hope not. Goodbye. It's been nice meeting you.

She left the courtyard, walking confidently on her nice legs and with a very straight back. His tea had got cold while they were talking. Damn, he said, out loud. It was a waste of a shilling. He ate the two pieces of madeira and decided he would have the hotel dinner later, and a good breakfast early in the morning before boarding the Palma. This evening he might even go to the pictures, if he could find a cinema open on a Sunday out of season; perhaps they would show the war in Spain on the newsreel. He would not go near a church for a priest's blessing; that might lead to an argument. He left the courtyard and the cold tea and went upstairs to his room.

The window of his room looked on to the back of a crumbling house, where washing hung on a line in a garden that was now a small jungle, like an abandoned cemetery, with weeds sprouting from cracks in the crazy paving. Torn curtains blew in the wind through broken panes. The whole town seemed deserted and there was not a sound in the afternoon except the occasional ship's hooter out at sea. The desolation of autumn was all around him.

York shivered. The bleak view through the window, and the blanketing silence, filled him with a vague depression. He felt adrift, and more alone than he had ever been. He was intelligent enough to realise that he might not come back from Spain. What could turn out to be his last day in England had been spent drinking two pints of ale and eating a pork pie, looking at an old boat that would take him to war, booking into a luxury hotel, and talking to a posh girl over a pot of tea. He had met only three other human beings; the barman, the desk-clerk, and the girl. It's just a bit of apprehension, he thought, natural enough with the unknown ahead of me. It was like going into some unmapped region. And then again, those poets like Rupert Brooke always wrote about the sadness of leaving England, as if it were some kind of heaven.

341

But York never took long to come out of an irrational depression. His reputation at Crawford's and among his few friends had been that of a likeable innocent who would do nobody a bad turn. You could rely on York, they said. Now, when he thought of the poor people everywhere and what he would be going into tomorrow, he felt refreshed and almost elated. How could he have possibly explained, to that girl, the happiness that comes from a commitment to something? He lit a Woodbine, and started whistling as be began to unlock his Gladstone bag...

Go Home, Davy Tuck

As a birthday present, Davy Tuck's father bought him a second-hand 1920 Briggs and Stratton Flyer, made in the USA, and the only five-wheeler car to be produced. Even by cycle-car standards, the vehicle was minimal: a frame of six wooden slats, cycle-type wire wheels with block brakes on the rear ones, two wooden bucket-seats and nothing else – apart from the 201cc single-cylinder 'motor wheel', complete with fuel tank, mounted centrally astern. To drive away, Davy just lowered this unit to the ground. If people asked him, he claimed 25 miles per hour and 80 per gallon for the Flyer, and said that at twenty quid it was a bargain. When he was working in the fields, he kept it in a rainproof shed at the back of his father's farm.

The extreme economy of this odd machine reflected both Davy's and his father's personalities, which were, to say the least, spare, if not actually non-existent much of the time. But Davy was very proud of his Flyer, which he drove around the twisting country lanes and into the nearby village: he enjoyed seeing the looks of amazement on the faces of the women shoppers and the mixed grins and frowns from the wagon-drivers.

One afternoon he left the farm to visit his girl-friend, Lucy. The weather was warm, and he felt good as he steered the Flyer, scattering the jays and swallows in the woods and the sheep cropping by the hedgerows. He saw a kestrel, unperturbed and single-minded, hovering above him for prey as he passed the lock-keeper's cottage; then along the towpath where the gipsy barges were moored, over an old stone cart-bridge across the Usk, down a short narrow lane, through a gate and up to the Sheaths' broken-down caravan, stranded like a large abandoned box in the middle of a field of stubble.

Jack Sheath, a widower who lived in the caravan with his daughter Lucy and worked as an under-gardener at one of the reservoirs, saw Davy through the window and came out to meet him. He was a big, awkward fellow with a round, reddish face, nearly always flushed from heavy cider-drinking, and a slyness about the eyes that marked him out as a scrounger or a shirker. He didn't much like Davy; he considered him to be uninteresting (meaning honest), and, if Sheath had been the kind of man to use such a word, devoid of 'respect'. What he really meant was that Davy didn't defer to him. Sheath, like most country people, was not one for overstatement or the more refined social graces, but he thought he knew a walking mistake when he saw it – and Davy, to his mind, was just that. Davy was aware that Sheath didn't care for him, but he couldn't be bothered about it, as he had better things to do; he was still young, not bad-looking in a fair, country-blown sort of way, and he possessed this remarkable and almost unique Flyer.

'Where did you get that thing?' Sheath asked, pointing a dirty finger at the vehicle.

'My old man gave it me for my birthday,' Davy said,

'What is it? Is it home-made?'

'No. It's called a Briggs and Stratton Flyer. American. There's not another one like it over here as far as I know. My father got it from a second-hand dealer in Brecon.'

'Where did he get it?'

'Dunno.'

Davy stayed in his bucket-seat as Sheath came up to inspect the car. 'Where's Lucy, please?' he asked politely.

'Dunno. Said she was going into Talybont.'

'What for?'

'How should I know? I'm not her bloody keeper.'

Sheath looked the Flyer over with a fake-expert's eye and the same expression of astonishment that Davy loved to see on the faces of the villagers. His eyeballs almost rolled in their sockets. 'I don't like it', he said finally. 'It looks just like a bogey.'

'It's faster than any bogey,' Davy said. 'I don't care what you think, anyway. I like it, it's my motor, and that's all that matters.'

345

'Lucy won't like it either.'

'How do you know?'

'I should know my own daughter. She won't, that's all.'

'Balls.'

'What?'

'Tell her I called, will you? Ta.' Davy switched on the ignition, revved up the motor-wheel and drove off, leaving Sheath with his mouth half-open and his flushed face reddening with fury. The irrational disgust he felt for Davy was equalled only by the intense loathing he felt for his superior at the reservoir, who was small, efficient, and drank weak tea.

'Where did you go this afternoon?' Davy asked Lucy Sheath when he saw her that evening in the Queen's Head, where she served behind the bar. He had penetrated as far as Brecon in the Flyer. The pub was noisy, full of cattle-dealers, farmers and hands. A few of them were leering at Lucy, who pretended not to see them. She was short, fat, blonde, and pink, with eyes like her father's that didn't stay on the face of the person she was talking to. She wore a rather low-cut pale blue dress, with sequins at the neckline, which gave more than a hint of what lay beneath.

'Where did you go?' Davy repeated.

'None of your business. You don't own me. We're not even engaged or anything.'

'I know. Do you want to see my new motor? I got it outside.'

'I heard about it from my father. He said it was a joke, and you're a laughing stock in it.'

'What does he know about it? He's not a mechanic.'

'Well, that's what he said. Looks like a bloody bogey, he said.'

Davy was not getting into that one again. Patiently he ignored her remark, and tried another tack. 'Would you like some trout I caught down by the lower bridge, Lucy?'

'No, ta.'

'They're nice trout. Rainbow.'

'I said no, ta.'

'Have you been seeing that Futtock again?' He was referring to the huge, violent son of an unpopular pig farmer, who had become rich on pigs and whose money spread like ripe manure over the neighbourhood.

'What if I have? What's it to do with you?'

'I thought you was my girl.'

Lucy sniffed. 'I'm nobody's girl.'

Davy gave up then, knowing when it was time to leave. He felt a bit sick inside, defeated, and decided to go home to have supper with his father, who was the only person he felt he could trust now. He had tried his best to be decent and kind, nice and reasonable, but the villagers stared and laughed at his Flyer. Mr Sheath didn't like him for some reason. Tom Futtock was a continuous menace, and Lucy was a

347

callous flirt. This was the way things went, when you weren't hard. If Davy had known about King Lear, he would have felt a kinship with the old man that day, being betrayed on all sides.

'Goodbye then, Lucy,' he said.

Lucy Sheath, a girl of limited feeling, said nothing, her mean little mouth firmly closed as she continued wiping the surface of the bar with a damp cloth, her large breasts bobbing up and down inside the tight blue dress and her fit body moving with the swing of the wipes. For a moment, looking at Lucy, Davy remembered the one occasion they had coupled, rather clumsily, down by the waterfall at Torpantau, late last summer when there were no picnic-parties about. Lucy turned away to serve one of the leerers. Then Davy left the bar.

'I saw a heron down by the shallows this morning,' his father said, placing a plate of bacon and eggs in front of him. 'And an oystercatcher taking a dip down by the canal, opposite the slope there. He was a long way from home, that one. How's the Flyer?'

'All right. Very good. It runs well.'

'You could go to Abergavenny and back in that for just a few pence.'

'Ay. I'll do that, next market day.'

'What's the matter, then?'

'Nothing.'

Davy ate the bacon and put one of the eggs on a

slice of bread, making a sandwich of it, but the yolk ran out through the sides and dripped on to his fingers, which he licked. He liked doing that, making the most of an egg. Then he drank a mugful of milk, sat back in his chair and rolled a cigarette. His father was still eating his bacon. 'I'll tell you, Pa,' Davy said, puffing at his fag. 'That old bastard Sheath can't stand the sight of me, and Lucy's been seeing that bugger Tom Futtock. We finished tonight in the Queen's Head.'

'Is that all?' his father said. 'I can't stand Sheath, either, or that Futtock. They should be both be thrown in the bloody reservoir. You'll meet somebody else. But I wish your Ma was still here to say something. I'm no good on that sort of thing.' He did not much care to talk at all, and seemed to welcome the end of his own sentences.

'That's all right, Pa. It don't matter.'

'Home's best, Davy. You can't beat it. We better mend that bit of fence tomorrow, and clean out the big barn. It looks like a shithouse. You got the Flyer anyway, Davy. You got that.'

Davy blew a smoke-ring. 'Ay, I got the Flyer,' he said.

No Peace for Dando

Before Gomer left the village to go to Port Talbot to seek his fortune in the steelworks, he said to me 'Shonni boy, I want you to keep an eye on Dando for me when I'm away. Look after him a bit, if you can, and give him this bottle only in a dire emergency, when he really needs it.' He handed me a medium-sized bottle of methylated spirits.

Gomer was referring to Dando Probert, a rodney who did odd jobs around the village and lived in an attic at the Top Hat Club, which was little more than a hole in the wall of a narrow passage-way off Minny Street. (One of my uncles, a very popular man, had spent most of his life in the Top Hat, trying to drink it dry.) Dando had been a deserter at the end of the war, hiding out with tramps and gypsies in Carmarthenshire and other counties. The redcaps never caught up with his scent, and even after the war they didn't come for him. It was said that Dando could have mingled with the sheep on the artillery range up in Epynt, and they still wouldn't have found him. He had done most of the disreputable things, including dope-peddling somewhere. When he wasn't on a mixture of rough cider and meths, he slept for long periods and forgot to eat. He was thought of as a character in the village, and tolerated as such. But

Gomer was very fond of Dando and did his best to keep him alive, buying him fish-and-chips or trying to cook a meal on the gas-ring in the attic. Dando's only other true mates had been old Pegleg Bevan the rag-and-bone man, who had died in the miners' home the previous winter, and a lurcher that was run over by a bus on the main valley road.

Gomer lived in a single room above the coalyard behind the Top Hat Club, and one Saturday he asked me to give him a hand when Dando was having one of his 'turns'. We had just come back from seeing a soccer match in Merthyr, followed by a good Chinese meal and a few pints in The Lamb – and Gomer, checking up on Dando, had found him blacked out in the attic. It wasn't a very pretty sight when I got there, but I'd seen worse. Dando hadn't spent the night in a rose-garden. He lay on a greasy caked mattress and was stinking the place out like a tomcat with the smell of cheap applejack and meths. The lethal purple liquid, after consumption and evacuation, always stank like unclean cats in a damp area.

'Doesn't he have trouble with rats here, Gomer?' I asked.

'I think so.'

Time was doing its job on the rodney, at an accelerated pace. He was not much more than a breathing skeleton as he snored and wheezed on the dirty pallet. I guessed that if Gomer and I couldn't pump some soup or milk into him, he would soon be gone from malnutrition. Eventually he would die from it, anyway, sooner or later. We stayed most of the night with him and the stench, and managed to get a cup of hot nourishing oxtail down his gullet. He didn't even say thank-you in the morning, when I went round to Willie's store for provisions and made him breakfast sops of fresh bread, sugar, hot water and cream off the milk. Then later we fixed a spare bed for him in the miners' hospital and they put some solids into him. After a few days he recovered sufficiently to be sent back to his attic, where he continued to indulge himself, procuring the cider from the club and the meths from the ironmonger.

I thought he was a lost cause, though I disliked myself for thinking this. I didn't want to let Gomer down, as I had promised to keep a brotherly eye on Dando, but I didn't know when a real emergency would show itself, or how I would be informed. Apparently this would come when Dando was no longer permitted access to the meths, and relied on my reserve supply. I hoped it wouldn't be during the day, when I was working in the shop. Common-sense told me that I was probably being party to slowly killing a man by feeding him that terrible liquid, but I had promised my good friend Gomer, who had his own reasons and was an older man whom I respected. You never went back on your word in the valleys. You could get away with a lot of things, but not your word. It was hard there, at that time, without much pity or sentiment among people, but you always felt part of a community. We kept to ourselves, among our own, and were highly suspicious of outsiders. I was only sorry that, in a situation like this, logic did not seem to matter very much.

'How's Dando doing?' I used to ask around the village, because I couldn't bring myself to visit that attic again.

The emergency call came sooner than I expected, not long after Gomer had departed for the Margam furnaces and big money. Dando had started a brawl one night in the Top Hat Club with a couple of colliers (his brains, or what was left of them, must have been scrambled, or he would have known better than to mix it with two tough face-men). When he was getting the worst of it, being punched all over the club, he ran out of the bar and up to his attic, where he began screaming his head off. The club-owner, Ivor, knew from Gomer that I had what Dando needed, and that he had been denied his ration by Pugh the ironmonger. So he rushed around to my lodgings in Pit Street and asked my landlady, Auntie Dallo, to wake me up. I wasn't asleep, and could hear them talking downstairs. 'Get Shonni out, Auntie,' Ivor said, quietly so as not to disturb the colliers off shift. 'Dando's havin' one of his bloody turns.'

'Is it bad, Ivor?' Auntie asked.

'He's a flamer, that boy, a bloody menace. We'll have to do somethin' about him, Auntie. I don't mind a joke but bugger a pantomime.'

Auntie Dallo called up to me, but I was already on my way down, still trying to buckle my belt as I held the precious bottle under one arm.

'I see you got the meths, Shonni,' Ivor said. He told me what had happened.

'All right, Ive,' I said. 'Everything's under control.'

'It bloody well isn't, boy. You wait and see.'

'Be careful, Shonni love,' Auntie said.

'Don't worry, Auntie.'

We ran down Pit Street, past the Picton and the Black Rose, like bats out of hell to the Top Hat. There was a small crowd outside looking up at Dando's grimy porthole-window, but he had stopped screaming now. Out of puff, I told Ivor to stay downstairs: 'Don't come up, Ive. He may get violent if he sees more than one.'

'Violent? He nearly wrecked my bloody club!'

I climbed the rotten back-stairs up to the attic. On the landing there were spots of blood from Dando's injuries. The door of his rat-hole was open, there was one weak naked bulb hanging under the skylight, and he was standing by the dust-crusted porthole, looking out.

He turned quick like a scared, cornered, skinny dog

when he heard my footsteps, and backed against the far wall. He looked more of a mess than usual. There was a lot of dried blood on his thin face, mostly around the mouth and nose, and on his torn shirt and jacket too.

'It's all right, Dando. Here it is. Gomer told me to give it to you.'

'I'll get the bastards,' Dando said. 'I'll get 'em.'

'Of course you will, Dando. Easy now. Here you are. Got any cider?'

'I'll fix the bastards.'

'Yes, Dando, 1 see you've got the cider. Here you are.'

Slowly he edged away from the wall, wiping his wounded nose with the back of his hand. He looked at me, his eyes blank. 'I only want a bit o' peace,' he said.

Then he grabbed the bottle out of my hand, pulled the cork out with his few remaining front teeth like an outlaw in a western, poured some meths into a cracked mug on the table, and added the scrumpo. He took a swig and lay on the mattress, with the bottles beside him. On the floor was a green crust and a piece of mildewed cheese, and a bit of onion. 1 gave him a screw of tobacco and some Rizla papers.

He didn't say anything else, not even Ta or goodnight as I shut the hardboard door and went back downstairs. Through the bar-hatch I could see the extent of the damage, and Ivor's wife sweeping up the broken glass. I told Ivor everything was under control and to let him sleep it off. He seemed unconvinced, shaking his head and muttering 'Bloody animal'.

I wrote to Gomer to tell him what had happened, and that I had done my duty. It seemed a proper emergency, at that moment, justifying my swift action. He replied that it was the right thing to do, in the circumstances.

But by the time Gomer came home on a visit – driving a second-hand Ford and wearing a new blue suit – Dando had not only disappeared from the attic, but from the village altogether. Nobody could trace him. Then about a month later a farmhand found him in a ditch as far away as Pentyrch, a bag of bones and dead from extreme malnutrition. At the inquest the coroner said it was death by misadventure, which could have meant anything, though it was no accident. Perhaps he thought it was impossible for anyone to starve to death in a welfare state.

Gomer was very upset, and wondered how Dando had covered the distance to Pentyrch on his own – what he had done on the way and where he had kipped. 'What a bloody fate,' was all Gomer said. For a while I felt guilty about that bottle of meths, but nobody blamed me.

Casualty

In a corner of the high room there was an elderly Marconi wireless set (the oldest I had ever seen) enclosed in a walnut cabinet. 'Can you get anything on that?' I asked.

'We can get the world, my boy,' he said. 'We have received Lloyd George and Adolf Hitler and Mr Nehru on that apparatus.'

The wireless was the only modern contraption he had. He disliked aeroplanes, motorcars and most other machines, and also lidos, the cinemas, jazz, and the general decline of manners. He belonged to the years before the world toppled in 1914.

It was a long time since I had seen him and I had forgotten how old he was now. He was complicatedly related to me by being the brother of the woman my mother's brother married. He had the aspect of a medieval Pope: his face was thin and distinguished, he always carried some silver stubble on his chin and neck that even the cut-throat couldn't defeat. That day he wore a smart grey suit, buttoned up, and a pearl pin in his royal blue tie.

He poured me a sherry, and a port for himself. 'Nothing more robust, I'm afraid,' he said. 'Only the drink of dons. Do you still gamble?'

'I play poker, and bet now and again.'

'You'll end like Fox – ruined by the dice-box and turf.'

In the cold house in Cowbridge he lived alone. It was built around 1880 and looked like a film set for a story about Jack the Ripper. A woman came in to clean twice a week and brought him provisions. He was a fair cook on the omelette level, and in the past we had shared delicious little feasts which he had rapidly whipped up, accompanied by two bottles of doubtful Beaujolais. He never went out, unless it was to go on warm summer days to the coast at Southerndown or to eat scones at a favoured tea-shop in Cardiff that had somehow survived the encroachment of the Wimpy empire. He was nicely slotted-in at peace and silence, reading Gibbon and Namier.

It was twenty years since he had taught history at an ancient and gloomy grammar school near York. During the holidays he wrote some good textbooks for schools and a volume of essays on secondary characters who blundered into the First World War, like the bloodthirsty Austrian, Conrad. I had learned a lot about history from him. He rejected the conspiracy theory, believing it all to be quite random and accident, but he was fascinated by adventurers of genius like Bonaparte, who wrote love letters from Russia to his doll Marie Louise back in Paris while his butchered legions were dying in the snow. 'How could men like that live with their consciences?' he used to ask.

'There was a reporter fellow here last week,' he said, 'from one of the journals. He wanted to know my politics and asked if I was one of Harold's men. I felt like a survivor of Hastings.'

He had told me his story years before. He came of turbulent stock, his father erupting over nothing at the table or marching out of a dinner party at some imagined slight. His mother was cursed with a bad temper, too, and migraine, but although she and her husband often had ferocious exchanges, they also had that peculiar bond which may exist between two people of stormy temperament. Sometimes even blows were struck and then she would retreat, whining, to the bedroom. At breakfast next morning the son would witness a gruffly affectionate reconciliation over the porridge and kippers, and all would be well again and the world stopped shuddering. During such intervals of calm, they would go on picnics together and behave almost like a normal family.

The one marshmallow part of his father had been a liking for verse, although he was unable to comprehend anything later than Tennyson. He was vaguely attracted to quotable bits of Eliot and Yeats and thought there 'might be something there', but on the whole he viewed modern poetry as the outpourings of unbalanced neurotics. He liked to declaim heroic verse, and when driving the family trap along country lanes in the Vale, flicking his whip at the hedges, he would spout 'The Charge of the Light Brigade' or 'The Burial of Sir John Mooreat Corunna' and similar stirring epics. His insensitive earth-bound wife dismissed all poetry and most novels as 'a nonsense'. But their son was a full-time contemplative, and early showed signs of an immense indolence. He did not possess the reinforcement of fortitude, he soon cracked under pressure, and tended to postpone decisions of a critical nature. The consequence was that he later became disappointed at every turn, things falling apart at a touch. Married twice and divorced twice, he had gone along with his wives in the invention of excuses for divorce. Life – anywhere for him – would have been an effort, too uninteresting and fatiguing to be properly coped with. It was a tedious arrangement at best, and not made to last. So he retreated further into history and the detailed examination of the motives of obscure dead men.

Solitary now, and comfortably austere, he had his books and his port and was perhaps content for the first time – cut off from people, unharassed by the demands of wives, and with enough in the bank to see him through. It was a tolerable loneliness he would have welcomed long before.

I told him my visit could only be brief, as I was on my way to meet a girl in Llandaff (she was actually a woman, but I always said girl to him, as he still regarded me as being about twenty-one).

'Why Llandaff, my boy?' I said she lived in Llandaff.

'Ah, as good a place to come from as any other. A fine cathedral there.'

No, I said, she shared a flat with two other girls.

'How strange.'

He had turned the Marconi on and we were listening to some Vaughan Williams – *Lark Ascending* I think it was. 'I like that and the *Theme of Tallis*,' he said. 'It's the only kind of sound I want to hear now.'

He was miles away and I might not have been there, yet I had a feeling of peace simply by being in his presence. I finished my second sherry and said I had to go.

He walked with me to the gate. 'You'll give my best to your mother?' he said as I shook the frail hand. 'Tell her I've finally reached zero.'

361

The Thinskin Award

'Who's this Carmarthen Thomas?' asked Duckham.

'He's a so-called playwright,' Stacy said.

'I know that, but is he any good?'

'Well, if quantity's got anything to do with it, yes. He's very prolific. He's written about fifty.'

'Good God. How many have been performed?'

'About five.'

'Where?'

'Mostly in small, out-of-the-way places. Clubs, town halls, that sort of thing. Why?'

'He's put in for the Thinskin.'

'Ah.' Stacy nodded. 'I'm not surprised. He knows about all the prizes going from here to Japan.'

'Has he ever won anything?'

'He got an arts council bursary once, I think, for an experimental thing up in the Midlands.'

Duckham the impresario and Stacy his lieutenant were sitting in the lounge of the Sandringham, weeding out applications for the Thinskin award, which was worth £500 and a trip to the States, sponsored by a firm that made contraceptives and women's tights. It was like the Pernod, Martini, Bollinger and other awards, put up by rich international concerns making vast profits that patronised the arts as a sop to their material consciences and to lose some of their tax. Their motives were not excessively noble and really had little to do with the pursuit or preservation of culture. But still the money was there, non-taxable, carrying a certain prestige among people who drank spirits or champagne or wore French letters or tights. The Thinskin was paltry, but it was Duckham's job to make recommendations, creaming off a fat fee for himself in the process. Usually he had a favourite in mind, one who came to heel like an obedient dog and would make a percentage for him with a popular play that was a load of crap.

Stacy, who advised Duckham on possible winners, like outsiders in a horse race, knew better than to push the claims of Carmarthen Thomas. A man who could write a five-hour epic about Oliver Cromwell with a cast of a hundred, to be produced in a castle with an elaborate set, and who had asked for Olivier or Burton to play the lead, must be either a genius or a lunatic. And Carmarthen was no genius. Stacy decided long ago that he was simply a colossal egotist, unrooted in reality, living in a world of his own and impervious to practical considerations. God knows what furies impelled him to write 50 unperformable plays, each of three-to-four-hours' duration or more that would have cost a fortune to mount. Thomas, he thought, like a hundred other no-talents, badly wanted a bit of fame

363

and his name in lights – not only a slice of the cake but the cherry, too.

'I'd like to meet him,' Duckham said, rolling his cigar from one side of his slack mouth to the other. 'Arrange it.'

Stacy was surprised, but he didn't show it. He was accustomed to Duckham's whims. Nothing seemed more incongruous to Stacy than a head-on collision between this greedy, soulless impresario and a mad, poverty-stricken Welsh playwright.

'I'll fix it,' he said.

Thomas wasn't big enough or good enough to be taken to the Napoleon or the Caprice, so he'd book a table at Asti's, a modest restaurant down town that was nice and quiet. For his job-reminders, Stacy kept a little book in which he used a form of abbreviated longhand: thus, 'CT l pf' became 'Carmarthen Thomas lunch pompous fart' – the 'pf' referring to Charles Otis Duckham Esquire himself. Stacy derived a childish pleasure, as befitted his childish public-relations mind, from insulting Duckham in a secret code only he could decipher. He had two obsessions: money, and the legal rape of women of any age, shape or description he could find. Duckham also had two fixations: money, and himself. They were both typical of their strange, concocted breed, messy products of their appalling time.

Carmarthen received his lunch invitation by letter one morning after he'd been up all night wrestling with the third act of another historical epic where he had to bring a bear and a pack of wolves into the action. It set him a problem, but he'd solved it. His eyes were bloodshot and felt as if particles of sand had been flung into them.

Apart from insomnia, he suffered from mild bouts of agoraphobia. He was often afraid to venture outside his room into the space, noise and traffic, and the jostling people. So he stayed at his table and wrote these interminable, unproducible stage plays. He kept himself alive on soup, bread, potatoes, sardines, Marmite, Bovril and tea. These were sufficient: unbalanced but nourishing. He spent most of his dole-money on posting heavy parcels of scripts to producers and theatrical managements all over the country. Some of these helpless folk had sagging cupboards full of Carmarthen's great wodges of words. He'd been at it for about 20 years, but felt that he still had a long way to go before he wrote the perfect drama, and all his endless, self-indulgent efforts were mere steps on the journey. Here in his room he could live in his fertile imagination, and make or break kings, move armies about, deal in patriotism, evil, loyalty and betrayal. His mind had become a jam of historical situations and fictional dialogue, his bizarre characters more real than his own dim landlady and his shadowy

365

neighbours. He had completely forgotten the existence of women, and used his roger only for its primary function.

A week later he arrived at Asti's restaurant for the Thinskin confrontation, wearing a long, old-fashioned belted raincoat the colour of green mildew. His dark face really resembled a hatchet, honed to a fine blade, and without that mack he could have passed for a corrupt night-club operator in one of those old Hollywood B-movies. The two smooth PR-sharks were already there. Duckham looked at him as if he were something the dustbin-men had deposited at the back door. On the middle finger of his right hand Carmarthen wore a gold ring set with a Buddha's head carved in green onyx, the same colour as his coat, and round his neck hung a facsimile of the seal of Glyndwr that he'd bought off a junk-stall in Cardiff.

'That's a very unusual ring and seal,' Stacy said, to make opening conversation, looking the perfect gigolo with his lotioned face and his silky blue suit.

'I only wear them when I go out,' Carmarthen replied, mysteriously. He kept his ankle-length coat on as they sat down and ordered the food. Duckham and Stacy chose truffled roast chicken, but Carmarthen asked for a pork chop with sprouts and boiled potatoes.

Duckham looked at him with distaste. 'This is on us, y'know, Mr Thomas,' he said. 'You can order what you like. The chicken is excellent.'

'No, ta. I like a pork chop.'

Stacy crumbled a bread roll with nervous fingers. 'What are you working on now?' he asked.

'A long one about Iolo Goch – Red Iolo.'

'Who's he?' asked Duckham, swimming in ignorance.

'He was Owain Glyndwr's bard. His poet laureate, you English would call him.'

'Do you always write long plays?' Stacy asked.

'Always. There's no point in writing short ones.' Carmarthen said it with such finality that it obviously ended the matter.

'Well, Mr Thomas –' Duckham began.

'Call me Carmarthen.'

Duckham winced slightly. 'Well, Carmarthen, what do you think of Beckett?'

'I've never broken bread with the gentleman. He's Irish, isn't he?'

'But his *work*. What do you think of his *work*?'

'He's just a sprinter. Too pessimistic. Just talking heads in garbage-cans.'

'And Pinter?'

'Don't know him. Not familiar with his work. Is he good?'

Duckham looked bewildered, lost for words, so Stacy quickly said: 'He's supposed to be one of the best.'

'Does he write long plays?'

'About medium length. Short ones, too.'

'Not worth bothering with, then. He's only a sprinter.'

The waiter came with a carafe of red wine, and within a few minutes Carmarthen had downed two glasses. 'What's this stuff called?' he asked.

'Er – Chateaubriand, I think,' Stacy said.

'It tastes like sheep-dip.'

Duckham shifted his bulk in the chair. He was well into his truffled chicken and ignored Carmarthen, whom he had already written off as a nothing. There was no percentage here. It probably smelled, too. Duckham felt like giving him a stick of deodorant and telling him to piss off.

Stacy felt decidedly uncomfortable in this barbarian's company, yet he also sensed that he was in the presence of a rough integrity – something which, like goodness, Stacy didn't fancy and rarely met.

Carmarthen was attacking his pork chop with gusto, and mashing the sprouts and potatoes. He took the chop in his fingers and gnawed the last meat off the bone. As he licked his fingers he said directly to Duckham: 'Are you going to give me the Thinskin, then?'

Duckham nearly choked on his chicken. 'What?'

Stacy intervened to stop his purple-faced boss throwing his plate at Carmarthen. 'You're definitely hot for it, Carmarthen.'

'Who are the other two?'

Stacy mentioned the names of a couple of time-serving ponces. Carmarthen looked hard at the other two and then returned to his last sprout. Do not con me, you hustlers, he thought. You pair of faggots, trying to dangle me on a hook with your bloody short lists. I don't live inside a filing cabinet. He knew all about Wankersville, where you kept your eyes and mind closed, your mouth shut except to utter safe, orthodox opinions, and where you used back-scratchers on your sucking cronies and a long spoon to sup with anything on two legs that resembled honesty. Stop conning me, he thought again, you two smart-arsed pigs. You're going to give that 500 quid to some poof sprinter who doesn't know the first bloody thing about writing plays.

There was silence at the table except for Carmarthen mopping up his plate.

'Would you like a sweet, Carmarthen?' Stacy asked. 'The gateau is delicious.'

But all Carmarthen wanted now was to get back to his small room on the other side of the town. Grab everything and run, when the vultures come. He'd have to walk, because he didn't have enough for the bus fare. He didn't have the Thinskin award either. But what he did have was a good free meal under his belt, four glasses of wine, and a further insight into the con. It made him feel glad to be Carmarthen Thomas,

369

unknown writer of long historical plays of genius, pure and unsullied. One day he'd be recognised, and not after he was dead. Comparing himself with these shiny wankers, he knew that he was clearly marked out for great things. This was all that mattered.

Carmarthen believed it, anyway. It was all he needed to believe as he belched loudly and got up from the table without saying a word – a bent half-truth against two total lies. He placed his last five pence on a plate between Duckham and Stacy, and left them sitting there with their mouths poised on spoonfuls of raspberry gateau as he strode purposefully out of Asti's in his long shabby coat the colour of green mildew.

Dic Tidy's Mistake

Tab's uncle, who was an eccentric and had some odd notions, used to say that men who tucked their shirts between their underpants and trousers needed watching with other men's women, because they had a quick-release method and were too smooth by half, while men who tucked their shirts inside their pants were safer, steadier, and undevious, probably preferring beer as a hobby.

Dic Tidy, who, according to Tab, belonged to the latter group, married a woman much younger than himself and was made to be cuckolded. He was called Tidy because his face was pink (some said from the gin) and soft, and he was always sprucely dressed, favouring pricey Donegal tweeds that he'd kept smart for many years, check Viyella shirts and wool ties, a gold Hunter in his waistcoat pocket, good Clark's brown boots, and sometimes sporting a plaid deerstalker with a red ribbon tying the earflaps. Another, not secret, concession to vanity was the dyeing of his grey hair with Tunisian henna – which led some unkind villagers to suspect, mistakenly, that he was a queer.

'Dic Tidy dyes his hair,' the grocer's wife said.

'Trying to keep himself young,' her customer said.

'Funny.'

Dic had received a grammar-school education at Cowbridge County and could speak well and knowledgeably on most topics. He was known right down through the south Vale for his sartorial elegance and his intelligence. When his father died, he took over the established family business, which was private printing and stationery, the only one of its kind for miles around. He had the local monopoly on letterheads, christening and wedding invitations, and funeral pew-cards, not to mention church, women's institute and British Legion newsletters. He was doing all right on his own, living comfortably in a flat above the business until, in his late 40s, he went berserk and married the buxom blonde cow from Cardiff. Dark Tab, his assistant and friend, who looked handsomely Italian, warned him against this alliance, sensing that it contained the makings of disaster, but Dic was fairly blinded by her looks and flattered by her interest, which was confined to his bank balance and nest-egg. He met her at somebody's wedding reception – she was a waitress for the caterers – and proposed to her the following week over a candlelit supper at the Fox & Hounds, when he slipped a second-hand emerald ring on her finger that he'd bought in Jacobs' pawnshop in Cardiff. Old Speedy Gonzalez had nothing on Dic Tidy when it came to rapid decision, putting thought into immediate action. But of the few choices open to him, in a narrow field, he made one of the worst. At the quick registry office wedding in Cardiff, with Tab as a witness and already getting the glad eye, from the cleavaged bride, a knot of well-wishers from the village thought Dic had acted while his mind was unhinged. ('He must be twp,' the grocer's wife said.) His only sister, Rachel, who was something straight out of a Victorian scrapbook, declined to attend the ceremony.

After a brief wet honeymoon in Tenby, they settled in the flat and it was soon apparent to Tab that all was not perfect in the Tidy household. For one thing, they stopped sleeping together after a fortnight. Tab found this out because he always got to the shop early from his digs and was in the habit of brewing a pot of tea at the back and taking a mug up to Dic in bed. This ritual went on even after the wedding, when Tab took in two cups and got the glad eye, but one morning he saw that they were in separate rooms, with the cow still asleep in the double bed and Dic, wide awake, demoted to a sleeping bag on a couch in the living room.

'You all right, Dic?' Tab asked, concerned for his friend and employer.

'She kicked me out,' Dic said.

'Why?'

'Said she was bored. It's a question of measurement, I suppose, with her.'

'You let her do that, Dic?'

'I'm past caring.'

'Already? It's only two weeks.'

'You can learn a lot in two weeks, Tab boy. She's taken me for a ride.'

'What are you going to do about it?'

'Nothing.'

Tab didn't know what to say, or do. He didn't want to remind Dic 'I-told-you-so' like a ghoul at an accident, but he *had* warned him about the possibility of calamity because of the difference in their ages and the basic frivolousness of the cow, who was as thick as two short planks. The only knowledge she possessed was carnal. She'd given up her waitressing, and now lay about the flat all day like an Edwardian mistress, drinking cheap Cyprus sherry and stuffing herself with Mars bars, Milky Ways and chocolate buttons. She was about as useful to society as a lesbian in a brothel.

Dic soon took to drinking a full bottle, instead of his customary half, of Gordon's gin a day, which he could well afford. When he was very drunk, and Tab partly drunk, in the living room in the evenings while the cow was with some bull in Cardiff or Barry, he liked to recite his favourite poet, Ezra Pound. Tab wasn't aware of it, because he didn't read poetry, but Dic – whose melancholy was extreme at this time – misquoted and mixed up old Ezra's lines, taking them from one Canto and putting them – somewhere Welshed – into another, yet oddly making sense: 'The living are made of cardboard,' he intoned. 'When one's butties betray each other, how can there be peace in the valley? The Pisan night is under wind, the hoar frost grips my old shed, the brambles are never still. I am at the end of my tether, a blown husk over the salt marshes of Gwent.'

Tab looked on bewildered at these outbursts, but allowed for Dic's state of mind, his despair at the marital shambles.

The weeks and months passed, and nothing changed, except that young Tab became slowly, magnetically drawn, against his better instincts, towards the sexy cow, who thrust her tits at him at every opportunity. First they kissed and felt on the landing of the stairs and at the back of the shop, then they had short-times on the bedroom floor when Dic was out or drunkenly asleep, later graduating to long-times in the bed itself. She couldn't boil an egg, so now and again Tab cooked a gravy-dinner for them to keep their energy up. While Dic was deeply sleeping off the effects of the gin on his couch in the living room, these two were taking extreme risks next door, and enjoying it to the full before Tab dismounted and crept back to his lodgings.

Surprisingly, Dic Tidy still remained true to his label and never had a piece of apparel or a dyed hair out of place. Dignity and self-respect would be the last thing to go, since that was the way he'd been brought up in Cowbridge by his strict English-influenced parents. He didn't let himself deteriorate. But inside he felt empty, hollow, and guessed that he was being cuckolded by Tab. It was an old story, one of the oldest, and as long as there were people in the world it would continue. They said the husband was the last to know, but he could tell by the glances that passed between his assistant and the cow, Tab's wearing of his best suit, and his irritating habit of whistling every morning like a bloody blackbird when Dic was having his corn-flakes – something Tab had never done before. Dic was no fool, and could smell infidelity and betrayal when they were there on his doorstep under his nose. He felt a bit like Dr Bovary. Old Flaubert had known a thing or two, for a recluse, about some women's appetites. The whole thing, to a person of Dic's fastidious taste, was beginning to take on the squalid appearance of an overheated French film. An unaccustomed harshness came over him.

'Why do you whistle like a bloody blackbird?' he asked Tab one morning.

'Eh?'

'Why do you whistle so much?'

'I don't know. Perhaps it's the weather.'

'It was pissing down outside and you were whistling like a bloody thrush.'

'I was a blackbird a minute ago. Make up your mind.'

Tab knew that Dic knew, he could sense it by the

unaccustomed brusqueness in his manner. He returned to his invoices, and Dic to designing a pew-card. Together they worked in silence every day, losing themselves in routine.

It wasn't long before Tab, exhausted, had served his purpose. He was continually short of sleep and yawning hugely. The cow moved out to investigate the potential of a garage-mechanic and then, appropriately enough, a cattle-dealer. There always seemed to be some local engines – randy bachelor, misunderstood husband, or lonesome widower – ready to look after her. She was often seen, by peeping toms who reported back, coupled in derelict barns, behind abandoned farmhouses, or on the back-seat of a car in the woods. Once she was spotted in broad daylight, in a Land Rover, with her legs in a scissors-grip around the back of the driver, who was going like a fiddler's elbow. Bets were taken in the Nag's Head on who'd have the screw of the week. The catch would come later, when she was older and started going to pieces, but at the moment she had nothing much to worry about. It would be some time yet before the crow's feet showed.

'I see Tab Hamer's bit has moved on,' said Griff the butcher to the landlord of the Tudor Rose.

'Ay,' said the landlord, who kept his own counsel. 'Who's rogering' her now, then?'

'No idea.'

'Loose piece, in' she? A sampler. Good riddance, as

377

far as Dic Tidy's concerned.'

'Ay.'

Dic carried on, stoically, neither condemning Tab nor forgiving him. He hadn't known his wife long enough to suffer like Othello. Everyone in the stifling village knew, of course, gossip and tongues wagging all day and night, but Dic didn't care. He said nothing, just kept the business running for his dead father's sake (he lost a few orders through the scandal), drank his Gordon's, ate alone in Llantwit, read Ezra Pound, and slept in his own bed again. He never mentioned divorce; perhaps he was waiting for her to grow older and come back to him, or perhaps he was sorry for her. Dic Tidy wasn't without compassion. Anyway, a quiet resignation to events was the attitude he seemed to adopt.

Everything went on as before, as if the cow had never appeared on the scene, except that Tab resigned from his job and what had become an impossible situation, out of embarrassment at the proximity of Dic and a belated sense of decency.

'I understand,' Dic said, as he paid him off, 'but I shall miss you. Off you go, then. And keep out of mischief.' ('Miss me?' Tab thought. 'After what I've done.')

The last time he saw his old friend was one wet summer day outside the Rose, sitting at a table with a glass of gin in front of him, staring ahead at nothing. Tab said later, with some remorse, that he'd never seen anyone look lonelier. Dic didn't have his deerstalker on, and the rain had made the dye in his hair run. It came trickling down his face in thin reddish-brown streams, over the eyelids and nose and mouth and chin, running down his neck into his collar.

The Seed of Dismemberment

A dialogue verse play for radio.

Place: Hampton Court.
Time: 1535.

Characters:
   Thomas Cromwell, English Lord Chancellor
   Rowland Lee, Bishop of Lichfield
   Thomas Vaughan, Welsh negotiator
   Barbara Fantham, Lee's mistress.

Note:
The basic historical facts are accurate, but I have invented Vaughan to put the Welsh case, and also Lee's mistress (though he kept a woman) to lighten the political discussion with some instinctive female wisdom.

The language is very updated here and there to pull away from the over-formality of 16th-century diplomatic discourse.

I would suggest a smooth, rather world-weary voice for Cromwell; a rougher but slightly fawning one for Lee; resonant Welsh accent for Vaughan; and frivolous but confident for Barbara.

MUSIC: appropriate serious Tudor, or Purcell.

Fade.

VAUGHAN: We are in the murk of 1535 at Hampton Court, built by the dead Wolsey for his corrupt Tudor, Henry, the eighth of that name – a monstrous greedy child, but intelligent, farting and loving himself on the throne of a powerful state given over the sick aristocrats and clever butchers' and grocers' sons. They are about to seal the fate of a small and ancient nation.

Aside: Do not be tricked by sophisticated scriveners excusing this royal mistake and his creatures for what they did. They were all cold manipulators from the egg.

Thomas Cromwell is chancellor of England: a subtle, conceited, and pragmatic lawyer with no doubts, only the bounding will of the renaissance. He has read his Macchiavelli. With him is Rowland Lee, dubbed bishop of Lichfield, his terror-hatchet in the Marches and mid-Wales who has already hanged about five thousand Welsh. *My* name is Thomas Vaughan, a last-ditch scrambler for crusts.

Fanfare of trumpets, distant clop of hooves on cobbles.

381

CROMWELL: The royal hog returns from playing in the sty. He is thundering about like he did with the Boleyn.

LEE: They should put him in a stud, Master Cromwell.

CROMWELL: You must remember, Lee, this king has a secret mission which he began as a boy: it is to destroy everything in sight before it can be built again, and I am his chief instrument.

LEE: Wolsey would have approved of his disciple.

CROMWELL: Wolsey was a big decayed thing in scarlet, crazed with ambition but gifted with a knife intellect.

LEE: He may have been a bladder of lard but he gave you a place in the sun. He made you what you are. What would he do about this Welsh thing, I wonder?

CROMWELL: It is a nothing place, a province not to waste time on, full of thieves and mongrels. Would God we could burn it from end to end.

LEE: We will put them through the hoop, I promise. I have been over to Llangollen chasing cattle stealers in the gorges. I like this work, Master Cromwell, being fitter for harness than bishop's robes, more comfortable at the head of my troopers than hunting heretics to the stake or chasing subtle formulas down the defiles of controversy. I think you would like my methods, being not affable to Welshry. We trap them in the glens and vales and hang them in batches at Shrewsbury. Soon it will be the king's dominion, and only their bastard tongue may remain with the passing of a statute.

CROMWELL: Who wants control of a territorial afterthought? You could have it, Lee, if I thought you wouldn't amputate it completely.

LEE: But such a strip of malefactors should be severed. Theft, murder, rebellion can only be stopped by a hundred gibbets.

CROMWELL: Henry must have this wing of his capon, Lee, no matter how thin. Our liege lord can be a deadly little turk if displeased. Wolsey and I often felt his displeasure like an earthquake ten corridors off.

LEE: Who is this fellow Vaughan?

CROMWELL: Some half-educated peasant from a loft in Glamorgan. They call him a negotiator, but he has a certain perished dignity like a weasel defending his hole. It is a sop to their pride and sensitivity, so I may throw him a few scraps.

LEE: Is he dining with us? We've got rainbow trout.

CROMWELL: (*chuckles*) No, give him horsemeat and leeks and a goblet of washing sherry, and a punnet of strawberries as a surprise.

LEE: If you look through the window Master Cromwell, you will see my piece of pleasure coming.

CROMWELL: Who is she, Lee, this apple-strumpet? Is that where you quench your lust?

LEE: Her name is Barbara Fantham, a middle-aged cleric's last attachment.

CROMWELL: I should hope so. You have run through the book. (*Pause.*) Greetings, Mistress Fantham.

BARBARA: Master Cromwell.

CROMWELL: We were just taking your clothes off.

BARBARA: I am flattered. Do you know of these things, Master Cromwell?

CROMWELL: Hardly, dear lady, I have experienced it, fitfully. Where power walks, tarts gather, regardless of one's looks. Lee is a corrupt bishop given to sensation between his thighs. I have my work cut out to ensure the sexual happiness of Henry. I am an observer of the royal animals and the randy Christian bishops of England.

BARBARA: It bores you, then?

CROMWELL: Indeed, yes. Furious appetites put us with the rats.

BARBARA: How unkind. Rowland's pleasure is my own pleasure in his terrible work. If I comfort him between sheets then it would seem he would be better the executioner of your policy. It is a kind of love to embrace a nice butcher, the expedient who makes history.

CROMWELL: Save me from the vanity of harlots! What do you think of the Welsh, Mistress Fantham? Do they set you panting and tapping?

BARBARA: I have met few gentlemen there and they do not put on frills or speak much English. Only their looks and bearing I would praise, dark and wild and dangerous they seem. Those who are fanatic for their red dragon strut like proud ramrods.

LEE: Men are fanatics until they win, then they are suddenly the government. The Welshry are swarthy thieves behind shutters, under hatches, ruined by their mad princes and liking the dark. It is my aim to keep them there. They had a chance of glory once and lost it, so they are meant to be trodden like cattle pancakes.

BARBARA: They are small people, but large in spirit. They claim they were outnumbered, and then our kings' greed ran them into the ditch.

LEE: Who loses opportunity deserves the gutter, and they always come at us from behind.

CROMWELL: Then *you* hang them in front.

BARBARA: The Welsh are not respectable, they are slightly animal like the bog-Irish, but then we have crushed their style.

CROMWELL: Quite. You are intelligent, Mistress Fantham. Lee is fortunate to have you... but leave me alone now to baffle this Welshman.

Short music.

Fade.

VAUGHAN: Thank you for the food and dishwater. It is thoughtful of Englishmen to provide leeks.

CROMWELL: You are a plodder, Vaughan. I've listened to you throughout supper and you've got peripheral vision which does not extend beyond Monmouth. You're nobody's fool, but you sniff villainy if an Englishman so much as breathes on a leek.

VAUGHAN: I guarantee it, two hundred years from now you will find no mention of Wales in the index of an English history book. You want our men and women to sift down the hour-glass, to sink quietly out of sight as if we had never been.

CROMWELL: You speak as if you possessed hindsight. Believe me, what we do here now, in this place, will clamp prosperity on your benighted land.

VAUGHAN: The sun still comes up over Harlech and the fords of the Teifi. We may be divided and tattered but you cannot wipe out a language or an idea. We are small but built for survival. You will not make English puffs of us.

CROMWELL: Don't hawk your rhetoric here, man. You foul fine minds with it. We are about the cool business of power from day to day. Your fancy speeches will not shake the rigour of cold fish.

VAUGHAN: Cold fish indeed! *Exactly*, Master Cromwell. Exactly that. You rob us of our language and our heritage in the name of what? Greater glory for the fat king? The expansion of his realm satisfies no one and nothing but himself. He would yield if faced by great power but attacks the smallest land in the kingdom which he misgoverns. It is a coward's way to show strength through violence. It will all blow back on you, even if centuries distant. It will blow back, believe me.

CROMWELL: Look at the evidence, Vaughan. You cannot support yourselves and you are collapsing into lawlessness and banditry. You are a difficult and bulging pimple on a healthy Tudor face.

VAUGHAN: Healthy! Jesu! Soon it will be a crater of syphilis.

CROMWELL: Strap your mouth, man! There is enough talent in this palace to run Europe and we are all realists here. You have a wilful indifference to realities which are quite obvious to me.

VAUGHAN: They say you follow the fat king because you are a jackal with sharp teeth and he is your lion.

CROMWELL: You are a parochial strawboy, Vaughan, the merest yokel. You see only Wales in the world.

VAUGHAN: If I am that, then you are a hypocrite gobbet of dung disguised in a silk stocking. You are an intellectual bully, sir! You cradle huge crimes in the name of effective action.

Slight pause.

CROMWELL: Have some wine. (*Sound of drink being poured/rustle of parchment.*) Now, let us get nearer the knuckle. See this, Master Vaughan? See those statutes? They are of a subtlety that your damned race will never possess. They are the logical alternative to the loss of Glendower. They are Henry Tudor's great experiment for Wales.

VAUGHAN: And we are the pigs.

CROMWELL: Goddam you, Vaughan! Would you rather be under the French? You raise the myth of racial purity to a religious symbol, you elevate the negation of human reason into theology. These transactions on parchment are called the Act of Union. They contain thirty-nine sections and they clearly state that those born within the Principality or Dominion of Wales will enjoy all the rights and privileges of the king's subjects in England. Our system of law will come to you, the lord-marcherships will convert to shire ground and the three of Gwynedd will remain untouched.

VAUGHAN: You are simply annexing us. This is not a settlement, it's rape. You move about under a snow of paper and change nations with it. You are corkscrew-devious in the bone.

CROMWELL: Yes, you must rise early to catch us.

VAUGHAN: You are sophists, cultivating skill in reason but degenerating into bloody quibblers. And what of the tongue? You will cut it out in all the courts of justice. You deny to my countrymen who are tried for life or liberty in their own land the elementary right of pleading in their mother tongue. Oh, we shall cling like ferrets to the oldest living language of culture in western Christendom.

CROMWELL: Your language means nothing to us. What is a language? One way to communicate among many. Use your eyes and fingers like the deaf and dumb, or learn the precision of Latin. The problem of saving the Welsh culture makes that of shoring up Venice seem a picnic.

VAUGHAN: What are these statutes but judicial murder, concealed as logic? Do you imagine you can fool all the Welsh who were eating smooth cardinals before breakfast? Provinces are nothing, and land is dirt, but there are people on them and they spit on crowns and sceptres.

CROMWELL: Have a care, Vaughan. We could dance you to the block for treason.

VAUGHAN: Death comes for us all, Master Cromwell. Even for your king and dukes he will not kneel or make reverence. *(Sudden, loud trumpet fanfare.)* What's that, for God's sake? The return of the Pope?

CROMWELL: *(amused)* No, no. Only our master going out to rut. They blow trumpets on his departure and arrival so that everyone knows he is still fit.

VAUGHAN: And *that* will rule Wales? *That?*

CROMWELL: Are you wived, Master Vaughan?

VAUGHAN: Indeed, yes, with six infants.

CROMWELL: You *have* been a busy Welsh buck. Let us hope they will grow wiser and more accommodating than their father, and thrive under England's roof. We can be generous to friends and give bounty to intellects in our service.

VAUGHAN: To creeping turncoats, you mean. I would sooner my sons were exiled to Caldey.

CROMWELL: They may be yet. You are obviously tired of life or you would not risk it so with that wild mouth. Go home and tell your lunatics that if you fight us it is the short path to ruin. You will not have a single hedgerow left.

VAUGHAN: Eyeball to eyeball then, Master Cromwell, we are locked. Your snail-view of the world is not mine. You see eternal excrement and the management of it where I see a glitter between the turds.

CROMWELL: To be blunt, which I have tried to avoid... you will not untie the knot once we have fastened it. We have been at this pastime too long. Soon the concept of Wales as a nation will cease to be a recollection, an ideal or a fact. And the very existence of a language will be a political offence, a reminder of difference, and a threat to the union. Have some more wine.

Drink poured.

VAUGHAN: Diolch... one day we will be banded together again, and knock you off your smug stool. Mark it, Master Cromwell. We are not provincial mice to be shuttled to history's wainscot. My meat may be stripped by maggots but my bones will rattle for Cymru. You and Bishop Lee cannot shift us to the margin.

CROMWELL: (*yawning*) Pooh! Pooh on it. It is over, Vaughan, and we have won...

Pause.

Fanfare.

VAUGHAN: The blaze of gold quartering is caught in a sun flood through the high window flashing all ways at once. Ancestors slabbed in marble on the walls, pearl, brocade and scarlet lions jumping in the lemon shafts. The living Holbein portrait hoists himself and his precious codpiece off his ulcered calves, thinking of bed and backgammon. Lee and Cromwell and a creep of courtiers, a slither of damp bishops ease to the long table. The pale black secretary dips the qu ill and hands it to the ruin: this once Golden Hope of the New Learning soon to queen again as easy as he split from Rome, and now with levity pocketing the hapless land to the west. Sun-slant catches his enormous ring-seal as he lifts his ruffed whiskers, shakes white lawn sleeves back from his wrists, scratches slowly on buff parchment, and impresses red wax with the ring, screwing it left and right thoroughly, for God knows how many centuries...

Solitary drum.

Bell tolling.

Fade.

Appendix

Thoughts from the Holiday Inn
(for John Tripp)

When you're dead, you're bloody dead.'
We both liked the punch of that one, John, said
Ten or more years ago by an author breaking
Through his fiction, kicking the rules, risking
All our willing disbelief to shock through
To the truth. B.S. Johnson, that sad and tortured man, knew
The whole thing to be by turns a joke, by turns the need
To love each other into something close to sense. We bleed,
John, we bleed, and time bleeds from our wrists.
Your death was shocking, and tidies up another lovely,
                                    angry (when pissed),
Poet of a man, who would not, for anyone, be tidied
                                    into respectability
Longer than an evening, or his allotment in some
                                    anthology.
There's too much to be said, by too many, too soon.
But from this lunchtime watering place, this unlikeliest
                                    of rooms,
Spare me the modest time and space – by Christ, you've
                                    enough
Of both in death old mate – to work things out, sound off –
About the months you've missed, the months that we've
                                    missed you.

You'd have seen this place go up, the skyline that you
                                                    knew
Transformed, jagged, blocked as urban planners brought
                                                    rationality
To what the coal century had grown and shaped to the
                                                    Taff's estuary.
We've needed you here, John, thrusting out our neck
                                            and stroking the chin
From a classy, fraying shirt to show the disdain we hold
                                            these people in,
These late-comers to a country and a nation in a mess.
They've given us the bum's rush today, John, I must
                                                    confess.
We checked out the place for next year's Literature
                                                    Festival
And sponsorship. As far as we could tell
It was a waste of time, for any management
Who'd given Sickle-Cell Research the thumbs down were
                                                    clearly bent
On profit, and to hell with charity, never mind cultural P.R.
Well fed and disappointed, we returned to the bar.
Still, they'd named the two big function rooms, the
                                                    'Dylan Suite'
And 'Gwyn Jones Room'. 'Don't know him,' said the
                                            manageress, with complete
Honesty. 'He's one of our academy's most distinguished
                                            senior members,'
I said, and thought, We do no more than blow upon the
                                                    embers,

398

We scribblers who'd want to claim
that everything in Wales for praise or blame
Is brought to life and fact and mythical creation
By that writerly mix of ego and the grasp of a tradition.
What use we prove the weight the world gives us, if any,
Is likely to be cheap and grudging, no more than a
                                        blunt penny
Flung to shut our mannered, metred whining.
Then, later, taken up again shining
From the rubbing our tongues and lives impart.
I hear you answer, John, 'It's a start, boy, some sort of
                                        bloody start.'
John, further down the Hayes, now I think of you,
                              haunting those benches
And passing a coffee or the length of a fag below the
                                        rich stenches
From Brains's brewery snugged in behind the Royal Arcade.
As the big internationals move in and build and build
                                        the shade
And sunlight shift position down the city's roads.
In spruced-up Bute (re-named, as Tiger Bay encodes
A docklands past we'd best forget or sanitise
In tarted-up pubs or tree-lined low-rise
Flats – *The Jolly Tar* or *Laskar's Close*)
The men who clinch the deals, the gaffers, the boss
With the tax-free Daimler, the Series Seven,
Square out the mazy city into real estate concepts,
                                        proven
Returns for their money. They are gilt-edged applicants

For Euro-funds, Welsh Development grants.
This hotel is for the likes of them. It stretches eve to eye
With the brewery's silver funnel, two hundred
                                        bedrooms in the sky
Starting at fifty quid the night. 'Fat cats,' I hear you say,
'And that's before your breakfast. Stuff the fucking
                                        pool, O.K.'
Tax payer's rage? John, even you, an occasional
                                        connoisseur
Of hotel fitments and glimpses of the soft life, would incur
A gullet-sticking at this pricey junk, mock-Grecian style
Arches, columns, thick marble-facings done in tiles,
Plush, deep divans around an open fire beneath a metal
                                        canopy,
Surrogate logs you'd hardly warm your hands upon.
                                        You'd see
Beyond, the indoor pool, functional, gaunt,
More marble, sharp angles with, each end, broken
                                        columns to flaunt
The facile version of classic decor money'll buy
And set down in a city anywhere, across a sky
Or ocean. Continent to continent there must be
                                        travellers
Who need the reassurance of such nondescript pools
                                        and bars,
To step off the plane or train, taxi down concrete tracks
To what the Telex reservation guarantees predictable:
                                        stacks
Of credit-cards accepted, pool-side temperature just O.K.

An in-house movie they choose and relay
To each room in American or English – God forbid
The native patois – (*These people down here, the Welsh, – did*
You say – a language all their own – an ancient tongue?
– King Arthur – well, I saw a movie when I was a kid, sung
The songs all that summer – Danny Kaye – got it!)
John, what kind of progress is all this shit?
They look the coal-miners and put 'em in a coal museum:
And the people drove down, coughed up three quid ten
                                            just to see 'em.
Tourists one-nighting en route the Beacons, Bath or
                                            Ireland:
'Cardiff – what's that?' 'The airport … it's halfways
                                            there. I planned
To break the trudge from Heathrow.' And what of the
                                            locals?
Lunchtimes bring yuppies of both sexes, the gals
Waft in like *Cosmo* covers, the men have knife-
Creased casuals, hook their index fingers through the
                                            keyrings of life.
And there's the midday nibblers, women past their prime
But dressed to the nines and painted, passing the time
Between Howells' upholstery and Hones and Jones with
                                            a small gin
And sandwich triangles of horseradish and smoked
                                            salmon,
Piquant, hardly fattening. Their cigarette smoke curls
Away with the suggestion of rope, these former good-
                                            lookers, girls

Who, thirty years before, bagged a man of promise or
                                              means
And moved up, to Cyncoed, out to Lisvane, a pool, lawns
Done by a man who brings his own machine and strips
His shirt in the long afternoons. They tip
Him with the last cut of September.
Their husbands arc on the board and successfully
                                        bored. 'Remember,'
They'd say, 'when we had that little detached in
                                              Newport,
And we'd spend Sundays, you mowing and me
                                        trimming.' 'I've fought
hard to get this far, and Christ, there's times I wonder,
'What for? What have we got? Where's it gone? Just
                                              blunder
On to the next rung, dinner party, contract, barbecue.'
'Love, you're working too hard. Is the company proving
                                        too much for you?'
John excuse this indulgence, that clumsy fiction, it's no
                                              digression
I'm still concerned to understand progression.
When working-class is all you've known
These rich fish cruise by bright-coloured (if overblown)
Distracting – but these too are tenants of the pool
You plunged your wit and pen into. Fool
No one was your aim, and at last came the anger of *Life
                                        Under Thatcher*.
But winos in the Hayes betray a watcher
Who'd sum up the whole state of things in verses.

It's too easy to shoot off steam in curses
That pepper the mark but fail to penetrate.
Guys with real assets, clever portfolios, are immune to
street hate;
They justify themselves in terms of respectability,
vision, advancement.
The world's an oyster if you lift your nose off the
pavement.
They've bought themselves out of the firing line.
Windows purr close, revs slipping the motor into fifth
gear, it feels fine
To loosen out along the motorway – weekends in Pembs.
Or, turning right, over the Bridge, a trim two hours to
dine by the Thames.
No one's rooted anymore, John, as you must have
known –
'The old man' coming to smith in Taffs Well in the 30s
where you'd grown
Up Welsh, not Cornish like him, in all but the language.
(The wounding of that loss, it seems, no achievements
can assuage.)
And, because of that, confused, determined and
concerned
As the rest of us, excluded from the *Gorsedd* but feeling
you'd earned
The right to sound off for this Wales – Taffs and Gwerin,
To voice the peculiar place of the eighty per cent. The din
Of justified protest settled after '79 – Welsh cheque
books, Channel Four.

The nationalist drummings the Sixties saw you working for
You realised later were too easy, too raw. like R.S.
you loved the country with a passion, an anger, but the
less

Misty, period-costume work will surely prove the best,
The more enduring; real poetry 'welcoming the rough-
weather guest'.

John, I would rather have seen your ashes ebb from
Barafundle

Bay. That grey day at Thornhill we watched your coffin
trundle

Behind the curtains to the kind of anonymity
You'd rail against for other 'botched angels', losers we
Turn away from, society's mistakes, the hard-done-to,
Underdogs you wanted to feel close to.

The glow of a cupped-hand fag was light enough to draw
You to some alley, a derelict huddled there against a door,
One of the Hollow Men, a voter with no vote
Wrapped in old woollens, *Echoes* stuffed inside an
overcoat.

'Cold enough, butt, eh? on the street. Here, have
yourself a cuppa.

Take care, old fella, and watch out for the copper.
Those bastards aren't for the likes of us,
They don't give a tinker's cuss
As long as things stay down and quiet, and everything's
neat.

You and me'll keep to the shadows, butt, and stay light
on our feet.'

404

I've a feeling poetry's not the thing most apt
To dissect society, or politicise an audience one
                                    imagines trapped
In wilful ignorance, lobotomised by the trashy press,
Disenfranchised by the soapy box, seduced by the caress
Of the goodish life in the second half of this softening
                                    century.
You, fellow sprinter, took your chance through readings
                                    – could be
Five or fifty listeners, in club, gallery, college, school.
But articles in the London nationals, plays on the TV as
                                    a rule
Work most action, albeit short-lived. We
Poets light shower-burning fuses or rockets you see
Flash and quickly fade as the moment's charged
And spent. John, you saw the first decade of this city
                                    enlarged,
Pulled into the dream-shape someone thought we needed.
At fifty-nine who's to say you'd not changed things, not
                                    succeeded
In stirring up whatever stuff this corner of the pool had
                                    in suspension?
Talk of booze, too little care taken of yourself,
                                    prevention
Of the heart's explosion that took you in the early hours
With McGuigan's fight won and the tele drizzling showers
Of grey flakes down its mute screen,
Won't bring you back. You slid away. The barely-tuned
                                    machine

Packed up. Unlike Dylan, no insult to the brain, John.
                                                Often we'd talk
Of going to the States, whistle-stopping, the Chelsea in
                                                New York,
Our tour for the Yanks, I could have rigged.
Yes, if I'd pushed it, we two in tandem could have
                                                gigged
Over there. Like a lot of the others, I chickened out, I
                                                suppose.
Pembrokeshire a couple of nights – you with no change
                                                of clothes,
Just a battered attaché, poems, toothbrush, fags –
Was the limit of my stamina for your ways. Memory drags
Such petty guilts to the fore.
Though I treasure and feed off that reading we did on
                                                the man o'war,
Reluctant sailors pouring export ale down us
To forestall the poetry (they did) drown us
With hospitality in the middle of Fishguard harbour
Until we staggered past the missiles in her belly's store
Up to the frigate's redundant forward gun-turret,
                                                officers dressed
In cummerbunds, and elegant women. The talk was
                                                veiled, but impressed
Words like 'Responsibility', 'Capability' and 'Global
                                                role'. 'Yes, but
What do you do with all this training? All the missiles,
                                                shit-hot
Fire-power?' I remember, he answered you with, 'We

can blow Fishguard
Away with each one, you know. We are, I suppose, a "hard
Fist gloved by our democratic masters".' John, before
                                    the evening ended –
You topped that with a poem scribbled on a cigarette
                                    pack. We descended
A precarious ladder to the launch with those lines of his
                                    and yours sinking
Into the night. And now, a decade later, the story has a ring
Any writer could tune. Perhaps that's what your
Sandeman Port inquisitor
Pointed to – after the jaunts and applause, the writer's for
Filling the void, putting structure into space, a kind of race
Against apathy and oblivion. Too grand, you say, too
                                    heroic? Let's face
it, John, we've both indulged in our 'intervals of heat'
On the page and off. Both been chilled by the thought
                                    one couldn't beat
The odds, stuck in Wales, chiselling verse, weak in the
                                    flesh.
We're out on the edge of the world's concern, no Wall
                                    St, no Long Kesh.
Unless the challenge here is also to connect radar dishes
                                    at Brawdy,
Hinkley over the water, Trawsfynydd, the poison
                                    brought in on our sea.
An *Anglo*, dipped in England's sewer should still
                                    produce the goods.
Albeit in 'invisible ink / on dissolving paper...' one loads

The futile quarto, pushes it out to travel or sink.
Standing here before the Holiday Inn, and its shiny O-3-O,
                                                    I think
How my grandfather, before the Great War, shunted
                        down to Wales on the G.W.R.
How arbitrary one's identity is: with voice and gestures
                                                    we are
Challenged to make sense of where and what we find
                                            ourselves. No
Border guards patrol the Dyke, no frontier seals us in at
                                            Chepstow.
Did you really ever want that, John, seriously?
From here I have to question that stance. Were you
                        quite as you appeared to be?
This locomotive worked the sidings in Cardiff and the
                                            junction,
Was scrapped at Barry and now is made to function
As an image of our hard-bitten history. 9629, freshly
                        painted green and black,
Her valves de-gutted, holds to her half-dozen yards of track:
No driver on the footplate, no steam, no destination,
This featureless hotel her final station,
Under the flags of Canada, Commerce and the Dragon.
I turn around. On the island in the Hayes a wino tilts
                                            his flagon
And light flashes from the moment.

                                            Tony Curtis

At Bosherston Ponds, Rain and Fog

Here in November with the slanting rain and the mist
it's hard to imagine Tripp slogging down these ruts
in his brogues, cake taken at the Trust tea room,
his head thick with historical cluck.
Furthest I ever walked with John
was bar to taxi and maybe back;
the ill tempered heartland of Wales
a matter for books.

Ahead I see the vees of duck crossing the bayou,
beyond, the smoke of sea above the dunes.
This place is an alien gate in time, somewhere lost.
If the long water held diplodocus or coelacanth
it would fit – the wet air here bends space.
The rocks jut just as Satan left them,
the stream leaks like a faulty heart.

The one church is locked when I get there and the
road back a drift of mud. I get JT to show me
the future. Fog, more fog, then the bang of winter.
Nothing new. I start the car but he won't get in.
This is it, boy. River of ghosts. I sail on out.

John Tripp wrote in the early seventies about Bosherston Ponds on the Pembrokeshire coast – a place which did not sound part of Wales. When I discovered them they proved to be every bit as alien as I'd imagined. And in the bad light absolutely full of ghosts.

Peter Finch

Coming Back with JT and Bob Dylan

Returning to Wales on the train. They used to call it
the 125 but they don't do that now.

There is downpour, always.
Fat rain hung over South Wales
like a diseased lung.
'There's many here among us
who think that life is but a joke.'
Dylan, walkman, bright chrome band
of earphones across my head
like a scar. Drove a shunter
once at Severn Tunnel. All the yards
now flat. Church with its spire,
stranger pointing a swollen finger.
Yellow rape bright in the rain,
land gouged by road and drain.

Tripp returning from foreign England
40 years back wanted border guards
to keep the place the same. But the terraces fail
and the tracks are crapped over with pitchmastic.
Jesus Saves – The Fuck He Does – white slapped
on a bridge side. Industry made hardcore
for car park. Half of Wales with a

411

chipboard wardrobe still overweight
still dying of wet heart attack.
'They stone you when you're fit and able'.
Two beers with JT's ghost in the swaying bar
full of men in bad suits who
sell and never go home.
Intellect and dignity buried.
The land leveed with golf, junk and garbage.
And God somewhere making it worse.

Peter Finch

Annotations

Farewell to a Shambles

Midsummer in Treslothan (pages 61-65)
Anglo-Welsh Review, Autumn 1973

a simmering stockpot: exemplifies the significance of food.

One of my uncles, Matthew: cf. the poem 'Craftsman'.

Ferret and Weasel (pages 66-69)
In ms from Fay Cornes.

Fay Cornes recalls: 'The farmer's son was Martyn Llewellyn, a neighbour and friend of my family when I was still living at home with my parents in Lisvane. My young sister had a pet rabbit and its food supply was stored in our garage. When I drove into the garage one night, a rat appeared from one of the food sacks and almost waved at me! The next morning I contacted Martyn (not a boy, but actually in his mid-twenties) to ask him to please come with his ferret (called Penelope!) which he did indeed always carry inside his shirt, in order to kill the rat. Thankfully, the "rat was torn in seconds".'

Farewell to a Shambles (pages 70-79)
Planet 28, August 1975. The last page of this was followed by Tony Curtis's poem 'The Last Soldier'.

Indonesian Interlude (pages 80-90)
Planet 22, March 1974

Yevtushenko: interesting that JT links the internationally famous Russian (born 1933, most famous poem 'Babi Yar') with three of Wales's leading Welsh language poets.

Minox: tiny camera favoured by Cold War spies.

End of a Guild (page 91-99)
Planet 24/25, August 1974

B. S. Johnson (1933–73): experimental English novelist who was Gregynog Fellow in 1970 and who organised the appearance of JT with John Ormond and Emyr Humphreys in the Penguin Modern Poets series. John Tripp had a mention in B. S. Johnson's *Christie Malry's Own Double Entry*, p. 81: 'Mr. Tripp the Welsh wizard waxed fiery every history lesson over the cunning of the English'.

Peewee Winch: JT delighted in twisting the names of contemporaries (here, Peter Finch), possibly to avoid legal repercussions.

flip dismissal: cf. the poem 'Who's in, Who's out'.

Fanny Willems: Fay Williams (now Fay Cornes).

Viriamu Lewis Slept Here (pages 100-108)
Planet 20, October 1973

Border Run (pages 109-119)
Planet 34, October 1976

Keido Rees ... Butt Griffin: again JT playing with names – Keidrich Rhys and Bryn Griffiths ... later John Ormond, Raymond Garlick and others.

The Way the Biscuit Crumbles (pages 120-130)
Planet 26/27, 1975

Radical Passing

Many of these were supplied by Fay Cornes (written, probably, between 1967 and 1974) from her large collection of John's typescripts, with which she helped him. Unless indicated these are previously uncollected, or out of print. These, together with the holdings of the National Library of Wales (supplied by Jean Henderson) number in the hundreds and are beyond the scope of this present selection. I trust that this sample may encourage further research and publications by others.

In a handwritten note on a copy of 'The Last Picture Show', which he sent me with other materials before a visit to my students in Barry, John wrote 'Here are 6 (published) fair copies – just a sampler, a taster to give a flavour. Most of my stuff is in illegible draft-form and I'd better keep those for Whitchurch Library!... I'll use these [poems] as a base for discussion, if U like – also read a sheaf of recent work – mention US influences (inc. *prose*). Leave it to U to control drift if it veers off... use of irony, satire instruments ("Because I do not seem serious, do not think that I am not dead serious").'

Jet to Palma (page 133)

On the typescript JT had pasted a clipping of a British Midlands airliner and a map of Majorca. It is signed and dated 25.iii.73 'with love always, Johnny'. He has drawn two stick figures at the bottom of the page; they hold hands and are labelled 'J' and 'F'. At the very bottom is 'LOVE IS... drinking long Bacardis and Coke together.'

Fay writes: 'A travel agent friend of mine offered me, at the last minute, a long weekend in Majorca in March. We only had a few days to get ready and John had to obtain a one-year Visitor's Passport. We were due to fly from Bristol but, because of bad weather, the holiday company transferred us to an hotel in Weston-super-Mare. (This hotel was infinitely superior to the one in Majorca.) We finally left Bristol Airport very early the following morning, just as the sun was rising (very stunning) and it was at this point that John started writing the poem about flying. The so-called "holiday" became a nightmare when John discovered brandy at 5p a glass! During his "brandy moments" he was determined to call on Robert Graves and, at other times, was threatening not to return to Wales. He thought he could survive very well on Majorca with brandy at that price! A professional photographer took a photograph of us arriving at Valldemosa, walking along but not speaking to each other! The reference to "LOVE IS..." is based on the cartoons by Kim Grove that used to appear in the *Daily Mail*! John thought they were wonderful and he was always making up his own captions. He also used to buy me the little books of the collected cartoons priced at 20p each in 1971!'

Radical Passing (page 134)
An elegy for radical politics, perhaps. *Clare College* is one of the oldest in Cambridge.

The Retreat in Gwynedd (pages 135-136)
Cf. the radio play *The Seed of Dismemberment* and 'Epitaph on Our Military Defeats' in *The Province of Belief*.

Patagonia (page 137)

the Carmarthen concept probably owes more to alliterative effect than any specific doctrine. Dago is an insulting term for native south Americans.

Prinknash Abbey (pages 138-140)

The monastery, near Gloucester, to which the Caldey Island Benedictines moved in 1929. They continued the perfume making which had begun in Pembrokeshire. Cf. 'Whitsun at Prinknash' (*Passing Through*). Fay Cornes confirms that they visited the Abbey in August 1972.

R. S. Thomas (pages 140-141)

Cf. the poem with the same name in *Passing Through*. JT takes from RST his gloomy assessment of modern Wales.

Edward Thomas (pages 141-142)

The London-Welsh First World War poet (1878–1917).

Peninsula Tour (pages 142-144)

Cf. the poems 'Barafundle' and 'At Bosherston Ponds' (*SP* and *CP*). JT loved visiting Pembrokeshire. Barafundle was originally called 'Boomer Hole' in the Fay Cornes ms. Here JT travels from the birthplace of Gerald of Wales to the western edges of south

Pembrokeshire, encountering the spoilations of both tourists and the military. The east blockhouse at Angle, one of the Milford Haven defences originally built in the sixteenth century and later modernised, represents the long military importance of this beautiful area.

Nash Point (pages 144-145)
A heady mixture of bully boy weather, and writer's retreat, cricket, foreign travel and the sense that Time is nibbling away at JT himself.

Pleasure (pages 145-146)
Despite its strained ending, this poem is a memorable celebration of pork and the sense of a tradition of Tripp family eating.

Craftsman (pages 146-147)
The craftsman sacrificed by war: cf. his uncle in the story 'Midsummer in Treslothan'.

West Welsh Tale (pages 147-148)
Carmarthen Ann: cf. Dylan Thomas's west Wales relatives and especially the poem 'After the Funeral (in Memory of Ann Jones)'.

Piggott: Lester Piggott (b. 1935), one of the greatest of British jockeys and an easily recognised diminutive man for JT's generation.

slitted the butcher for a copper: an image of her parsimony: she haggled aggressively over the cheaper cuts of meat.

broth and duff: rural soup, similar to cawl, followed by a fattening pudding: another example of JT's use of food as an indicator of status and human relationships.

Solva: picturesque north Pembrokeshire fishing village. The county is always regarded by JT as a beautiful, restorative place: see also 'At Bosherston Ponds' in *SP*, and 'Barafundle' in *Passing Through*. Much of the anger in 'In Defence of the West' in *SP* is focused on the threat to Pembrokeshire.

crocked Alvis: one of the most notable of mid-century British cars. An Alvis, together with the *gold half hunter*, denotes his previous wealth and status.

a / bisexual epileptic gravedigger: the grotesque elements underpinning this poem are clearly informed by the work of Caradoc Evans (1878–1945), the Cardigan-born writer whose collection of short stories

My People (1915) scandalised Welsh society by its portrayal of an ignorant, superstitious rural community. See 'Caradoc Evans Revisited' in *CP* and *SP*.

Village Circuit (pages 148-150)
the old Rialto: an art deco cinema which closed in the 1990s.

A story teller: the poet, critic and fiction writer Glyn Jones (1905–95).

Meic: Meic Stephens, poet and critic who directed Literature in the Welsh Arts Council in JT's time. Tripp was not always respectful of Meic's position and undoubted erudition; he was once sick, deliberately, in Stephens's car after being generously given a life back to Whitchurch after a poetry reading.

The Journey (pages 150-152)
A gilded memory of meeting Jean Henderson, who lived in the Pentyrch area and served as a Conservative councillor.

Gwaelod-y-Garth (pages 152-153)
From here JT may have looked down on the site formerly of his father's forge.

Trust (pages 153-154)

deerstalkers and tweed suits: JT saw himself as a conservative in some matters. Signed and dated 'Whitchurch. Dec 75'.

Writer in Schools (page 155)

JT needed schools visits for the money, but here he seems to celebrate his perceived empathy with the girls.

Recital (page 156)

Pulteney Bridge places the reading in Bath. JT and Fay visited the Pump Rooms in August 1971.

Who's In, Who's Out (page 157)

Ian Hamilton and Edward Lucie-Smith are satirised here. JT attended Lucie-Smith's poetry group in the London days. Cf. 'The Last at Lucy's' from *The Province of Belief*. JT felt a mixture of pleasure and guilt at being in or on the edge of such circles: 'in a blue of ethical indolence / on the long bent furlong of doubt' ('Exiles' in the Bryn Griffiths anthology *Welsh Voices*, London, Dent, 1967).

Tiff (page 158)

JT typically crafts a poem out of his pub research.

Sleeper into Waverley (pages 159-160)

JT sees in Edinburgh the tourist traps and clichés he would hate for Wales. Fay Cornes recalls: 'This poem is based on a terrible overnight train journey to Edinburgh when we were unable to sleep on the sleeper! At 6.00 am "my host compatriot" was D. Myrddin Lloyd, (Chief?) Librarian at the National Library of Scotland, George IV Bridge, who very kindly gave us a tour of Edinburgh "at this barbaric hour", before taking us to his house for breakfast. A reading had been arranged by the Welsh Arts Council and the Edinburgh Welsh Society who presented "An Evening of Poetry Reading by Anglo-Welsh Poets". The other poets taking part were Raymond Garlick, Roland Mathias and Harri Webb and it took place on 3 September 1970 at the Roxburghe Hotel. The following day Harri Webb and John were invited to give a reading at the Traverse Theatre.'

Kestrel (pages 160-161)

Nature's 'vast blood arrangements' is particularly memorable. On another Cornes typescript JT has written 'Tomcat and other Poems – an adult guide to some animals and birds', so he clearly had considered a collection of such poems.

Taffy (pages 161-162)

In the NLW mss collection and the Cornes collection. Fay Cornes writes: 'I have found my copy (hand written on a scrap of paper) of "Taffy" – second line was originally: "His cold soft nose and whiskers" but "cold" and "nose" are then crossed out. I found it in my first scrapbook, i.e. started in 1970. My Welsh Terrier of that name had died in January 1970, aged 14, and when John and I started going out the following month, I had obviously told him all about my dog. My family and I lived in the country and the dog had complete freedom to go where he wanted which included being out at night. I think he was the father of many a dog in the surrounding farms! Re. the mention of vol-au-vents, my parents had given a cocktail party and the left-over food had been thrown into the field the following day for the birds. Taffy had spent most of that day burying every vol-au-vent individually and very gently. John had found the story amusing. Cf. Welsh Terrier in *SP*.

Northern Railway Blues (pages 162-163)

Dr Zhivago: one of the most successful film adaptations of a novel in the 1960s; it was a film JT admired.

Masks (pages 163-164)

my sagging Hamlet: JT's self-deprecation hangs here, as elsewhere, between the confessional and the self-centred.

Four poems from *Intervals of Heat* (pages 164-169)

This was the collection of some eighteen poems that JT asked me to publish in the late seventies in the small press, Edge Press, which I had been running and whose authors had included Mike Jenkins, Alan Perry, Madeleine Mayne, myself and Charles Simic in his first UK appearance. The press ran out of steam and the project slipped quietly away. The title page has 'Intervals of heat – a sheaf of soft pornography' and the name 'Lloyd Llewelyn' is crossed out for John Tripp's name to be typed instead. John handwrote: 'Here it is – hope you enjoy and have a giggle. All more or less true – reminiscences of a misspent but pleasurable life. (I suggest a hand-on boobs pic. for cover, or something wilder as in *Penthouse* etc) p.s: 3 of the screws are in Pembs. settings.' JT sent the first manuscript to Y Lolfa, not long after they had carried a picture (in a Welsh-language magazine) of Cynon with a nude woman sitting on his lap. Y Lolfa turned down the manuscript.

One of these poems, 'Lady of Devizes', was included later in the pamphlet *For King and Country*.

Conceit of Power – as with many of JT's sexual poems it is the man who fails or is guided by more knowing women. The influence of Dylan Thomas is clear. The original title in manuscript was 'Disaster'.

Military Ram – JT's National Service, as with many others, was an education and an unconventional training for life. At the bottom of the page he has typed 'Note: It is said that the term "a nice piece of crackling" originated as a description of the fine buxom women who were attached to the catering units of the British Army; another name for them was "camp followers". Also a "bobby-dazzler" (flashy in appearance) was usually the girlfriend of a redcap (military policemen) who was not the soldier's favourite.'

Zip – an honest dipping of the Tripp toe into fetishism. His typescript had a photo of a woman's thigh-length boots pasted in the margin.

Jane Russell at the Old Beeb – surely a poem written from life. *Polaroids*, sunglasses, worn for sophisticated effect at that hour.

Dream of Lush Ladies (pages 170-172)
A remarkable weaving of sex and food with, again, uncharacteristic but effective homage to Dylan Thomas's language. Cf. 'The Seasons of Women' in *Diesel to Yesterday*.

A. E. Housman (pages 172-173)
JT acknowledging the strength of the traditional; also locating that thread of English poetry which, like

John's father, passed through the British wars. From *The Inheritance File*, published by Peter Finch's Second Aeon Press in 1973. With illustrations by Martin Dutton.

English Crow: a laureateship in animal history (pages 173-175)

Homage to Ted Hughes, who was Poet Laureate in JT's last year, but who is seen in such a role over a decade before by JT. Tripp's many animal poems attempted to emulate Hughes's visceral style, red in tooth and claw. From *The Inheritance File*.

Passing Through (pages 175-177)

An afternoon spent with Jean Henderson (from *Passing Through*).

Connection in Bridgend (pages 177-178)

As much as 'On My Fortieth Birthday', this poem is JT's anticipated signing off from the business of writing, and life (from *Passing Through*).

At the Rainbow's End

At the Rainbow's End (page 181-186)
Planet 5/6, 1971

Living on the Strip (pages 187-197)
Planet 9, December 1971/January 1972

Barn: the Welsh language monthly magazine covering all aspects of culture in Wales.

The Prince of Wales: now the largest pub in Wales; see Dannie Abse's *Goodbye Twentieth Century: An Autobiography*, pp. 146–7. His play *House of Cowards* was performed there in 1963.

Castro: the Cuba Crisis of 1962 almost brought the world to nuclear disaster: it still resonated for JT.

Gwyn Thomas: the influence of Gwyn Thomas (1913–81), novelist, short story writer and broadcaster, is clear in much of JT's work.

The English at the Eisteddfod (pages 200-210)
Planet 18/19, 1973

Aimez-vous Solzhenitsyn? (pages 211-218)
Planet 23, 1974

August 1914: first published in English in 1972.

Spirit of a Union (pages 219-237)

Published in 1985 in the WUW's Future of the Word annual Register, edited by John Osmond. The chapter had two photographs of groups and individuals at the conference.

my companion: Jean Henderson was with JT.

the college: this was Coleg Harlech.

John Arden (1930–), whose *Serjeant Musgrave's Dance* is one of the outstanding plays of the immediate post-war years.

Owen Dudley Edwards (1938–) is the Irish writer and academic.

Dafydd Elis Thomas (1946–), now Lord Elis Thomas and the Presiding Officer of the National Assembly of Wales. How JT would have enjoyed that.

Meic Stephens: JT's relationship with his Whitchurch neighbour Meic Stephens was colourful and ambiguous. See previous note for 'Village Circuit'.

Planet: the magazine was relaunched and continues to this day.

Janet Dubé: born in Fulham but settled in Wales with her journalist husband for four decades. Works now for the Red Cross.

Robin Reeves (1941–2001) was the second editor of *The New Welsh Review* and guided that magazine for ten years until his death.

Jaci Stephen: later to become the successful journalist and TV critic.

helicopter: in his *Stepping Stones* autobiography by interview Seamus Heaney squashes this myth, which was current at this time.

Metaphor Men: another crack at Craig Raine and the Martians' school of poetry.

Fringe Diversions

Richard Burton: A Biography (pages 241-245)
Anglo-Welsh Review vol. 21, no. 47, 1972

See the note about the Burtons in *The Seed of Dismemberment* annotation.

Killhope Wheel (pages 246-248)
Anglo-Welsh Review vol. 20, no. 46, 1971

Jon Silkin was a frequent visitor and reader during my undergraduate days at Swansea University. He would roam the campus and press copies of *Stand* magazine into your hands.

Mercian Hymns (pages 249-255)
From the same issue of *AWR*.

Another World (pages 256-259)
Again from that issue of *AWR*. JT was a generous contributor – there was a small fee, but he kept the books of course.

Round the Poets (pages 260-279)
Planet 16, February/March 1973

Glyn Hughes: when he won the first Welsh Arts Council Young Poets Prize it was because Meic Stephens, the Literature Director then, and the judges did not realise he was, in fact, not Welsh and from Yorkshire. In 1974, when I won together with Duncan Bush and Nigel Jenkins, I was grilled on the phone by Stephens, who did not wish to repeat the mistake. I had just moved back to Wales from teaching in Yorkshire.

B. S. Johnson: now acknowledged as one of the most radically innovative of post-war British novelists. He committed suicide on the eve of his fortieth birthday. See also the note to 'End of a Guild'.

Gleeman etc. (pages 280-286)
Anglo-Welsh Review vol. 24, no. 52, 1974

George MacBeth (1932–92) was the voice of poetry on Radio 3 for many years. He was a prolific poet and editor. His *War Quartet* of 1969 was a strong influence on the present editor's work. He died tragically early from motor neurone disease.

J. P. Ward taught the present editor in the PGCE year at Swansea University. He organised an experimental poetry event in that year, 1969, the sort of concrete work that JT so opposes in this review. J. P. Ward has a number of more conventional poetry collections from Seren Books.

Brief Encounters (pages 287-292)
Anglo-Welsh Review vol. 25, no. 54, 1975

Goronwy Rees (1909–79) resigned from the Principal's post at Aberystwyth University after four years, in 1957, when it was revealed that he had known of Guy Burgess's work as a spy for the

Russians. He made a full confession of his involvement with the spy ring in the year of his death. His two volumes of autobiography, *A Bundle of Accidents* (1960) and *A Chapter of Accidents* (1972), are both fascinating memoirs of the post-war period and written with great style.

Wide-Eyed in Babylon (pages 293-295)
Anglo-Welsh Review vol. 25, no. 55, 1975

Ray Milland (1907–86) was a crack shot in the Household Cavalry before taking up acting. He had a later career in TV in America, where he had lived for most of his adult life; he died in California.

Come Out Wherever You Are (pages 296-301)
Anglo-Welsh Review 61, 1968

The Loved Ones (pages 302-307)
Arcade 5, 5 January 1981

JT was an avid TV watcher; he died on the settee of the house in Whitchurch after watching a boxing match. 'Of the heart's explosion that took you in the early hours / With McGuigan's fight won and the tele drizzling showers' ('Thoughts from the Holiday Inn').

Arcade, a short-lived fortnightly current affairs and cultural magazine for Wales, edited by John Osmond, which ran from October 1980 to March 1982. JT was the regular reviewer of television programmes.

Vincent Kane left the BBC in 1998 after a long, successful career in Cardiff and London.

David Parry Jones: after retiring from TV he has published a number of books on Welsh rugby.

Bob Humphrys [sic] died in 2006 at the age of 56; he was the brother of the Radio 4 presenter John Humphrys.

Fringe Diversions (pages 308-313)
Arcade 11, 3 April 1981

In my limited experience: JT worked in the BBC at Llandaff before going to London. At one point he did sound effects for a children's programme.

Grand Slam: JT at his most prescient: the film is constantly repeated during rugby seasons on BBC Wales TV.

Alun Richards (1929–2004): editor of the *Penguin Book of Welsh Short Stories* (1976). The novelist and

short story writer from Pontypridd who scripted the
very successful TV series *The Onedin Line* also wrote
on Welsh rugby.

The Shrewd Goat Recaptured (pages 314-320)
Arcade 12, 17 April 1981

Lloyd George: see the poem 'Lloyd George' in *SP* in
which he is 'the genius of his time', though 'For the
Somme he paid the butcher's bill'.

As an indication of the importance of *Arcade* it may be
noted that this issue, for example, also had Jan
Morris's 'Thoughts at My Mother's Funeral'; Dai
Smith on novelist Ron Berry; Ned Thomas on Florence
and Savanarola; Moira Vincentelli on women's images
of men; Raymond Williams on the need for a new
impetus for the novel in Wales; Philip George (Phil
George) on Haydn James and the Swansea
Philharmonic; shorter pieces by Duncan Bush, Euryn
Ogwen Williams and Nigel Jenkins. The feature article
was on the state of Welsh-medium schools in Mid
Glamorgan.

The Life and Times of David Lloyd George: a nine-part
dramatisation which was popularly successful, due in
no small part to its unforgettable theme music by
Ennio Morricone.

Philip Madoc: the Merthyr-born actor (1934–) with a long and successful career in film and television; despite this he is frequently referenced with regard to one minor, comic role as the U-boat captain in a 1973 episode of *Dad's Army*.

Elaine Morgan: born in 1920. One of the most distinguished writers from Wales, winning BAFTAs and Writers Guild Awards. She had previously done extensive television writing, including *Doctor Finlay's Casebook*, *Testament of Youth* and an adaptation of the Richard Llewelyn novel *How Green Was My Valley*. A feminist, she gained an international readership with *The Descent of Woman* (1972).

John Hefin became Head of Drama for the BBC at Cardiff. In 1983 he initiated the first drama series in the Welsh language and later founded the Welsh Film Commission.

Frances Stevenson (1888–1972), later Countess Lloyd George of Dwyfor; LG's letters to her were published in the selection *My Darling Pussy* (London, Weidenfeld and Nicholson, 1975, edited by A. J. P. Taylor).

Rachel Thomas ... Paul Robeson: Rachel Thomas (1905–95) played Mam in the television version of

How Green Was My Valley and had co-starred in *Proud Valley*, the 1939 film, with Paul Robeson (1898–1996). Robeson visited Wales many times and had a special relationship with the south Wales mining communities with whom he sang and acted.

A. J. P. Taylor (1906–90): the first television historian whose face-to-camera talks had wide appeal. His wife sponsored and was a lover of Dylan Thomas.

Thomas Cromwell (1485–1540): Tudor politician who, as Chancellor, was instrumental in enacting Henry VIII's Reformation. Executed by Henry. See also JT's radio play *The Seed of Dismemberment* and 'Rowland Lee to Thomas Cromwell' in *The Province of Belief*.

Life of Brian: the Monty Python film, released in November 1979, was banned by Swansea Council as blasphemous. This decision was not finally revoked until March 1997.

Saunders Lewis (1893–1985): writer, teacher and political activist; founder of the Welsh National Party, later Plaid Cymru.

No Peace for Dando

Apricot Sponge with a Sage (pages 323-326)
Planet 15, 1973

Last Day in England (pages 327-342)
This and the next two stories are taken from the Alun Books pamphlet *Last Day in England* (Port Talbot, Alun Stories no. 1, 1979).

Casualty (pages 357-361)
Planet 17, April/May 1973

The Thinskin Award and Dic Tidy's Mistake (pages 362-379)
These were the first two of four stories published in *The Thinskin Award* (Barry, Edge Press, 1978), in a short series of pamphlets published by the present editor.

The Seed of Dismemberment
(pages 380-394)

Thomas Cromwell, First Earl of Essex (c.1485 to 28 July 1540) served as Henry VIII's chief minister from 1532 to 1540. Cromwell rose to power from humble beginnings in London. He was a principle figure in the

Reformation and the acquisition of Church lands by the Crown. He is a legitimate figure for JT's perceptions of an England intent on the exploitation of Wales. This is, it would appear, the most successful of JT's play attempts. The cast was an impressive one: Ray Smith, Bernard Hepton, Ray Handy and Christine Pritchard. It was produced by Lorraine Davies. JT handwrote a set of stage and set directions on the NLW ms, even down to costume colours: he obviously had stage ambitions for the play as well as its radio appearance. One section of the play, from 'The blaze of gold quartering is caught in a sun flood... screwing it left and right thoroughly for 400 years', was extracted as a poem in its own right as 'Henry Signs', for the proposed collection *Fwrrwm Ishta*. The title refers to a pub in Machen – 'the sitting bench'. This was included by John Ormond in *SP*.

Note that NLW has several short plays in manuscript from the same year. 53/7: 'A Patriot for Supper'; 53/8: 'Inquisition at Beddgelert', rejected by both the BBC and the Welsh Theatre Company; this play has arguments against the perceived monopoly of the Welsh language; 53/9: 'Border Stop'; 53/10: 'The Hot Seat'; 53/11–12: 'The Fallen, a Play for Television'; 53/13: 'Be This Her Memorial', a one-act play based on the short story by Caradoc Evans; 53/14: 'Cadi Hugh', a one-act play based on a short story by Glyn Jones; 53/15: 'Wil Thomas', a one-act play based on a short story by Glyn Jones; 53/16: 'The English Maid', based on the short story 'As It Is Written' by Caradoc Evans; and 53/17: 'The Welsh Private's Wench, or Where the Dregs Went', a one-act play. From this period of the early seventies there are a number of play ideas and incomplete drafts, including one from 1973 for a film shown on BBC on St David's Day 1974, called 'Eagles in Exile' and concerning Polish exiles in Wales.

Of these, few are successful and I believe that none was used professionally. In the NLW mss most of these plays have detailed directions by JT as to how they should be staged, costumes etc. He evidently took this work seriously: there are annotations on an *Echo* newspaper article (1 September 1977) about Richard Burton and Elizabeth Taylor attached to 'The Fallen: a play for television' (1972), indicating that he still held ambitions for the play some time after writing it. Robert Barton says: 'I worked as a haberdasher's apprentice in Bridgend and I was an oil-monkey in Margam. I played stand-off for Llanelli Thirds. I played Romeo in Ponty, Lear at Stratford, Sir Thomas More with O'Booze, "The Lion in Winter"...'. Wyn, the 'ex-script-writer friend', remarks, 'As Gwyn Tomo said, you were a sexual athlete of Olympic standard, sire... You were a veritable king of shaft, a prince of thrust.' Barton says, 'Yes, I liked a tussle in the straw.' And to 'Kate': 'There is a pong in the court of Denmark.'

'A Welsh Private's Wench' has some good barrack room humour: 'I am yours to command. I am never bored, sir. I darn my socks. Sew my buttons, whitewash the coalhouse, and salute anything that moves. But I have been put in the Welsh hut, sir, with the Taffs. They are awful, sir. It is full of bookmakers, actors and spongers, and smells of feet. They are the despair of every colonel and chaplain from Colwyn Bay to Penzance. But none, sir, none, has dared to do what Kippo Lewis has done... The despicable Kippo has had this fair dumpling. This flower of the English aristocracy beside him after light out, in his bunk.'

Appendix

Thoughts from Holiday Inn (pages 397-408)
First published in *The Last Candles*, Seren, 1989, and included in the anthology *The New Poetry*, ed. Hulse, Kennedy and Morley, Bloodaxe Books, 1993.

Gwyn Jones (1907–99): novelist, story writer, anthologist and academic; translator of *The Mabinogion*.

The man o' war describes the evening with JT which I fictionalised in the story 'H.M.S. Cassandra', in *Considering Cassandra: Poems and a Story*, Gwasg Carreg Gwalch, 2003.

At Bosherston Ponds, Rain and Fog (pages 409-410)
JT was very fond of this remarkable man-made water system in south Pembrokeshire. See 'At Bosherston Ponds' in *SP*. 'I lose all strut. / Skidding along slotted planks, the bridge shakes / as my flimsy tenure shakes. / I look out / at sheer rock and sloped dune, stretches/of water lily'.

Coming Back with JT and Bob Dylan (pages 411-412)
Both Peter Finch poems are uncollected.

border guards: see 'The Diesel to Yesterday' in *SP*.

Acknowledgements

This book would not have been possible without the help and encouragement of several people and organisations: I wish to thank Jean Henderson, John's last partner and the copyright holder of his work; Fay Cornes for her John Tripp poem manuscripts, conversations and photographs; Peter Finch of Yr Academi, whose Gwyn Jones Lecture commissioning led to my recent work on John Tripp and who has written a foreword and contributed two of his uncollected poems; staff at the National Library of Wales; the Welsh Writers Trust who awarded a research grant; the University of Glamorgan and my colleagues for sabbatical leave; and all at Parthian Books.